The World Class Inventors Handbook

Stephen E. Moor

ISBN 978-0-692-53644-5
Published by World Class Inventors LLC

Book design and layout by Stephen E. Moor
Cover design and artwork by Robert Cipolla Graphics
Back cover photo by Jaclyn Moor

Printed and bound in The United States of America

Other books by Stephen E. Moor
The Greed of a Dime

For more information about the author and videos:
Please go to World Class Inventors.com or look me up on You Tube.

DEDICATION

This book is dedicated to all the inventors who have come before me.
To all the starry-eyed dreamers yet to follow, both great and small.
May the pursuit of living out your dreams keep you all the days of your life.

FORWARD

I am so pleased that you happened upon this book.

I promise not to disappoint! What I do promise is to bring you to the next level.

My goal is to bring you to a place where you must be as an inventor.

After reading this book through, keep it handy and consult it often before making your next move.

Follow it diligently and your chances of becoming a successful inventor will multiply greatly.

CONTENTS

INTRODUCTION & Authors Qualifications and Background 1

Chapter 1
AN INVENTOR'S PRIMER
Part I

The Springboard 9
It All Starts with an Idea 10
Do You Know Why They Issue Patents? 11
What Inventing is Not 11
There is Nothing New Under the Sun 12
Claim It 12
A Time to Dig 13
Keep It a Secret 15
Is It a Good Idea? 16
Research 17

Chapter 2
AN INVENTOR'S PRIMER
Part II

Marketing Trends 20
You're the Visionary 23
Not Invented Here 24
Soften the Blow 28
It's Your Dream so Live It 28

Chapter 3
CLAIM IT

Intellectual Property Formation 30
Document Your Ideas 32
An Inventors Notebook is Critical 33
First and True Inventor 35
The PTO and Memorialization 41
Patent Pending 44
Walk Tall and Carry Two Big Sticks 47

Chapter 4
SOME IMPORTANT THINGS

Market Trends are Very Important 50
Claims 51
Framing Your Claims 53
The Castle and Your Claims 54
Your Claims and the Examiner 57
A Tale of Two Examiners 58
Loose Lips Sink Ships 60
Memorializing Your Idea 63
Prototypes 65

Chapter 5
CONSIDER YOUR OPTIONS

Your Options 70
Consider the Internet 70
Consider a Patent Lawyer or Agent 71
Consider an Invention Service 72
Consider a Patent Search 73
Provisional Patents 73
Consider Going it Alone 74
Who are You Going to Choose? 76

Chapter 6
CHOOSING YOUR TEAM
Part I

The Good, Bad and the Ugly 77
General Qualifications of Patent Practitioners 77
Some Important Qualifications 78
Patent Agents 79
Qualifications and Abilities are Two Different Things 80
The Right Specialist for the Job 81
Steady as You Go 82
Ah, Law Firms 82
The Pecking Order 83
Some Good Questions 85
Foreign Protection 86

Chapter 7
CHOOSING YOUR TEAM
Part II
It's All in the Claims 88
The Patent Search 89
The PTO's Job 89
Attorneys are My First Choice 92
The Attorney and You 93
Retainer Agreements 95
How Much is this Going to Cost? 96

Chapter 8
MOUNTAIN CLIMBING
Things You Should Know 97
Inventor's Waivers 97
A Honey Do List 101
The Right Negotiator is Critical 103
Inventor or Entrepreneur 104
Are You Ready? 105
What's a Royalty? 108
The Reason Why You Would License 110
Monopoly, Oligopoly or Free Market 111
The Outright Sale 113
Make It and Market It Yourself 115
Pros and Cons 118
Trade Dress and Marks 119
Two Real World Examples 120
A Homework Assignment 123

Chapter 9
THE PSYCHOLOGY BEHIND ROYALTY RATES
Beginning the Valuation Process 124
Licensing is the Norm 125
What Licensing Is 126
Some Good Psychology Never Hurts 126
Humility, Diplomacy and Vigilance is Key 129
How You Conduct Yourself Matters 130

Chapter 10
A ROYALTY RATE PRIMER

Establishing a Value 132
The Manufacturer's Pre-tax Profits 134
Goldscheider's Rule 143
Now What's Your Share? 145
Pricing it Right and Splitting Up the Profits 147
Royalties vs. Reality 149

Chapter 11
MOUNT MARKETING

Who's Going to Make the Phone Ring? 151
You have the Ability to Market 152
A Marketing Tutorial 152
How May I Direct Your Call? 155
One Call at a Time 158
Resistance to Change is Normal 161
The Basis for Your Invention is Critical 162
Making it Come Alive: An Overview 166
The Second Trend Wave 169
A Bit of History 172
My Last Two Companies: A Case Study 173
Purolator's Dynamics 176
Fram's Dynamics 177

Chapter 12
PRE-LICENSE AGREEMENTS

What You Sign Matters 181
Setting the Stage for the Pre-Licensing Phase 181
An Overview of the First Document 182
An Overview of the Second Document 184
Pre-License Agreements are Like Stop Signs 186
Why All the Caution? 187
Controlling Law 190
Some Things to be Mindful Of 196
Just So You Know 199

Chapter 13
LICENSING AGREEMENTS
Who's Invited to Your Meeting? 202
You had Better Come Prepared 204
A Very Important List 206
Turning the Tables 212
Aftercare 216
Some final Thoughts and One Last Lesson 217
Believe in Yourself 219

EPILOGUE 220

PREFACE

When I set out to write this book, I envisioned that the both of us were sitting on the front porch on a warm summer's evening enjoying a cold drink.
You shared with me that it was your dream to become an inventor one day.
As the light faded and the stars came out, you began to ask me what it was like to be an inventor.
Then you asked me the really big question, "So what was the journey like getting there?"
As the night grew long, you still had many questions left unanswered…, to which I had the answers.
In keeping with that spirit, this manual was born.

Introduction

So, you want to be an inventor?

You have a great idea, but where do you begin? Is there a straightforward roadmap out there for an aspiring inventor to follow? Quite frankly, as far as I'm concerned there hasn't been one until now.

I understand where you're at, and I can relate to your desire to become an inventor. Perhaps it's in your genes, and we'll soon find out. No matter what, your time to act is now.

If it's your destiny to become an inventor, then I certainly don't want anyone talking you out of it, because some people will try. And I especially don't want the forces lurking about to separate you from your idea, because that's a real possibility as well.

My mission is simple. I want to help you preserve your dream and I want to watch you walk in your destiny as an inventor.

At this juncture, I realize just how overwhelmed you might be as you consider the inventing process. As you know, there are many avenues out there for you to choose from. So which one are you going to pick?

The way I see it, here are just a few of your options:

- There are numerous postings on the Internet for you to consider.
- You could jump right in and contact a patent lawyer and pay him a minimum of $300 per hour and let the meter run for a good 15 hours or so. But let me assure you of something before you run out and do that. Upon the completion of this expensive process, it doesn't necessarily mean that you will be any closer to becoming an inventor.
- You could hook up with one of those free invention services, because on the surface it seems like the easiest way for you to accomplish your goals. But in the end, you could wind up paying them several thousand dollars for their help and in many cases it could be much more than that before it's all over. They'll happily produce a pretty binder for you, laced with the expectations that your fortune is just off on the horizon… and they may even promise that a lucrative licensing deal with a notable manufacturer is just waiting on you. Really now, if it was that easy, wouldn't everyone with an idea become an inventor?
- You could spend hundreds of dollars on a patent search, or you could try and do it yourself on the Internet for free. In either case, the results may not tell you a darn thing as to whether your idea is patentable, and more importantly, whether it's marketable or not. Chances are, the outcome of such a search will only just serve to confuse you.
- You could consider enlisting the services of a registered patent agent, who by the way isn't a lawyer. After all, you might be trying to save yourself some money instead of using a certified patent attorney. The result; you may wind up getting what you paid for.
- You could file an inexpensive *provisional patent application*, but what will that really get you? The application lapses in a year's time. You don't have to make any claims. And you don't have to adhere to the same criteria as a *non-provisional patent application.*
- Finally, you could go it alone. For sure that's the least expensive option of them all, especially if you're looking do this on the cheap. And today with the aid of the Internet, that's a rather obvious choice.

I'm sure that you are a fairly confident individual, or you wouldn't have dreamt of becoming an inventor in the first place. After all, inventors are an independent bunch. They are a very special breed and can accomplish almost anything if they only put their minds to it. Right?

How hard could inventing be anyway?

Allow me to give you a bit of advice, before you consider any one of your many options, "Only fools rush in where angels fear to tread." The simple truth is that there are plenty of opportunities to get things wrong in the inventing game and you certainly don't want that.

Above all, please don't get sucked in by all those people out there who are clamoring to help you out with your idea.

Coming up with an idea is one thing. Yet inventing and receiving a *valid* patent is quite another. And making money from your idea is much bigger than both of those things put together. Inventing is certainly way more complicated than just having someone, or some service evaluate your idea!

So why not spend some time with me and I will take you through the process personally. Together we will explore all of your options, plus so much more. I promise that by the end of our time together you will be properly informed and ready to begin an inventing journey all your own. As for those of you who have already begun the inventing process, or any of you who are in the midst of marketing a valuable idea… stop! Take a breather and check out what I have to say before proceeding any further. You'll be glad that you did.

Qualifications

My name is Stephen Moor, and I'm an inventor with over 20 years of inventing experience. My experience has been in the world of automotive oil filtration. During the course of my inventing journey I have approached the biggest automotive oil filter manufacturers in the United States. I did this as a sole inventor and I did so as a total industry outsider. To make myself perfectly clear, I was a backyard inventor just like you. I had but one objective, and that was to license my patented technology to one of the key players in the oil filter business and to see my product come alive on the shelves of the major automotive retailers around the United States.

As the facts bear out, my two patents created the Fram Double Guard and the TRT oil filters that were marketed throughout North America, beginning in the 1996 timeframe. These two patents in conjunction with my trade secrets were also responsible for laying the groundwork for subsequent models that Fram would later introduce, all of which began an unprecedented period of innovation for the Fram oil filter division.

The oil filter business is an industry where over 500 million oil filters are sold each and every year, in just the USA alone.

To keep things straight, Fram was wholly owned business unit of the AlliedSignal Corporation. In 1997 AlliedSignal merged with Honeywell International and took on the Honeywell name since it had significantly greater name recognition than AlliedSignal.

In 2011 Honeywell sold off their Automotive Aftermarket Division, which included the Fram oil filter business to Graeme Hart; New Zealand's wealthiest man for 950 million dollars.

My two benchmark patents are; 4,751,901 & 5,209,842. These patents were so revolutionary, that they created an entirely new oil filter category for additive treated oil filters.

As of this publication I have been cited a combined 84 times in the United States Patent Office's prior art, and that number has been going up all of the time. The fact is, nearly any individual or corporation who wants to file for an additive treated oil filter must cite at least one, or in many cases both of my patents in order for the PTO to consider their application.

This fact makes me the most influential inventor in this multi-billion-dollar industry to come down the pike in the last 45 years.

Composite oil filter

Patent # 4,751,901 filed 10/13/1987 issued 6/21/1988

The USPTO provided only 6 citations ranging from 1937, '38, '76, '77 & '78 as the prior art for this application. None of the prior art citations were from oil filter manufacturers. So if you follow the chain of this invention, my idea certainly wasn't on anybody's radar screen during this time.

Since its grant, my '901 patent has been cited some 61 times by companies such as Exxon, Cummins, Baldwin, Wix, Harvard & Lubrizol from 1991-2011.

AlliedSignal / Honeywell has since been granted 10 US patents that have incorporated my trade secrets and they specifically cited my '901 patent 10 times as the justification for their patent applications.

Oil enhancing multifunction oil filter

Patent # 5,209,842 filed 2/3/1992 issued 5/11/1993

The USPTO provided only 3 citations ranging from 1975, '77 & '85 as the prior art for this application. Again, none of the prior art citations were from any of the major oil filter manufacturers. The lack of prior art citations definitely bolsters the fact that this patent was another category game changer.

Since its grant my '842 patent has been cited some 23 times by companies such as Exxon, Baldwin, Fleetguard, Lubrizol & Mann and Hummel ranging from 1994-2012. AlliedSignal / Honeywell has been granted 10 additional patents that have incorporated my trade secrets and in due course they cited my '901 patent 10 times in order to justify their patent applications.

I personally devised the marketing, manufacturing, and the critical co-branding strategies for the Fram Double Guard oil filter. I laid the groundwork for the trademark licensing deal that was consummated between DuPont and Honeywell in order to employ DuPont's Teflon® in this filter. My rational was simple. It was critical that my product display both the Teflon name and logo on both the product and the packaging in order to bolster consumer recognition and confidence.

Now this may seem trivial by today's marketing standards, but in the mid 90's co-branding was not a common occurrence whatsoever in the world of marketing. This was the first time that Fram or its parent AlliedSignal had ever co-branded a product using another industry leader's unique ingredient and trademark. I developed this marketing plan in order to gain huge dividends derived from a trademark that had enormous brand power.

Just so you know, at the time, AlliedSignal manufactured their own version of Teflon, but it could not be referred to as Teflon. It would have to be referred to as the generic compound; Polytetrafluoroethylene or PTFE. Only DuPont owns the Teflon® name, and nobody no matter how big or small can use it without first obtaining a license from them.

My filter products were sold nationwide in Walmart for over a decade and were so disruptive that they had to be repackaged in theft proof packaging since over 750,000 oil filters were stolen off their shelves during its first few months of retail life.

I should at the very least be the co-inventor of an additional 17 patents that both AlliedSignal and Honeywell filed without my knowledge nor my consent. They did this indirect violation of US patent law 35 USC §115&116, contract law and The Uniform Trade Secret Act.

So what did I do?

Better yet, "What would you have done?"

As for me, I sued Honeywell International. At the time they were a 30-billion-dollar corporation and I sued them in US Federal Court as a Pro Se plaintiff. That means that I had no lawyer by my side.

IP Lawsuit: Moor vs. Honeywell formerly known as AlliedSignal.

02-CV-03142 JAG filed in the US 3rd District Court, Newark, NJ vicinage.

To put things into perspective for you, Honeywell had 250 in-house attorneys on staff. And as if that wasn't enough firepower, they hired a very connected Newark law firm in order to help them navigate through the halls of the Newark Federal courthouse.

The law firm of Kirkland and Ellis was brought in to bat clean up, as they were Honeywell's lead defense firm. They fielded a team of 1,100 lawyers and at the time, they were ranked as the 9th largest law firm on the planet.

To my utter dismay, I settled just four days short of my scheduled jury trial on September the 6th 2006.

Once Upon a Time

I began my journey as a bright-eyed backyard inventor just like you, but my experiences have changed my perspective about an inventor's journey. As you've already begun to figure out, I've been through the inventing process full circle. Therefore, I already know about the stuff that's been keeping you up late at night.

Right about now, you might be wondering, "How am I ever going to get my foot in the front door of a major company?" Well you can rest assured that I'm going to teach you a thing or two about that.

Just so you know, during the inventing process, I had come up with all of the elements necessary to create and support a patented product that would enjoy a long life-cycle. As a result of developing a brand new technology, I had amassed a healthy amount of trade secrets pertaining to the proprietary materials and the specific manufacturing processes needed to produce these products. Because trade secrets play such a crucial role in the development of any new product, I plan on thoroughly teaching you about trade secrets and how to properly handle them. Trade secrets *are not* part of your patent; therefore, they must be handled in a totally different fashion. In fact, they are governed under an entirely different set of laws.

In addition to that, here's something else that the *Voices* on those invention help sites aren't telling you about. It is of supreme importance that *you* understand how to formulate a cohesive marketing plan that's capable of sustaining any new product that you might develop for the duration of its life cycle.

The fact is; it was my marketing plan and my vision that enabled the Double Guard to grace the shelves of Walmart, and the many other automotive retailers for over 10 long years! I need not remind you that Walmart is the largest retailer in the world and that if your product appears on their shelves, then you've made your mark as a product innovator.

That said, I'm going to let you in on another little secret. The inventor's odyssey can be more akin to walking through a minefield than anything else that I've ever attempted. When I first began my journey, I was rather clueless as to what would actually lie ahead. I was self-taught and that is exactly how many costly mistakes can be made.

As we all know, "experience" can be a brutal teacher and I know about this first hand. Being a self-taught inventor is definitely not the best path for you to follow and that's the reason why I have decided to use my intellectual property lawsuit as the backdrop for this teaching.

What is truly best for you, or any fledgling inventor is to be properly mentored, but mentors in the field of inventing are non-existent.

Here's just a small sampling of what you need to know as an inventor...

First and foremost, you need an accurate, yet simple outline that will enable you to take your kernel of an idea and grow it to maturity in the form of a patent or a properly trademarked product.

Next, you need to be able to take your product into the marketplace where it can generate an income for you based upon its sales. The trick here, is that you need to do all this without committing any one of a multitude of common mistakes that can derail you at any point along the way.

Do you realize that making any sort of mistake during the licensing and pre-licensing stages could potentially set you up for total disaster later on?

Believe me, it's not inconceivable that you could have your patent and its valuable rights ripped right out of your possession if you've been either *too sloppy or too trusting* during the journey. Becoming too trusting is a boat sinker. Bottom line, you need to do things properly from the moment that you first get your idea, and if you don't, you may find yourself having very little recourse once the mistakes have been made.

Unfortunately, you heard me right. The fact that you could get yourself into some serious hot water at any twist or turn during this process is a common thread that will run throughout the entire length of this teaching. I dare say that nothing will be taught without paying careful attention to this reality.

There are truly many things that you need to know before you begin your journey. It is especially important that you respect the fact that the inventing game is not for the uninformed. My best advice to you, is that the inventing process is that special something in life that requires a good mentor if you truly want to become successful.

So here is your opportunity to be taught, challenged, and honed by someone who is willing to share his intimate knowledge in a no-holds-barred fashion concerning the entire process.

Of course the choice is yours. Should you decide to pass on my offer, I think that it's only fair to inform you ahead of time, that many of the backyard inventors in America that have come up with *valuable ideas* wind up getting their inventions stolen after presenting their *patented ideas* to an interested party! Just spend some time on the Internet and look up the myriad of intellectual property lawsuits and find that out for yourself.

So here's what I've done for you. *I've taken a complex process that is both very foreign and mysterious, and boiled it down to its most elementary parts. Most importantly, I've taken the inventing process and its intricacies and put them in front of you when you need them the most... before you ever begin.*

Some Background and Some Friendly Guidance

As for my background, I received my first oil filter patent in 1988. I received my second oil filter patent in 1993. I entered into a license agreement with AlliedSignal's Fram oil filter division in 1995. I filed a lawsuit against Honeywell in July of 2002, which settled on the eve of a Federal jury trial in September 2006.

Do the math. I come out with an 18-year "Nantucket sleighride." This expression harkens back to the days when fishermen in double-ended dories were towed around in the open ocean by giant whales with harpoons sticking out their backs. The outcome wasn't always pleasant for the men being dragged about in the dories, since many of them were lost at sea and never to be seen again.

This analogy holds perfectly true for any inventor who attempts to wrestle back his patent rights from some powerful corporation once they have been misappropriated. By the way, the word misappropriated is a nice glossy legal term that means stolen.

The take away message here is this; it doesn't have to be that way for you, because I'm on a mission to debunk all of the disinformation that's been so popularized of late about inventing. Towards that effort I have developed a blueprint for you to follow, beginning from the very moment that you get your idea, to the time in which you sign your license agreement and everything in between. I will flesh out all of the options for you, and in the end; I am going to suggest which option makes the most sense for you to follow.

During our journey together, I will always give you my best explanation as to you why I am advising a certain course of action and why I would counsel against others.

Along the way, I will share some of my many experiences with you and tell you where I've been magnificently right, and where I went terribly wrong.

So let me ask you something, "What expert have you consulted lately that is willing to admit where he's gone terribly wrong and then explain to you why?"

Besides all of that, I will provide you with the essential details that you must be aware of long after the ink is dry on your license agreement and beyond. *Yes, there is much to know about inventing.*

I have even included a section for those company employees that may have already signed an inventor's disclosure agreement as a prerequisite for employment.

The last thing that I want to do, is to prop myself up as some kind of brain surgeon or nuclear physicist, because I'm not. As a matter of fact, I'm far from it and that's a good thing, because I'm going to explain this process to you as if you never got past the sixth grade.

I graduated from the University of Connecticut in 1982 with a BA in Psychology. I've been an over-the-road truck driver who's logged over 300,000 miles. I've owned and operated my own rigs on two separate occasions and I've trucked though all 48 states. On the opposite end of the career spectrum, I built a career that spanned over 20 years selling properties on the Jersey Shore as a full-time straight-commissioned real estate agent. And through it all, I've probably held more menial jobs and done more physical labor than most of you. Though I'm rather proud of my ability to perform hard physical labor, it was that way of life that drove me to try and find a better way. The way out for me was to follow my dream of becoming an inventor.

Inventing to a large degree has been a liberating force in my life. I credit my inventing success for providing much of the financial freedom and the creativity that I now enjoy. Above all else, I had a burning desire to succeed as an inventor. I was fortunate enough to have uncovered just enough information that enabled me to understand and survive the inventing process without being formally taught or mentored. Looking back, I was blessed not to have been completely destroyed in the process, because *what I invented was exceedingly valuable*.

Here's the very cornerstone of this book. If you should be fortunate enough to come up with a valuable idea, and I don't care whether it is patentable or not, chances are, your intellectual property could come under attack. This teaching above all else is going to open your eyes to the various means that will enable you to either prevent, minimize or put to an early end any of those possible attacks on your intellectual property.

Much to my regret, I'm out about 30 million dollars in lost royalties! All the many wonderful things about becoming an inventor aside, in the end it's really about the money, now isn't it? Therefore, I want to teach you how to keep all of what rightfully belongs to you.

If I only knew then, what I learned after going through a hard wash cycle. If only I had done certain things differently. If only I had been given the opportunity to know what lie ahead in the process. However, there was no *World Class Inventor's Handbook,* nor Stephen Moor on the Internet to guide me through the process back then. I can only wish there was, but as I can tell you from experience, that wishing is for fools and being ultra-prepared is for winners.

So there you have it. I dare say this book is about as close to getting personally mentored as you can get on the subject of all things inventing. If you can find a world-class inventor in the flesh to take you under his or her wing, then by all means you should go for it!

As for me, I know the inventing game. I spent over 20 years at it. I know the process from the inside out. I know it from the boardroom to the courtroom. From my garage to Fram's worldwide research centers. From the shelves of Walmart, Pep Boys, and AutoZone and beyond.

I certainly know how to place a value on an invention. Therefore, I can teach you how to calculate what a fair royalty rate is and how to evaluate the worth of your invention. You don't need anyone's help to do that.

I can counsel you as to whether you should sell your idea outright to a manufacturer or whether you shouldn't. Furthermore, I can give you sound advice whether you should manufacture and market the product yourself, or whether you should seek a licensing deal instead. With regard to licensing, I'm going teach you from my vantage point what licensing is all about, and I promise not to spare any horses on this subject. Obviously, I know the art of how to get your foot in the front door, because I'm still an expert at that. So you can expect that a highly informative marketing game plan will be coming your way as well.

I know how to defend myself in the most complex legal scenarios imaginable, and I have a better than healthy grasp of intellectual property law and how the legal system actually works in the inventing game. As such, you need to be in possession of this sort of information, well before you ever venture out to hawk your new idea. And I'm going to ensure that you have it. Most importantly, I am going to challenge you how to think like a seasoned inventor before you ever become one.

Lastly, I am going to provide you with personalized counsel as we go through this process together, sharing with you the kind of information that you won't find from any other single source.

So if this is the type of information that you have been searching for, then you needn't look any further. That's just a smattering of what *The World Class Inventor's Handbook* has in store. So accept my invitation... climb aboard, and allow me the privilege to become your mentor!

Chapter 1

AN INVENTOR'S PRIMER

Part I

The Spring Board

As you've no doubt already discovered, the world that I'm about to share with you can be rather complex. It's also a high stakes game where the amount of information is so immense that an entire library could be filled to the brim with materials about the subject. That said, I thought that you would benefit if I provided a general introduction to the subject.

The word *primer* as defined, means *the very first principles of any subject.*

The word primer goes to the heart and soul of what we're about to explore during these first two chapters. With that in mind, I'm going to give you a general lay of the land in preparation for the many important details that will shortly follow.

My hope is that every single one of you who is about to explore this book has come upon an idea that will become the basis for something incredibly valuable! You see, it's one thing to dream up an idea and it's quite another thing to slave over something and perfect it. Yet, it's an entirely different universe to properly protect your idea and then be able to successfully market it.

It's going to be my privilege to teach you about all of these things.

Here's the key.

- You must *protect* your idea every step of the way or in the end you may wind up with nothing.

Unfortunately, the world that we live in is greedy. Therefore, *if* your *intellectual property* happens to be capable of generating significant amounts of money, then your idea is vulnerable to an attack.

That is why I have taken on the mission of *reverse engineering* the inventing process for the aspiring backyard inventor. I want to teach you about inventing from the perspective that what you are about to invent *is* something valuable. And I want to prepare you well in advance that an attack on your idea is *not* out of the question.

Whether you know it or not, this is a major hurdle that plagues *every* modern day inventor who's come up with a valuable invention. In my opinion, if you are going to go through the trouble of inventing something valuable, then you may as well do it the right way from the very beginning. That of course means protecting your idea. Although *patents* are an essential piece of that protection, they are not the only part. So I'm going to cover the entire spectrum of protection as we journey along.

I'm certainly not about to discount the fact that there are legal remedies afforded the inventor should he or she suffer an attack on their idea, because there are. However, don't let the *Voices* out there or your lack of understanding about these matters lull you into complacency about the inventing process. What you may not know, and what the V*oices* aren't telling you, is that these remedies are very time consuming, very expensive and they will leave you emotionally devastated.

Therefore, as an inventor, it's your mission to avoid having your idea attacked in the first place. Simply put, an attack on your idea will rob you of your joy and any potential future earnings.

The best way to approach the art of inventing, is to simply know what the rules are before ever stepping onto the playing field. Whether you realize it or not, inventing is the big leagues and by the time we're finished, you'll have an understanding of why.

As I've already shared, I've been through the fiery furnace of an intellectual property lawsuit. An intellectual property lawsuit is not only the highest test of one's patent, but of an inventor's mettle as well. In a desire to put that horrific experience to good use, I have employed it as the springboard from which to teach you all about the inventing process. In my estimation, there is no greater real-world mechanism by which to teach you about the inventing process. The bright spotlight powered by a Fortune 38 company, and the experience of dueling it out with one of the most powerful law firms on the planet happens to provide the perfect backdrop to expose in high definition the important nuances of how the inventing and patenting process actually works.

Just so you know, I filed my lawsuit Pro Se for a reason. It wasn't because I didn't have a good case. And it wasn't because I didn't seek out the proper legal remedies either, because I did. The facts are, I had a very solid case and I conducted an exhaustive search for legal representation that spanned nearly a year and a half. During that time, I presented my case to not only the US Patent Office, but to some of the biggest and most successful intellectual property litigators in the country.

After all of that searching I began to realize something really scary. If I wanted any semblance of justice, I would have to represent myself. So allow me to fill in some of the blanks for you.

If you've been stolen from, the US Patent Office for the most part is going to wash their hands of any accusations of foul play and when they do get involved, their involvement is limited as to what they can actually do. Instead they will politely direct you to the Federal Court System to obtain resolution for your matter, because that's what the Federal Law requires. That's simple enough.

What about hiring an IP law firm on contingency?

Please don't count on that option, since finding one that will represent you on a contingency fee basis is about as rare as finding a hen's tooth.

OK. So how much does it cost to hire a law firm to wage an intellectual property lawsuit against a formidable adversary?

I can tell you from experience that you better have between one to two million dollars' liquid to mount a serious legal campaign.

Again, my sentiments bear repeating. If you have come up with an idea that is valuable, and if you are lax about any aspect of inventing process, you could easily lose your patent rights without ever being aware of it.

It All Starts with an Idea

Ideas can come to us in many ways and they can take shape in many forms. Your idea may have dawned on you one day as a whimsical vision, or it may have hit you square in the head like a brick. It doesn't really matter. What matters is that the idea originated with you and not with someone else.

- Patentable ideas that are worth big money are indeed rare!
- Patentable ideas that are worth big money are certainly worth protecting.

Most patents granted to backyard inventors rarely generate a dime for their owner's. So please don't be under the false impression that just because you've invented something that you're automatically going to get rich. It doesn't work that way.

The bottom line; if your idea is not revolutionary, beneficial, practical, useful or profitable to everyone who comes into contact with your *proposed* widget, then it is worthless. I'm not trying to be the bearer of bad tidings here, but think about what we're actually doing. We are inventing! We are dreaming and we are trying to profit from our ideas against some mighty powerful odds!

Do You Know Why They Issue Patents?

I would like to give you my take as to what patents really are, and why they get issued. Simply put, *a patent is an idea that is protected.* An idea that has you so personally convinced of its value, that you want to both protect it and exploit it, all at the same time. An idea that in your heart and mind is so lucrative, that you're willing to take the necessary courses of action to protect it, before ever exposing it in the public square. An idea that you're so pregnant with, that you're willing to pursue it despite the expenditure of time, capital and energy necessary to see it come true.

In short, *a patent is your very personal vision!* The point of this whole exercise is that one fine day, your idea is going to enter the public domain and you're going to make money off of it. Hopefully, lots of money.

You see it doesn't really matter how you got the idea, as long as it originated with you and that's the key.

And if that's not so, then please explain to me why there are Federal Statutes on the books, which govern the formation, the protection and ultimately the enforcement of those ideas that we call patents and trademarks?

That's what it's all about folks. Patents can *sometimes* be a very precious commodity. And they *always* require hard work and a considerable investment from any inventor who desires to obtain one. Therefore, to the backyard inventor like you and I, they are always personal. I care very deeply about that aspect, and you should too.

What Inventing is Not

I don't know what you think inventing is, but I feel it's important that I tell you what it's *not*. Prior to our meeting, you may have previously subscribed to the notion that inventing was just about tinkering in your garage on some gadget. And in part, that's what is.

Or perhaps, inventing to you is a bit more sublime, such as lying on your back in a tree-lined meadow, where you're lost in some dream about a gadget that might make you rich. And in part, that's what inventing is about as well.

Even so, those two idyllic pictures taken at face value are just myths; like the Easter Bunny and the Tooth Fairy. Inventing is so much more than that. Although those are great pictures that conjure up warm feelings about the art of inventing, I have to break it to you; they are only the tiniest part of the inventing process.

The great Thomas Edison once said that, "Inventing is 1% inspiration and 99% perspiration," and from where he stood as a man who made a living from his inventions, he was absolutely right.

But sadly enough in our age of bank scandals and celebrated cheats on Wall Street, things have changed dramatically. As compared to Edison's times, intellectual property lawsuits have become even more of an aspiring art form. Fighting over patent rights has risen to meteoritic heights and patent litigation is a goldmine for IP firms. Therefore, it's something that all backyard inventors should be keenly aware of from the start.

The patent process and the opportunity to make significant money from your idea is more akin to tiptoeing through a minefield than tiptoeing through a field of daisies. Therefore, unlike the inventors of Edison's era, you should be spending a great deal of your perspiration on keeping your invention safe.

There is Nothing New Under the Sun

Now that we've established that you've come up with an original new idea, we can begin. In order to keep the inventing process in context, I'd like to start off by sharing a few words of wisdom on the subject.

An Old Testament quote taken from the book of Ecclesiastes states, "There is nothing new under the sun." There happens to be a lot of truth in that statement if you think about it.

From a modern scientific standpoint, one doesn't have to look any further than Albert Einstein's 1st Law of Thermodynamics, which puts it yet another way, "Matter can neither be created nor can it be destroyed." In either case, whether you consider the biblical principal or the modern day scientific fact, nobody on this planet has ever been capable of creating any new matter.

So let's make this clear. By the act of inventing, you're not creating any new earthly or cosmic matter. Rather you're taking the elements that have already been created and placed here on this planet, and by the power of your intellect, you are able to combine them in such a manner as to make something unique and purposeful out of their combination. At that point you are inventing and hopefully your invention is now worth protecting. Your goal now, is to take that new invention and properly turn it into a patentable opportunity and to ultimately make a lot of money from it.

You've got an original idea; so let's explore what's next.

Claim It

- The very first thing that you must do with your new idea is to claim it.

Although this may sound simple enough, don't underestimate its importance. The first thing that you must do is to take your idea and claim it in your heart. As you will soon discover, much of what you will invent takes place in your heart and not in your head.

So let's establish the fact that what you're about to work on is your idea and that you've come by that idea honestly. Honesty is another very important principal and there are some things that you should know about it from the start. First and foremost, this idea must have originated with you and must be yours. Getting wealthy from your invention is a noble enterprise, if it's done the *honest* way. That means integrity must always come first! If you compromise your integrity in the process of inventing, then you're stealing! Stealing will not only result in your failure, but it will bring upon you some serious heartache, not to mention that a tarnished reputation will be in your future.

In the event that you should happen to be collaborating with someone else on the same idea, that's okay too. Just so long as the both of you have acknowledged your partnership upfront, because you will both end up being *co-inventors* one day. We will explore the legal foundation for that statement when we discuss the importance of 35 USC §115&116.

Whatever the case, now is the appropriate time for you to take ownership of your idea. As American citizens we are fortunate to be able to partake in a system that encourages us to exploit our ideas and make a profit from them if we so choose. Nobody else should be able to interfere with your opportunity to do so. But as with anything that may have potential value, we must be proactive and take the necessary precautionary steps to protect what is ours.

Therefore, it's going to be *your responsibility* to protect that idea and to keep others from stealing it from you. One of the things that we must consider up front, is how do we go about preserving our rights of ownership under the US Patent System.

In a perfect world, the patenting process should protect our ideas from the intrusion of others, but as we'll explore along the way, that's more of an ideal than an absolute fact. As we move further along, I'm going to teach you how to protect yourself under this system.

Just so you know, through all my many years of research, I never crossed any ethical line of behavior. I never committed any act that could be viewed as industrial espionage and I never entertained stealing someone else's idea. I always held myself to the highest ethical standards and now I am advising that you must do the same.

A Time to Dig

- You must be smarter than the next guy and you must be willing to outwork your opponent.

Once again it's time to share some personal experience with you. When I was doing my research in the field of oil filtration in the late 80's and early 90's there wasn't an Internet to speak of. At least there wasn't one that I was aware of, nor one that I had access to. In turn I did all of my research manually in various local libraries, using the Thomas Register® and other resource materials. I also traveled and used college libraries, including technical, as well as some of the best engineering libraries in my state. I joined scientific societies, and availed myself to many of those types of resources. I even went so far as enlisting the services of the National Laboratory Consortium of the United States of America and sought out their assistance. In my quest for information, I was in contact with some of the great field laboratories, such as Los Alamos, Belvedere Air Force Base and The Argon National Laboratory to name just a few.

The point is, I sought out the information vital to formulation of my patent. I scoured the planet for information. I did all of this digging, so that I could be sure of two things:

- First you need proof that your idea is rooted and grounded in reality and that your idea is viable. In a word, you need to assure yourself that your patent will do what you say it will do.
- Secondly, you need to know beyond any doubt, that your idea's market viability will be profitable enough for you to gain the interest of a potential licensing partner.

Let me point something out. You must become your harshest critic. You alone are responsible for setting the height of the bar that you must clear. In addition to that, you must do this long before you ever begin to file for a patent or contemplate hawking your idea to business or industry.

In that regard, *I spent years* trying to get the inside information regarding the size and the characteristics of my intended market. In my particular case, the information that I sought after was closely held by the oil filter companies and was not available to the general public. Yet through hard work and determination, I slowly but surely began to acquire the necessary bits and pieces of the information that I was seeking. Over time, I was able to put together a rather realistic picture of my intended market and as we move along I will show you how this actually occurred.

So keep this in mind during your research. Some of the information that I will be directing you to compile will be accessible, and some of it won't. Nonetheless with the advent of the Internet, it's still going to be so much easier for you to research any idea that you may come up with. There is an incredible proliferation of information right at your fingertips, so there isn't any excuse for not conducting the proper research.

Depending on your particular invention, you might have to dig like heck in order to find the necessary information that you need. Depending on how complex your idea is, you may not come up with too much information at all, simply because it might not be readily available in the *public domain.* If that's the case, you may only wind up with is an educated guess with regard to the information that you're seeking.

Yet don't let that stop your forward progress! Because if an educated guess is all that you can come up with, it's still far better than being clueless about the basis of your invention. Again, depending on what you are inventing, an educated guess might be all the information that you will have to go on in the early stages of development.

Just so you know, in early stages of my inventing phase, an educated guess was all the information that I had to go on. In my particular case I never stumbled upon the Holy Grail, nor was I lucky enough to have unlocked that one door capable of providing me with everything that I was looking for in one single and convenient source. So in my case, I had to conduct research in many areas to be able to obtain the necessary information that pertained to the materials that I wanted to employ in my product and the very same thing held true for the marketing data that I needed to justify entering into the marketplace as well.

- The key is, don't look for convenience and expect to dig.

This is what I'd like you to grasp. Over time I had acquired enough information along the way that permitted me to move forward with my idea. This in turn allowed me to fill in some of the blanks as I moved along. So depending on your invention, you may have to progress along in a similar fashion. Sometimes as inventors, things aren't always going to be perfectly spelled out for us; therefore, we must always forge ahead despite not having the luxury of acquiring all the pieces to the puzzle at the same time.

Just so you know, in my particular case, I was nearly always right and I'm not saying this to brag. Actually, I had done so much digging and investigation that it wasn't too terribly hard for me to justify nearly any of my conclusions when it came time for me to hawk my invention.

So what I'm telling you here is this; if you've done your research in an exhaustive manner and all you've got to go on is a strong feeling in your gut, …so be it. At least you'll know it's there as a result of all of your mental prospecting and not just some hair-brained scheme that you conjured up while lying on the couch watching television.

Conclusion. "Should you follow your gut instincts?" Sometimes. Both prospectors and inventors do when they're following a hunch. I know that I did. Sometimes you'll be magnificently right and sometimes you'll be dead wrong. Again, this is something that you might have to do at various points during your odyssey, so be prepared for it, because very few things in life are spelled out in black and white.

Keep It a Secret

- One of the first rules of protecting your idea is to keep it to yourself.

  Isn't that the exact opposite of what the *Voices* out there are advising?
  Some of the *Voices* are extending you an invitation to just email them your idea for a quick evaluation. That's yet another option for you, but as far as I'm concerned, that's just plain crazy, especially if your idea is potentially valuable.

  Now keeping a secret may sound simple enough, but you might want to ask yourself, "Are you good at keeping a secret?" Because the moment that you begin blabbing about your idea, a couple of things are going to inevitably happen to you.
- First. Someone else might claim, appropriate, abscond or steal your idea. They may either file a patent or bring it to market before you do. Then you'll be out of luck.
- Second. Human nature being what it is, you might run the risk of being talked out of your idea way before you ever get it off the ground.

If you think about it, we humans have a tendency to be skeptical and often times negative when it comes to embracing other people's creative ideas. The Wright Brothers and their magnificent flying machine comes to my mind right about now. At the time that the Wright Brothers were inventing their flying machine, the general public thought that human flight was crazy. Perhaps that's one of the reasons why the Wright Brothers conducted their flight experiments in relative secrecy in the sand dunes of costal North Carolina. You see, given enough time and exposure in a negative environment you too, can run the risk of being talked out of your idea before you ever get it going.

Does that sound familiar? Has something like that ever happened to you before in some other area of your life? If you're being honest with yourself, the answer is - of course! Well, inventing is no different than acting on a creative idea. Inventing starts in the heart, you may have thought it starts in the brain, but it really doesn't. So guard your heart!

Allow me to prove this to you. Have you ever had something so wonderful and so good happen; that you thought your heart was about to explode? Of course you have! And from where did that feeling of joy emanate? Well it sprang up from the center of your being, not your head. Check it out next time, and you'll see.

Anyway, when your idea arrives you might want to climb the nearest rooftop and tell the whole world about it. But when it comes to inventing, my advice is don't. You certainly can rejoice privately, but end it there.

Remember, it's going to be your decision who you will share your secret idea with, and with whom you won't. I realize that at some point you must confide in various people about your idea, but for now, it's best for you to be very secretive about your new idea. As the process moves along, I'll let you know how to properly disclose your idea.

At this point in the process, it's best to keep your secrecy level bordering on paranoia. Therefore, I want you to ratchet up your secrecy level to the point where you actually believe that one false move could result in having your idea robbed.

In reality this is quite true, because at this juncture, your idea is really nothing more than... well, an idea. The only thing protecting your idea at this moment is your secrecy. Think about it. Except for your prudent secrecy, there's no mechanism in place to protect your idea.

So allow me to interject a thought. After all, that I've just shared with you, why would you ever consider contacting a total stranger to evaluate your idea without being armed to the teeth? The answer is, if you're thinking clearly, you wouldn't.

Aside from that, *you* still have lots of soul searching to do. There's much work that lies ahead before it's even realistic to consider bothering someone else about your idea, because quite frankly, your idea might just be worthless. So let's find out.

Is It a Good Idea?

What does soul searching have to do with inventing anyway? Actually, quite a lot!

Just because *you think* that you might have a good idea, and you want to trumpet its merits, doesn't guarantee in any way, shape or form that it's patentable, marketable or valuable! My advice to you early on is to keep your enthusiasm level high, but keep your expectation levels metered, because we still have a few tests that we're obliged to take.

Let's first start off by being brutally honest about your idea. Simply put,

- Is your idea realistic?
- Will others rush out to buy it once it hits the market?

Do you have any idea how many people have approached me with the most ridiculous ideas that they *think* will make them rich?

Just so you know, in my all my years of inventing, there hasn't been one person who's ever approached me about an idea that has *ever* followed through with their idea to the point of either receiving a patent or having it produced for sale.

The reason for that is quite simple. To obtain a patent or to produce and market a saleable product requires two things:

- Follow-through. Gobs of it.
- Realistic concept.

With that in mind, let's consider the Wright Brothers once again. I want you to go back into the archives of your mind and replay the video clips of some of those early flying machines. Play back in your head all those wacky ideas of how people thought they could fly. Now compare those ideas to that of the Wright Brothers concept of a bi-plane design.

Well inventing in many ways is a lot like that. You have to be realistic about what you're inventing. So the next step in the process, is that you must be honest about the viability or the practicality of your idea. Then you must decide whether your idea merits pursuing or not, because it simply may not be worth pursuing at all.

Research

As you begin to research your idea, do it under a cloak of secrecy. Remember, at this stage secrecy is the rule. You don't want anybody to know about your idea, except perhaps your mate or your dearest friend. I'll leave that up for you to decide whom you might want to share your secret with. Later on you'll have plenty of time to bounce your idea off of other people, but for now, you're a long ways off.

Now would be the appropriate time to take a real hard look at your idea and see if it fits into our capitalistic markets and society. In plain terms,

- Can your idea be manufactured in a practical manner?
- Can it be marketed to a big enough audience?
- Are the profits going to be big enough for everybody involved in its manufacture and marketing to have a fair share of the profits?

As we explore this topic in much greater detail, I'll explain how the sharing of the profits works. For the time being, you must begin to ask yourself; is there anything like this presently on the market? And I don't mean for you to take a casual look, so that you can justify going forward with the project either. I want you to look as if your life depends on *finding* your idea out there. I want you to be able to discover a similar patent or a similar item that already exists somewhere out there, because if it does exist, you're at a crossroads and I'll explain to you why.

First of all, don't panic if you happen to find something similar to your idea out there, because in a way, that's a good thing! Keep in mind that presently in the real world there are not that many *stand-alone inventions*. And chances are, your idea isn't going to develop into a stand-alone invention either.

Once again, Thomas Edison comes to mind. It's a known fact that Edison invented the first incandescent light bulb. Prior to his invention, there was *never* an incandescent light bulb. There were both gas and oil fed lamps of all types, but these were all open flames and none of them utilized a metal filament. Besides that, there were certainly no sealed glass bulbs to speak of, and none of them were fed by electricity.

That should give you a good picture of what a stand-alone invention looks like. The Patent Office refers to those stand–alone inventions as *pioneer patents*. Which again, is a patent for an invention covering a function that has never been thought of before in its *class*; and therefore it's a wholly *novel device*.

The terms that apply here are not what's important; what's important is the concept.

The question is this. Has your idea ever been put forth in the history of mankind? The overwhelming odds are that *some variation* of your idea has already been thought of, patented or produced and utilized before. So please, don't get disheartened if some *form* of your invention has already appeared before.

As for me, I didn't invent oil filters. I didn't create the category of additive treated oil filters either. What I did, was to invent two very *novel and distinct* additive treated oil filters and their applications that were more advantageous than the previous applications documented in the *prior art*.

The key is, you may proceed with your *patent application* so long as your *exact idea* has not ever been exposed anywhere in the world before. That includes its use, its sale or its description in a published article.

The plain and simple fact is this. There haven't been many Thomas Edison's in the history of the world and there aren't many light bulbs being invented for the first time either. So you need not set your goals that unrealistically high.

Yet as we all know, even the light bulb has gone through untold variations over the last hundred years. As a matter of fact, we are all witnessing one of the greatest improvements the light bulb has ever undergone… the advent of LED's.

So here is perhaps something that you may not have considered before. All of those improvements that the light bulb has undergone can be referred to as inventions in their own right. Furthermore, many of those improvements put forth regarding the light bulb were patented improvements as well. Quite naturally, some of those patents were either more significant or more revolutionary than others. Hence some of those improvements have proved to be more valuable than others at any given time during its development.

Nonetheless, after the original creation of the light bulb, all patents that would be related to the original light bulb would fall into that category.

So let's agree, Thomas Edison invented the first incandescent light bulb and it is a fine example of what a stand-alone invention is. Any subsequent patent[s] granted for the light bulb would be classified as either a *utility or design patent* that would be based upon what Edison had initially invented.

As a result, all inventions both great and small, share something in common. Allow me to break it down for you further. In its most basic form, Edison's light bulb concept employed a metal filament that glowed white-hot. Furthermore, it was surrounded by a sealed glass container in the form of a bulb, which in turn gave off light generated by a revolutionary new power source that they called electricity.

Notice something here. All of these elements existed as either separate materials or natural occurring phenomena long before Edison's discovery. Yet he was the first person or *inventor* to have ever combined all of these various elements together for the first time, for the specific purpose of making light. He took all those various components and made both a useful and novel device out of them and he in turn invented the lightbulb.

By the way, that is one of the criteria that United States Patent and Trademark Office's employs for the granting of a patent.

- The invention put forth must be novel, useful and purposeful.

I hope you now understand what I meant, when I started out by saying, that there is nothing new under the sun. There are just new ideas and purposes for the materials that have already been produced by others, or raw materials created and placed here on this earth long before we arrived.

Thomas Edison didn't invent light and he didn't invent electric current. He didn't invent glass or the various metals that he employed in his light bulb either. Other people had discovered all of these raw materials and phenomena long before Edison dreamt of incorporating them into one fixture. However, it was to Edison's ingenious credit that he was able to take all of those materials and combine them in such as fashion as to produce a novel, useful and purposeful invention capable of producing light. Now that's inventing!

As just pointed out, patents are the purposeful combinations of materials that already exist. Now let's take a quantum leap forward. If by some miracle, you could create those materials out of nothing, which would be an extraordinary feat indeed; then you would be elevated to the level of Creator, and not just referred to as the inventor.

In any event, people still depend on the product that Edison gave birth to well over a century ago. And should you be fortunate enough to invent something that people are still using a century later that would certainly qualify your idea as a stand-alone invention as well.

So my advice to you is simple. Don't be concerned if you wind up at the crossroads, because *some version* your invention already happens to be out there. Because after Edison's *initial* invention of the incandescent light bulb, many inventors have come down the road and improved upon his light bulb and got rich!

I hope that it's become clear to you that you don't have to be an Edison to be a successful inventor. You are not obligated in any way to come up with a first time, stand-alone concept to qualify as an inventor either, because you don't and I certainly didn't either!

You will be in good company if your invention just happens to be significantly better, or significantly different than someone else's original idea. One of the secrets of a good patent is to come up with an improvement that is significant enough to draw a new wave of consumers to purchase your product. That's how you are going to profit from your idea. So for the time being, that's all you need to be shooting for.

Chapter 2

AN INVENTOR'S PRIMER

Part II

Marketing Trends

Begin to ask yourself the following questions:

- How much better is your idea than what's already out there?
- Is there room for your idea to compete against what's already available?
- Which way is the market going relative to your idea?
- How big is the market dollar volume-wise?
- How many units are sold annually in the USA?
- Who's buying this product?
- What is their social as well as their economic strata?
- What is their ethnic makeup and their income levels?
- How do you plan on getting your invention out there?

After you get your initial idea, you must begin to fine-tune it. Your first order of business during this evaluation stage is to address these questions pretty much in the order that I've just presented them to you. These questions will help enable you to get a handle on your ideas potential worth.

In order to do so more effectively, I want you to begin to view your idea as a tangible product or a widget. For those of you who might not be acquainted with the term; a *widget* is a *thingamajig* that you can touch and feel.

For some inventors you might be inventing a much-improved product or device. For others, you might be inventing an entirely new manufacturing process. And for yet others, you might be developing some new plant variety. In any case, begin to see your idea now as a material object.

The Patent Office breaks down patents into three separate types or categories:

- ➢ Anytime this symbol appears, it denotes a direct quote from the USPTO.
- ➢ **Utility** patents may be granted to anyone who invents or discovers any new and useful process, machine, article of manufacture, or composition of matter, or any new and useful improvement thereof.
- ➢ Utility patents are granted for 20 years in duration, then the protection expires.
- ➢ **Plant** patents may be granted to anyone who invents or discovers and asexually reproduces any distinct and new variety of plant.
- ➢ Plant patents are granted for 20 years in duration, then the protection expires.
- ➢ **Design** patents may be granted to anyone who invents a new, original, and ornamental design for an article of manufacture.
- ➢ Design patents last 14 years in duration, then the protection expires.

On June 8, 1995, utility and plant patents grants were extended from a 17 year grant to a 20-year grant. This applies extension applies beginning from the time in which that patent was granted and is subject to that patent being current with the appropriate maintenance fees.

The point is this; your idea must become real enough for you to begin work on it in earnest. If your idea does not become real, you simply will not work on it.

One of your primary objectives is to figure out which way the market is going. Is the demand growing or shrinking for your widget? You have to be aware of the market trends, because in all likelihood, it is going to take you *years* from the time in which you first get the idea, until such time that your product actually reaches the marketplace.

I liken the market trend for any particular invention to that of riding a giant wave. Try to conjure up a picture of a huge wave off on the horizon.

- Is the wave out there forming?
- Is the wave still building in size?
- Is the wave out there coming closer to the beach and about to crest?
- Is it beginning to break?
- Has the wave already broken?
- Is the wave beginning to lose its momentum?
- Has the wave already reached the beach and lost nearly all of its power?

Only you can judge where you happen to be on the marketing trend wave that you're attempting to ride. If the trend's wave for your idea is already dying out, I'm sorry to tell you, time will have already run out long before you'll ever get your product to market. So please, don't underestimate how long this patent process may take. You should know upfront that the patenting process at the very least will be measured in multiple years, and not months.

➢ Currently, the average patent application pendency is somewhere around 24 months. Applications received in the U.S. Patent and Trademark Office are numbered in sequential order and the applicant will be informed within eight weeks of the application number and official filing date if filed in paper. If filed electronically, the application number is available within minutes.

As a consequence, your research concerning which way your widgets trend wave will be developing must be calculated for the long term. And by long term, I want you to try and see out five years at the very least. However, looking ahead ten years is much more realistic.

I am not playing to your ego, but the cold reality of it is this, if you are truly going to be a successful inventor, then you'd better see what is coming up around the bend with regard to your invention's intended market. That simply means that as far as your invention is concerned, you had better be become somewhat of a *visionary.*

Here's a quick way to validate whether your idea is realistic or not. Go to the PTO's website and pull up some related patents in the field that you hope to capitalize upon. At this time don't be too concerned if you haven't fully formulated your idea yet, because you have to start somewhere. Pull up several patents and make a note of when they were applied for and when they were issued. Notice how long it took from the date the application was clocked in, and compare it to the date that the patent was finally granted. You will clearly see that the PTO will hold onto your application for years before it ever grants you a patent. I refer to this block of time as the *examination period.*

Keep in mind that the application date does not take into account the block of time that the inventor has spent perfecting his idea before filing. The time that it takes the inventor to develop his idea, prior to ever filing the patent application is something that I refer to as the *incubation period.* In many cases the incubation period can also be measured in years as well. The length of time required to do this will depend upon the complexity of the invention and the inventor's particular circumstances.

I don't want to get to far ahead of myself, but if you go back and re-read the last paragraph, I just told you that it can take years to fine-tune your idea before you might be ready to file for a patent. It is important to note that a *provisional patent application* expires in one years' time and then must be followed up by a *non-provisional patent application* for the exact same idea in order for your idea to be protected. Much more on this later, but I want to open your eyes early to the process.

Also, be mindful that it can take a considerable amount of time to get your product to market. Again in most cases, this could be measured in years as well. I happen to refer to this block of time as the *marketing period.*

Just so you know, this is how it went for me. My first patent had an incubation period of approximately a year and a half, and my second patent had an incubation period of about a year.

The PTO granted my first patent in only nine months and granted my second patent in fifteen months. Keep in mind the timeframe was in the late 80's and early 90's. Remember the information age is growing at an expediential rate and therefore the backlog at the PTO may continue to increase the amount of time that needs to examine the applications submitted.

After my second patent had been granted, it took me well over two years before I secured a licensing deal with AlliedSignal. It then took AlliedSignal and I working together nearly a year to develop the Double Guard and prepare it for a public launch.

All told, this process took me a good nine years, beginning from the time that I got my first idea, to the time that my product made its public debut in Walmart. From that point forward, my invention enjoyed a ten-year life cycle in the marketplace.

In no case can anyone who aspires to be published inventor and expects to profit from his or her idea, view this process as either being easy, or a quick way to get rich. So once again, most of what the *Voices* are selling you in this area is pure fantasy.

The inventor's time clock can be broken down into three distinct time periods:

- The incubation period.
- The patent examination period.
- The marketing period.

So if you have any aspirations of taking your idea to the next level, then you can count on investing a considerable amount of both time and energy to make this happen. Here's a general outline of what the inventing and patenting process looks like.

- First. The inventor must come up with a worthwhile and viable idea.
- Second. The inventor must subject his idea to a thorough an honest evaluation. If there is suitable proof that his or her exact idea has never been exposed anywhere in the world before, he/she can proceed to the next stage.

- Third. A rough draft of the inventions *claims* will be drafted.
- Fourth. The *summary of the invention* along with its claims will be *documented and memorialized* by the inventor.
- Fifth. The building of a suitable *prototype* of the invention will be undertaken. Although the PTO *does not* require prototypes, the inventor should embrace this process to prove to himself that his invention not only works, but that it can be manufactured in a real world environment.
- Sixth. A cost analysis should be performed to figure out what it will cost to produce the new product. At that time the inventor should try to get a handle on what manufacturing processes may be involved in the production of that product as well.
- Seventh. The patent application for the proposed invention enters the patent office's system and attains for the first time, the status of *patent pending*. Just so we're clear, when your patent application first arrives at the Patent Office and your application has been clocked in; it then enters the pending stage. A patent that is pending is *not* the same as a patent that has been granted!
- Eighth. After the inventor's patent application has proved to the satisfaction of the United States Patent and Trademark Office that his/her invention is unique, novel and purposeful *over* all the other similar US patents, which have previously been granted in his class, a patent is finally *granted*. With that grant, the inventor receives an *exclusive right* that restricts others from using it for a specific amount of time. For both Utility and Plant patents the grant is now twenty years. Design patents provide a coverage period of 14 years, not 20.

After all that has been accomplished, then and only then, can you unequivocally refer to yourself as a published inventor who has been granted a United States Patent! Believe me folks this is no small achievement, yet it's just the beginning of what it's all about.

As you can see, it's a marvelous progression to go from a wisp of an idea to a tangible widget. And it is even more impressive yet, to wind up with a US patent with all of its privileges.

You're the Visionary

As we begin to move forward, let's not lose sight of the basics.

- If your idea isn't practical, profitable, marketable, and timely, you'll just be spinning your wheels.

In plain terms, you must become a visionary when it comes to your widget and its intended marketplace. And from where I stand, only *your* personal research and *your* gut instincts can determine that. After all, this is *your idea* and not someone else's. You are the one who is going to be responsible for living with this idea and nurturing it. Nobody else, regardless of how hard they may try, will ever get as close to your idea as you can.

So my question to you is this. If you are planning on leaving the role of visionary up to someone else, such as an invention service or any number of other intermediaries, how are you ever going to become an expert in the field of your invention? This is yet another area where the *Voices* are selling you blue sky.

So you have to ask yourself,

- Who's going to be best suited to know where your widget fits in the universe called *the marketplace*?
- Who's going to make it?
- How simple, or how complex, is your widget going to be to manufacture?
- Who's going research how much it's going to cost to make your widget?
- Who's going to be able to market it for you?

Do you really think that a *stranger* is going to exert the same kind of effort to get their foot in the front door to market your widget? Based upon my experience, I don't believe that a total stranger can. I'm not saying that it's impossible, just improbable.

In the final analysis, who's going to be the *master salesman* with regard to the marketing of your widget? When it comes to inventing, being a visionary goes directly hand in hand with becoming a *master salesman.* And yes…, you will develop into a master salesman before this process is all over.

- So, will you produce your product in the USA?
- Or will you produce it overseas, or south of the border to save money?

Hint. If you're going to manufacture or market your product outside the US borders, it will have to be patented over there as well in order to protect it. If you don't, your widget will stand a good chance of being pirated to death before it ever gets off the ground.

So for the time being, it's a safe bet that the United States has a big enough market, and has enough buying power to make any inventor with a truly great idea wealthy beyond his wildest dreams. Going past our borders for the first time inventor will complicate matters tremendously. In addition to that, obtaining foreign patent rights will escalate your costs dramatically as well.

In my opinion, America is still the "Disney Land" of the world. Despite what the experts might be saying to the contrary, this country still remains the most coveted marketplace on the planet. So as a matter of course, the USA is going to be the marketplace that I'll be focusing on.

Just so you know, I never filed for foreign patent protection, for the aforementioned reason.

As you can see, these are just some of the many questions that you should begin to ask yourself as you prepare to launch out. I realize that since you haven't done any of this before, at face value these concepts may appear a bit basic, but don't let their simplicity lull you into a false sense of reality. Contrary to appearances, these are areas of paramount importance for you to consider, because they are going to become the foundation for all of your inventing. Just remember, if your idea isn't practicable, profitable, useful and truly novel… then you haven't got a thing.

Not Invented Here

While the mechanics of evaluating your product is still fresh in your mind, I would like to introduce a rather strange phenomenon that an inventor *could potentially* face once he/she has been granted a patent. For the most part this can occur in a marketplace that is entrenched in a specific technology and as a consequence, controls both its development and deployment.

Allow me to give you a personal illustration. During my marketing phase, I placed a phone call to the worldwide headquarters of Fram oil filters in East Providence, RI. Not only did I have to get my call past the switchboard operator, but I also had to know before ever placing the call where I wanted it to go. That in of itself is something to consider and I will explore this in much greater detail later on.

Based upon my prior experience, I knew that I needed to have my call directed to the marketing department, where hopefully, an *open-minded individual* would field my call. I was also keenly aware, that I would only be allowed a few precious moments to grab this person's interest or my call would miss its mark. This exercise is no different than clicking on a website and having it immediately grab your attention.

So if you're lucky and your call actually gets put through to the right department, you can only expect a brief moment to get your idea across. This is yet another reason why you must know your material inside and out and be able to present it with passion.

Again, appearances may be deceiving, because on the surface this process may appear way too simple, but take my word for it; there is a myriad of details and hours of preparation that go into making such a call. So it bears repeating, you *must* not only be a *visionary* to get this far in the process, but you darn well better become a *master salesman* if you have any hopes of selling your *patented invention* during a cold call.

So...how about reversing our roles for a moment? I'd like you to imagine what it would be like to make a phone call to the world leader in oil filtration and then present your concept to someone on the other end of the line who happens to know the oil filter marketing business from the inside out. The very idea of selling a stranger on the other end of a phone line a revolutionary concept during a cold call may sound crazy, but that's exactly what you're building up for.

So... was I nervous? Was I nearly terrified? Was the fear of failure nipping at my heels? Was this a do or die moment for me? *Of course it was!*

And when your moment arrives, you'll be going through that same gambit of feelings and emotions as well! This is my point; you must know your idea and be able to promote it on the level of a master salesman, because chances are, you'll only be getting one shot. If you fall short, you can count on the fact that the opportunity to make another fresh cold call will be lost forever. There are simply no do-over's when it comes to making a good first impression!

In the event that you fall short and blow your call, your only hope of moving forward is that you have more marketing leads to follow.

So why I am getting so far ahead of myself and spending time on this topic now? Because only a visionary with a burning desire to make his/her dream come true can effectively communicate the potential of a new idea to another person, especially when that person happens to be on the other end of a phone line.

Now let's complicate matters. What if the other person has a *closed mind* concerning your idea? Don't forget that's a very real possibility to consider.

Allow me to let you in on a little known secret. Business and industry in many cases are not necessarily looking for new ideas, and especially not yours!

So don't lose sight of the magnitude of the exercise at hand. The day will come when you'll be attempting to market your patented invention either over the phone or eye-to-eye with a total stranger. Depending on your particular invention, you might be trying to introduce your product to an industry representative that may not take too kindly to any new ideas that are born *outside* of their corporate ranks. Especially if it happens to be coming from an industry outsider like yourself! This barrier is known in the inventing trade as *not invented here* or *NIH*.

Whether or not you've ever heard of NIH doesn't really matter, because it exists in various forms. Later on, I will give you a vivid account of my personal dealings with NIH, but for now I want you to settle for a couple of good examples of how it works.

As consumers we are fed only what each particular industry wants to feed us. For example, Microsoft with its computer operating system is a perfect illustration of how a dominant manufacturer is able to spoon-feed their product[s] to the general public. That scenario has led many participants in that market to accuse them of conducting business in a monopolistic fashion and one only needs to look up how many anti-trust lawsuits Microsoft has been named a defendant in to see if there's any truth behind that observation.

If you need further convincing that NIH is real, then consider our gas guzzling automobiles. The price of crude oil is routinely over $100 a barrel. Consider the economic chaos that this situation has spawned on the American economy. This economic malaise has all been foisted upon an entire civilization, because newer and better fuel saving technologies have been barred from the automotive marketplace for decades now. The two offending monopolistic industries in this case is big oil in cahoots with the US automakers. Arguably, these two groups have intentionally kept the doors shut to new innovations created outside their domain, because it would threaten their business model. I mean their profit margins.

Just so you know, in my particular case, there were at best only five oil filter manufacturers of any note in the entire USA that I could potentially license my patents to. All of them were huge, experienced, monopolistic, and closed minded to product innovation in the oil filter market. As a general rule, they would never consider using an industry outsider's patent to base a new line of oil filters on. The possibility that they would ever take an outsider's idea and make a flagship product from it was particularly unthinkable. In fact, to my knowledge, it hadn't ever been done prior to my achievement.

What made my penetration into their marketplace such a big deal is the fact that what I invented fit into the category of what is known as the *original equipment manufacturer*, or *OEM*. This meant that my widget would have to be universal in its use. It would have to fit nearly every car model in operation, both old and new and it would have to be totally interchangeable with the oil filter that originally came with the car. All told, thirty-two separate filter models had to be manufactured to accommodate this market.

In addition to that, because it fell under the OEM parts classification, my product would have to be warrantied against any product malfunction or engine damage that could occur as a result of its use. It was truly a very significant achievement for someone outside of such a rigid industry to be able to go out and sell an OEM class invention to a tier-one automotive supplier such as Honeywell!

I just shared all of this with you, because I want to make it clear that there is so much to know about the art of *your* sale. As a result of my personal experience, I cannot for the life of me fathom how some intermediary representing you can waltz your idea right through all those impediments, just because their commercial or promotional materials says they can.

So from my vantage point, you need to begin getting comfortable with the fact that you're going to become the visionary where your invention is concerned. One of the surest ways to do this is by conducting your own extensive research on what you are inventing. Once you become an expert about your widget, you'll be able to defend your idea based upon the facts that you have gathered, and not based upon someone else's preconceived ideas of what your invention is.

The only other way that I know of achieving success in the inventing field is for you to latch-on to some expert who is willing to mentor you along the way concerning your widget. And since that isn't very realistic, be prepared to be self-taught about your invention and its intended marketplace.

So understand, becoming a *visionary* and *a master salesman* during this process isn't something that you're going to learn overnight. It only comes as a result of living with your *dream* for quite some time.

Just so you know, this is one of the only areas where being a self-taught inventor is a good thing.

Right about now, you may be wondering, how am I supposed to be able to accomplish all of this? My answer is simple. Did anyone teach you how to breathe? Of course not!

Well inventing is a lot like breathing. Once you begin to eat, sleep and drink this idea of yours, and once you begin to obsess over it, you'll have no worries. As the odyssey progresses, you'll grow into the roles of both the visionary and the master salesman. It just happens.

In case you might be wondering where all this self-actualization fits in, let me just say that you'll need to become all of this and more as a prerequisite for filing a proper patent application.

To recap,

- Identify the market and see where your product fits in.
- Evaluate your costs of production.
- Evaluate your products potential profit margin.
- Most importantly, what segment of the population is going to buy your widget once it becomes available for sale?
- How long do you expect your inventions market trend to last?
- Can you envision on the time-horizon, that your market will be there and ready to embrace your idea some three to five years down the road?

As a result of *living your invention*, you will gradually become an expert on your widget. This will enable you to lead your team forward with regard to both the patenting and licensing process.

You heard me correctly. There is going to be a *team* that is going to come together during the latter part of this process and at the appropriate time, you will assume the role as the team leader. It's all very exciting!

Again, right about now you might be saying to yourself. I never dreamt that inventing would require that I become both an expert and a master salesman? And as far as becoming a visionary and a team leader, I never contemplated that either. After all, I'm no Edison!

That's quite all right. You see early on, I'm sure that Mr. Edison didn't know that he was all of those things either. Not by any stretch of the imagination did he ever see it! Yet over time Edison grew into his role of inventor. Subsequently, so have the millions of other people who've since followed in his footsteps. I know that I did, and that's why I am passing this information on to you.

Soften the Blow

The last thing I want to do is to discourage your efforts at becoming an inventor, so what I have to say regarding NIH is exceedingly important. NIH is prevalent and very real *the more technically advanced* your idea is and the more technically entrenched that industry happens to be when it comes to conducting business the way that it always has. Unfortunately, the ground rules for entry in this environment tend to be the toughest here. That isn't to say you shouldn't take a run at the roses, because you darn well should. I did and I succeeded in a very big way.

Trust me, a valuable idea is often a once in a lifetime occurrence and accordingly, you should play the hand that you've been dealt, because if you want it bad enough you can make it happen.

On the other hand, if your idea is a *soft sell* like toys, cookware, hardware, fashion or everyday consumables such as the many little devices that make life easier and more convenient for the general population, well that's an inventor's dream come true and you should definitely go for it with both barrels!

So my advice for you is this. Just relax and take in everything that I'm sharing with you.

No matter what your idea is, I have a feeling that inventing might just be the missing piece of the puzzle that you've been seeking and perhaps inventing might just be that special something that you've never been able to quite identify with until this moment. I truly hope that's the case.

If it's in your genes to become an inventor, then I encourage you to sit back and enjoy the ride. Given enough information and encouragement you'll certainly rise to the occasion and do whatever is required in order for you to succeed. In my opinion, inventing is a terrific and an exciting journey and there are few experiences like it in all of life, so savor it! If you really have a good idea coupled with the potential to make a lot of money, there are few things in our mortal world that can propel you forward like your dream!

It's Your Dream so Live It!

Believe me when I tell you, that after a while your inventor's journey is going to possess you. And when it does, it's going to burst forth as your *dream*!

"Oh my God," you might be saying! "So that's what has been rattling around on the inside of me." I would have to say, *yes!* It's been your dream all along and you probably didn't even know it, because realistic people aren't supposed to indulge in their dreams. But I am going to tell you otherwise. Dream and learn how to dream big!

Look back with me for a moment and notice how this all began to take shape. In the beginning, it all started off as a wisp of an idea. And now look at it! It's morphed into a material widget that's on its way to fitting into a market trend that's building right before your very eyes! A market trend that you just know is eagerly awaiting the arrival of you and your patented product. Over time the inventing process and its possibilities will begin to possess you and before you know it, you'll have been divinely overtaken! This is truly one of the ways that dreams are born! Isn't that fantastic?

Ask yourself a couple of questions. How many people do you know that actually have a dream? I mean a realistic dream! How many people have the privilege of pursuing a dream where they could feasibly make a significant sum of money in an honest way? Not too many, right?

Maybe now you can begin to fathom what motivated me to file a lawsuit against Honeywell in Federal Court as a Pro Se plaintiff without having one ounce of legal training.

All I can say to you is that they stole my dream and I wasn't going to let them get away with it… at least not without a proper fight.

Here's the lesson. The process of becoming an inventor will be much more empowering and meaningful if you will allow this wonderful pursuit to become *your dream.*

Just so you know, I dreamt of becoming an inventor and now so must you.

The key is to have a real dream, and to let it possess you. Inventing is as close to the purest form of empowerment that I know of. My hope is that sometime in the not too distant future, you too will be able to look back and see how your kernel of an idea has matured into a concrete and tangible invention that is worth a lot of money.

Now let's step down from the clouds for just a moment and take a look at the flip side of this coin, because the last thing I want to encourage is any self-delusion.

Just because your idea has become your dream, it does in no way guarantee your success. Let me make this crystal clear to you. Just because you have a dream about an invention does not in any way guarantee that you will obtain a patent, or make one thin dime off of it. But like I said, being propelled by your dream if it's realistic… does indeed help!

If your dream is realistic, then in large measure it's going to be your dream that will become the rocket fuel that will propel you ever forward during this odyssey. Your dream will put you in a position where you won't take *no* for an answer, especially when you know deep down inside that you are right.

Just so you know, there will be many "no's" that you will have to face along the way and personally, I faced a ton of them.

You are about to embark on a journey where quitting can never be an option, a journey that will offer you many opportunities to throw in the towel and quit. However, the type of success that you are looking for will not allow for that!

The fear of failure will taunt you incessantly, and you'll have to beat back those fears constantly, because every step forward will be yet another step into the unknown. That's just something you are going to have to master over time, and believe me you will. The purpose behind this teaching is to remove as much of the unknown as I can for you.

I know of only one thing strong enough to accomplish all of this and it can be summed up in a word… *faith.* As an inventor you must have faith in yourself and faith in your dream. And personally speaking, I placed a great deal of faith in God to get me through all of it.

I hope that you'll consider what I'm trying to communicate here, because in the final analysis, it will be the faith that you place in your dream and in yourself that will supply the courage necessary to take on this marathon of Olympic proportions. So as we begin to prepare for the next level, I suggest that you bring that dream along with you, because I know that you'll be needing it. In the end, if you've been realistic and diligent, there's no earthly reason why you cannot succeed at the inventing game.

Chapter 3

CLAIM IT

Intellectual Property Formation

Intellectual property is an idea or a concept that has its origins in the mind or the intellect of an individual. If those ideas are original to that individual, they have the power to make that person the inventor of that given idea. See 35 USC §115

However, it is important to note, that before an idea can be considered to be someone's *intellectual property*, that person must first comply with the various legal protocols in order to formally document their *property of the mind.* There are several means for an individual to publicly document his intellectual property. They are *patents, trademarks* and *copyrights,* which are all governed by the USPTO.

In addition to that, there are *trade secrets* that are also considered to be intellectual property and are protected under the law as well. However, trade secrets are not formally registered with the PTO like patents, trademarks and copyrights are. The way in which trade secrets derive their protection under the law is totally different. They are governed under the *Uniform Trade Secret Act.* To date, 47 states participate under this act including the District of Columbia and Puerto Rico. As for the three states that have not adopted this universal code, they are still governed by their respective state statutes that govern the protection of trade secrets.

In 2014, Massachusetts has introduced a bill to join the 47 other participating states. At this point, only the states of North Carolina and New York haven't put forth bills to participate under Uniform Trade Secret Act.

See www.Uniformlaws.org/Act.aspx?title=Trade+Secrets+Act

Trade secrets can be protected by either one of two ways. The first way, is for the owner of the trade secret to keep both the details and the corresponding applications a closely held secret. Therefore, whether it's the formula for a product such a Coke®, or a special manufacturing process to make the heat resistant tiles on the space shuttle, the details are kept *proprietary.* The word proprietary means the same thing a *closely held secret.*

The second way, is for the owner to enter into a *confidentiality agreement* with the receiving party regarding the use of those trade secrets. The *receiving party* in this case might be a manufacturer who for example is allowed to use those trade secrets during a specific manufacturing process. At any rate, the *furnishing party* is the inventor. And that inventor would enter into a *secrecy agreement* with the receiving party who in this case would be the manufacturer. The key to this exchange is that both parties expect to receive a benefit from sharing the trade secrets in the form of shared profits. The profits that would be generated would directly be attributed to the *competitive edge* that the trade secret information would provide to the manufacturer and the holder of the trade secrets.

- Intellectual property is a made up of creative works or ideas that must be embodied in a form that can be shared or can enable others to recreate, emulate, or manufacture them.

As we progress further, I will be covering the various other forms of intellectual property, as well as the kinds of protection that they can afford the inventor.

- The truth is, protecting your intellectual property rights by means of just obtaining a patent is not nearly as straightforward as some of the *Voices* would have you believe.

Throughout the rest of this teaching I will frequently be using the term *intellectual property* and I will often times abbreviate it as *IP*. Aside from that, it is very important for you to understand that *all* of your *thoughts* and *ideas* relating to your invention will fall under the broad category of IP.

However, it's vital that you understand that not all of your IP will end up being neatly encapsulated in your patent and here's why:

- First of all, your patent can only hold so much information regarding your invention.
- Secondly, your patent is not going to contain everything that you have learned about your invention.
- Thirdly, patents purposely do not spell out in explicit detail how to produce the covered invention.
- Patents are built upon the claims, and it is those claims that make your patent novel over all of the patents granted before it.
- Most notably, the trade secrets embody the means by which the patented invention can be produced; the patent itself does not necessarily instruct how the covered invention can be produced.
- Last but not least, the process of inventing is *fluid* and not *static*. Simply put, new information is generated all the time.

As soon as you think that your invention may be in its final form, invariably you will come up with yet another improvement of one sort or another. Whether it be for its design, its manufacture or its raw materials.

Therefore, this information whether it be an overflow of ideas, secret processes or materials, is referred to as your *trade secrets*. Since your trade secrets cannot be tied up in a neat little package like your patent claims can, they will require extra special care for their protection. Because of their nature, these trade secrets must be well documented and kept a strict secret. The only time that an inventor would ever divulge his trade secrets to anyone would be under the protection of either one of the following:

- Non-Disclosure Agreement — *NDA*
- Confidentiality Agreement — *CA*
- Trade Secret Agreement — *TSA*
- Proprietary Information Agreement — *PIA*
- Test Marketing Agreement — *TMA*

I will explore the scope of these agreements as we progress forward. At that time, I will basically tell you everything that you might need to know about them.

Keep in mind that central to the debate is that one person is claiming over all others, that a specific concept has originated in his mind, and not in the mind of someone else. Therefore, the inventor of that idea wants to be granted exclusive control over that idea or concept and bar all others from using it. This is done so that the holder or the owner of these ideas can gain a competitive advantage over their competitors in the marketplace. This pertains to both patents and trade secrets equally.

As you can imagine, there is a lot at stake here.

Document Your Ideas

We have already established that inventors must devote considerable amounts of both time and energy to insure that their inventions are viable. Therefore, it's not inconceivable that an inventor could easily become lost in those pursuits and put aside documenting his inventing activities. Since many inventors may not be aware of how important documenting is with regard to both the formation and preservation of their intellectual property, they may not put forth the required effort to do so.

It is of the utmost importance for all inventors to record all their inventive thoughts and ideas. Strong documentation will do two things:

- First. It will enable you to better *formulate* your ideas, because putting your ideas down on paper has a way of making them come alive.
- Second. By putting your ideas down on paper you will develop a record. A written or a recorded record is one of the most valuable assets that an inventor has to substantiate his or her ownership of an idea.

The simple truth is that sometimes an inventor can get too caught up in his dreams and disregard the possibility that an *intellectual property lawsuit* might be lurking around the corner one day far into the future. This can especially hold true if the inventor has developed something valuable, because *only valuable ideas get attacked, not worthless ones!*

One of the key elements that will assist you in repelling such an onslaught will be strong documentation. Perhaps you've never thought about inventing in quite this way before, but if you plan on inventing something valuable, you should begin to adopt the practice of documenting.

Just so you know, I was oftentimes lost in the pursuits of gathering information and working on the practical aspects of my inventions. As a result of focusing so intensely on the viability aspect of my invention, I didn't document my inventing activities nearly to the degree that I should have. When I was actively engaged in the process of inventing, the mere thought that I would wind up having my intellectual property stolen right out from underneath me by my licensing partner one day was inconceivable. So to be honest with you, I never prepared for that eventuality like I should have! Therefore, keep in mind that the individual who becomes a successful inventor these days will not achieve this status by mere accident. Becoming a successful inventor will happen on purpose. It will be the result of following a carefully executed plan that consists of a set of well thought-out and calculated set of activities. Chief amongst them is strong documentation. Strong documentation will be your best insurance against a highly contentious intellectual property lawsuit that may not rear its ugly head, until years on down the road. Our goal is that you do everything right from the very beginning, so that an attack on your IP *might* be repelled or avoided altogether.

My goal is to make sure that you protect yourself today, for a battle that could pop up years after your patent gets granted. Or in my case, after you have entered into a licensing agreement.

This simple analogy will illustrate why the basic mechanics of inventing should not be ignored. Let's take your health for example. Specifically, let's talk about maintaining a healthy heart. When the American Heart Association says that you *can* suffer a heart attack during your lifetime, they aren't saying that you are personally guaranteed to suffer a heart attack. What they *are* saying is that if you do not engage in a heart-healthy lifestyle, you'll be increasing your chances of having a heart attack at some point during your lifetime.

The point is, the possibility of a heart attack is real for every one of us. However, if an individual chooses to take some basic precautionary measures along the way, a heart attack in many cases can be avoided all together. To me, that sounds like straightforward advice and not a scare tactic.

Likewise, throughout this instruction what I'll be sharing with you will be analogous to maintaining your heart's health. An intellectual property lawsuit isn't necessarily waiting for you at the end of your inventor's odyssey, just because you have invented something valuable!

However, if you don't take some basic precautionary measures as you journey along, the probability that your intellectual property may suffer an attack of some sort will increase dramatically. And that's not a scare tactic either, it's just a fact.

Disclaimer. In the terrible event that you do suffer an attack, you will be in a far better position to repel the interloper, provided that you have systematically documented everything that you have invented.

As the saying goes, "if you fail to plan, you plan to fail."

An Inventor's Notebook is Critical

So how should we go about the process of documenting our inventing activities?

Start out by recording your idea in an *Inventor's Notebook* and by keeping it handy. From now on, I want you to record all of your inventing activities; beginning from the very moment that idea enters your mind.

- An Inventor's notebook is a conventional, witnessed, permanently bound, and page-numbered laboratory notebook or notarized records as evidence of conception of an invention. This method should provide a more credible form of evidence than that provided by the mailing of a disclosure to oneself or another person by registered mail.

As you can see, the best method for recording your idea is by using a notebook with numbered pages that cannot be easily tampered with and by having your formalized idea duly notarized. These notebooks are available for purchase on the internet if you're so inclined, however any notebook configuration will do just fine.

Consistency and discipline are the keys to success here, and not what style of notebook you are using. Unfortunately, many people might have a tendency to be gun-ho in the very beginning, and then soon slack off and document almost nothing. A little friendly warning; don't get lazy or sloppy with your notebook, because down the road it has the potential of becoming one of your best friends.

Every time you do something on your invention, summarize what you did. Record the date and time, names and places. You don't have to rewrite "War and Peace", but good solid bullet points will do just fine.

When you inquire about information, record it. When you receive materials regarding your invention, record those activities and put those materials away for safe keeping. That includes the packaging and the envelopes that the materials arrived in. You never know, but someday those postage marks on the various envelopes and packages that you've been putting away might come to your rescue.

When mailing things out, make it a practice to use Certified Mail, return receipt requested by the US Post Office. Whatever shipping service you may choose, be sure to get a delivery confirmation slip that can prove that the party on the other end has received your correspondence.

If you send and receive emails, print them out and record them along with any responses that you may receive. It's a very good practice to immediately print out every email and file them.

If you cannot bear the thought of writing by hand, because the keyboards and the keypads in your life have taken you over, I understand. So if you must, use a word processor and keep a journal that way. But the same rules apply! Make sure that you document your work product and get your original idea notarized. Just remember to back up your notebook and burn backup disks regularly.

In the event that you should happen to upgrade your computer by purchasing a new one, or in the case that you replace your hard drive for any reason, store your old hard drive by keeping it in a safe place. Be mindful that your hard drive and your original entries will now be looked upon as the physical notebook. Should you ever get embroiled in litigation, there is a good possibility that your hard drive will be gone over by a highly trained professional. So keep your entries in their original form and do not go back and rewrite over them. Just write another entry as if you were using a pen and pad.

Just so you know, I would prefer that you journal in a notebook, because it is so much more concise and will eliminate all this extra confusion with regard to when each entry was actually created.

The best court fights take place over what's been written down on paper, so take a hint.

Look my friend; from now on begin to view your inventing activities as if you were a miner prospecting for gold and about to stake a claim of a lifetime. At this point in time, I want you to act like your idea is the gold that is still hidden below the ground and has yet to be mined by anyone. And for now that includes you as well, because you've yet to officially receive any patent protection.

Therefore, your idea has to be carefully guarded if it has any chance of making you any money. During the inventing process you must stake your claim, which means that *you must get there first.* One of the major ways of accomplishing this is by accurately documenting your invention along the way in your inventor's notebook and by getting your *formalized idea* notarized.

For example, a miner first scouts a piece of ground to see if it's even worth prospecting. Then if he believes that the ground will produce enough gold to make him rich, he runs to the claim office and files his claim.

- As an inventor, you must do the same thing by researching your idea and making sure that your invention is viable.
- As an inventor, you must identify the market trends and make sure that your invention is in synch with the present market trends.
- A miner then runs to the local claim office to stake or record his claim. You must do the same thing.
- First. By recording a detailed description of your formalized idea in your inventor's notebook.
- Second. By getting your formalized idea notarized.
- Third. By filing a formal patent application with the USPTO.

You must do that, in addition to documenting every bit of your inventing activities as you journey along through the entire inventing process.

After the miner has gone to the government's claim office and has officially filed his claim for a specific piece of ground, he then returns to that piece of ground and drives stakes around the perimeter of his claim. He does this in order to tell others that this particular claim belongs to him and that others should stay out.

You must do the same thing concerning your invention. You do this by filing a patent application with the United States Patent and Trademark Office and by furnishing them with the appropriate details and the particular claims that you are making about your invention. In effect, you will begin the process of telling others that this invention is yours. At this point you've begun the process of telling the world that this invention belongs to you and that nobody can use this invention unless they receive your expressed permission to do so.

The miner has a gun loaded with bullets, which will enable him to defend his claim against all-comers.

Likewise, you as an inventor must not only have your patent application on file with the PTO, but you must also have a well-documented inventor's notebook in your possession as well.

Look at it this way. The patent application is the gun, and the inventor's notebook provides the bullets to that gun. Without an inventor's notebook you will have a gun, but you will lack the necessary bullets to fire at any would-be thieves should the situation arise. In my personal experience, having patent without having a solid inventor's notebook is the beginning of a fool's errand.

Building an inventor's notebook is the very foundation of where it all begins. And here is where the attention to detail will be your best friend should a challenge to your patent's origin or its validity ever arise. This also includes your trade secrets and your IP portfolio as well.

First and True Inventor

At this time, it is appropriate that I direct you to the United States Code. The US Code is the body of law, which contains the Federal Statutes or the laws of our land. The US Code is the body of law that governs patents, trademarks and copyrights. As inventors we want to specifically focus on the statutes that will govern both patents and trademarks.

The following provides the legal definitions taken word for word from the federal law, which governs the sanctioning of patents. In legal terms, this is what I meant before about claiming your idea. And in case you might be wondering, this is the standard that's used by both the Federal Judiciary and Patent Office regarding patents.

It is in your best interest to become acquainted with these definitions and begin to understand what they are telling you. I highly suggest that at some point early on, you print them out from the web site and keep them as a handy reminder of what you are supposed to be doing.

The following is taken nearly word for word from Cornell Law School's website, which happens to be one of many sites that posts the U.S. Code.

USC Title 35 Part II Chapter 11 §115 & 116 refers to authorship and ownership of an invention.

[§ is a symbol for section]

- §115Oath of applicant

  The applicant shall make oath that he believes himself to be the original and first inventor of the process, machine, manufacture, or composition of matter, or improvement thereof, for which he solicits a patent; and shall state of what country he is a citizen.

  Authors note. When you make your patent application there will be an affidavit that you will need to sign and truthfully swear that you are the first and true inventor. If some other person is collaborating with you on the patent, then the idea is not 100% yours. In which case §116 will pertain to you. If that's the case, then you and the person whom you are collaborating with must file for the patent jointly. *Authentication of one's idea begins with the oath that you declare that you are the first and true inventor.*

- §116 Inventors

  When two or more persons make an invention jointly, they shall apply for patent jointly and each makes the required oath, except as otherwise provided in this title. Inventors may apply for a patent jointly even though:

  they did not physically work together or at the same time,

  each did not make the same type or amount of contribution, or

  each did not make a contribution to the subject matter of every claim of the patent.

  If a joint inventor refuses to join in an application for patent or cannot be found or reached after diligent effort, the application may be made by the other inventor on behalf of himself and the omitted inventor.

- §100 Definitions

  The following is how the U.S. Code defines Definitions:

  USC Title 35 Part 2 Chapter 10 §100

  Section 100 Definitions

  When used in this title, unless the context otherwise indicates-

  The term "invention" means invention or discovery.

  The term "process" means process, art or method, and includes a new use of a known process, machine, manufacture, composition of matter, or material.

- §101 Patentable

  The following is how the U.S. Code defines Patentable:

  USC Title 35 Part 2 Chapter 10 §101

Section 101 Inventions patentable

Whoever invents or discovers any new and useful process, machine, manufacture, or composition of matter, or any new and useful improvement thereof, may obtain a patent therefore, subject to the conditions and requirements of this title.

- §102 Conditions for patentability; novelty and loss of right to patent.

The following is how the U.S. Code defines Conditions for patentability; novelty and loss of right to patent:

USC Title 35 Part 2 Chapter 10 §102

§102 Conditions for patentability; novelty and loss of right to patent.

A person shall be entitled to a patent unless-

(a) the invention was known or used by others in this country, or patented or described in a printed publication in this or a foreign country, before the invention thereof by the applicant for patent, or

(b) the invention was patented or described in a printed publication in this or a foreign country or in public use or on sale in this country, more than one year prior to the date of the application for patent in the United States, or

(c) he has abandoned the invention, or

(d) the invention was first patented or caused to be patented, or was the subject of an inventor's certificate, by the applicant or his legal representatives or assigns in a foreign country prior to the date of the application for patent in this country on an application for patent or inventor's certificate filed more than twelve months before the filing of the application in the United States, or

(e) the invention was described in

1- an application for patent, published under section 122 (b), by another filed in the United States before the invention by the applicant for patent or

2- a patent granted on an application for patent by another filed in the United States before the invention by the applicant for patent, except that an international application filed under the treaty defined in section 351 (a) shall have the effects for the purposes of this subsection of an application filed in the United States only if the international application designated the United States and was published under Article 21(2) of such treaty in the English language;[1] or

(f) he did not himself invent the subject matter sought to be patented, or

(g) 1- during the course of an interference conducted under section 135 or section 291, another inventor involved therein establishes, to the extent permitted in section 104, that before such person's invention thereof the invention was made by such other inventor and not abandoned, suppressed, or concealed, or

2- before such person's invention thereof, the invention was made in this country by another inventor who had not abandoned, suppressed, or concealed it. In determining priority of invention under this subsection, there shall be considered not only the respective dates of conception and reduction to practice of the invention, but also the reasonable diligence of one who was first to conceive and last to reduce to practice, from a time prior to conception by the other.

I cannot stress enough, how important these definitions are. You should treat these statutes as the bedrock of your inventing process. Besides, it doesn't take a rocket scientist to understand their meaning.

Just so you know, when I had set sail on my inventing journey, I hadn't a clue as to what I had just showed you. The reason was simple. There wasn't an Internet that would enable me to instantaneously look them up. So in order for me to know about this stuff, I needed to locate either the proper law books or find a law library to search these things out. Besides, I was inventing and didn't realize the impact that these laws would play in my endeavors. However, when I finally got wind of what Honeywell was doing behind my back, this was one of the first places I went to in order to get clarification on what was actually happening to me from a legal standpoint.

Now might be a goodtime to see if the *Voices* out there are mentioning anything about the application of the law with regard to inventing?

As a consequence of my lack of knowledge, I wasn't aware of the big picture.

- It is one thing to come up with a great idea.
- It is quite another thing to be able to put it in the proper form.
- It is yet quite another thing to be able to hold on to your idea and keep it for your own.

Knowing the law is one of the best tools that you have at your disposal. So please, don't just gloss over this stuff and view it as just some legal mumbo jumbo, because it's not! These statutes are the rules of the game, whether you agree with them or not. Again, I would highly recommend that you explore Chapter 35 in its entirety if you're *even considering* inventing at this time.

There are many reasons why I am suggesting that you become familiar with Chapter 35 of the US Code. For instance, in the unfortunate event that the validity of your patent was ever challenged, or in the event that someone else infringed on your patent, one of the greatest battles that will ever be waged over your patent will be; *who got the idea first!* And that's despite the fact that the Patent Office rules have now changed to *who files first is awarded the patent*. As an inventor who's been attacked, it is going to be your burden to prove a few essential things:

- That you got the idea first and that your notebook can prove it.
- That your patent application date with the USPTO can prove that you filed it first as well.
- That your patent claims are not ruled *invalid as obvious*. This means that one or more of the inventors cited in the prior art *could have anticipated* your present claims during the construction of their patent claims.
- That your trade secrets are the product of your intellect and therefore have originated with you.

It's in your best interest to build an airtight case that will support your inventorship well in advance of you ever needing it. Be aware that any party that attacks either your patent or your trade secrets will immediately and intentionally try to bury a judge with minutia in order to cover up their crime. So remember, understanding these facts will serve you well, should your licensing partner decide to do to you, what Honeywell did to me.

Therefore, I want you to forget about the concepts of "innocence before being proven guilty" or "the defendant has the burden of proof." Or the plaintiff [which will be you], "should be viewed in the most favorable light by the court." Trust me, depending on your judge and the circumstances that you may wind up facing, these legal concepts may not necessarily apply so neatly.

In the event that the patent game turns ugly, your hard drive may be gone over with a fine-tooth comb. It's also not out of the question that ink and handwriting specialists may be called in to examine your notebook as well. Therefore, any alterations that you make to your data during the fury of litigation could certainly be turned against you, and make you out to be the liar!

This tactical move by your adversary will have the effect of taking the pressure off of the real thief, and turn the spotlight of accusation on you.

A friendly warning; if there is enough money at stake, the sky is the limit as to what could actually occur during an intellectual property battle. Just be mindful that the bigger the adversary, the more millions they will be able to throw at you. I calculate that Honeywell spent on the order of 5 million dollars defending themselves against me.

My advice is this, be thorough all the way through the process, and you won't be prone to give into temptation to stretch the truth at any point..., even under pressure. So let paranoia be your guide during the dotting of the I's and the crossing of the T's in your journal. It will serve you well later on.

In the spirit of being an honest instructor, I would like to share what my particular strengths and weaknesses were in this particular department. So before going any further I want to tell you that I wasn't really aware of the importance of keeping an inventor's journal. Oh I knew about having an inventor's journal, but I glossed over its immense importance.

Just so you know, the notes that I kept were in the form of handwritten drafts and revisions of my patents. This is because I pretty much wrote my own patents in book form on yellow legal pads. I have to say that the paper trail that I generated certainly did help me. Perhaps by dumb luck, many of my handwritten drafts contained my claims as well as other important evidentiary facts that pertained to my invention. However, what I had in my possession was a far cry from the inventor's notebook that I'm urging you to develop.

Here's a key. Save every scrap and every botched entry. Do not discard any thought that you have put to paper. You may never know until way later how immensely valuable your written thoughts regarding your invention might be. Again, I want to stress the value of good organization.

Just so you know, now that I'm in the position to know better, my inventor's notebook wasn't up to par. The fact is, my inventor's notebook was pretty sketchy at best. During my life, I had never been inclined to keep a journal or a diary. There was only one time that I was ever forced to keep a diary, and that was for a college psychology class. I can still remember how much of drudgery it was for me to keep it current. I guess that lack of desire to document my activities spilled over into my inventing world as well. The fact is, I never kept what I would classify as a proper inventor's notebook by my present day standards. To be sure, that was one important weapon that my arsenal was missing!

But to be fair, I have to laugh as I share this with you. During the lawsuit Honeywell's inventor's notebook's had to be turned over to me during the discovery period for my analysis and inspection. And I have to tell you, their notebooks were even more pathetic, and their entries were virtually non-existent. Oh they introduced a few feeble pages during *discovery*, but that was hardly what you would expect from an engineering powerhouse that can lay claim to tens and tens of thousands patents. And any subsequent claims to the ownership of the IP was clearly lacking.

Here is yet another key, for all you backyard inventors. Perceptions are very important! Especially if someday you find it necessary to institute a lawsuit against some industrial behemoth and accuse them of stealing your intellectual property. In Honeywell's case, being a Fortune 38 company and having a war chest brimming with unlimited millions of dollars to throw at any legal contest had a magical way of making their behavior look way more proper than it was. And their persona of being the "gleaming city on the hill" translated all the way down to their pathetic inventor's notebook and the judge's perception of this case.

Just so you know, I was put through hell to prove that I got there first and that they stole my IP; including, but not limited to my trade secrets. Honeywell was in blatant violation of 35 USC 115&116, our NDA's and our licensing agreement. My original complaint filed with the court accused them of patent infringement, breach of contract, unjust enrichment, fraud in the inducement, tortious interference with advantageous business relationships and misappropriation of trade secrets amongst other things.

Here's my point. I have only God to thank, because somehow I managed to save every envelope with their postmarks, since I really didn't know exactly why I was doing it. Let me tell you that *did* help establish my time line of who got there first. In addition to that, I saved every letter and correspondence and that helped me immensely as well. Like I told you, good documentation is similar to a miner staking his claim and it will establish who gets there first.

I am a fanatic for certified mail and always have been. Maybe it's because as a teenager when I was applying to colleges my father had drummed it into my head that if I ever needed to mail something important, I should use certified mail; return receipt requested. According to my dad who was a mailman, it was the only piece of mail that the Post Office never loses. So during my inventing odyssey I used certified mail whenever necessary. This also helped me establish my case of who got there first. By the way, it wouldn't hurt to take a tip from the lawyers; they are big fans of certified mail as well.

Another plus for me was memorializing my invention with a notary of the public. This bit of documentation was so foundational that I used it as an exhibit in my legal complaint. However, when I first memorialized my invention, I did *not* mail a copy of this to myself via certified mail.

I am advising that when you first memorialize your invention, you should send a copy of your invention to yourself via certified mail. Upon receipt of the envelope do not open it. Keep it sealed in the original envelope and put it away for safe keeping until such time that you would need to bring it forth in a legal dispute. Again, you should do this in addition to getting your idea memorialization notarized. Had I done this little mailing exercise, I may have gained some additional clout in the eyes of the court.

I also had plenty of notes that documented some important names, dates, times and places. I also had reams of paper phone records. All of this was a huge help. Again, it established a time frame as well as sources of my trade secrets. I also had the proprietary chemical additives and their Material Handling Data Safety Sheets sent to me from DuPont and as well as other vendors that were in my possession long before I ever disclosed any of my trade secrets to Honeywell. Again, this helped me immensely for the very same reason. I got there first.

Taken together, all these various things enabled me to prove my case, but you should do all of this *and more*!

This is key,

- Your well-kept and well-documented inventor's notebook means more than all of this put together.

I repeat, your well-kept and well-documented inventor's notebook means more than all of this put together, because it is contained in one neat and concise document. The legal impact of a properly documented inventor's notebook in my opinion is off the scale.

Perhaps if I had put together a properly documented inventor's notebook and I had been able to throw it down on the table at the time in which I was accosted, the entire patent grab and the lawsuit that followed might never have manifested. That's a very real possibility and that's just one of the valuable aspects that this notebook can provide you!

In every lawsuit of this type, there is a little something called Summary Judgment. Either party can file it, and both parties are mandated to respond to its accusations. Here's my point. If you have a great inventor's notebook, and you slam it down on the table, there is a very good chance that the other side's counter suit will be thrown out of court based upon the lack of facts verifying their position. For one thing, if you were the first to invent, the first to document your trade secrets and the first to file the patent application; your notebook should bear all of this out. So what will the other side's notebook have to say regarding these same issues? My guess is nothing. Remember, though Honeywell wanted to steal, they were at a loss to fabricate their own inventor's notebook.

Of course possessing a notebook like the one I'm urging you to develop is not a hundred percent guarantee of success either, but in light of all that I've experienced, I would have loved to have had the opportunity to brandish a nice thick one for them to try an attack.

My point is simple. At the time I was clueless as to how important these simple things were, and because of my ignorance with regard to proper documentation, it helped Honeywell to perpetuate a much longer and drawn out pre-trial period specifically designed to wear down their opponent.

So from my perspective, if you cannot discipline yourself to keep an up-to-date inventor's notebook, don't bother becoming an inventor. And that goes double for any one of you that has developed a multi-million-dollar idea, because the hell that you might have to pay down the road simply won't be worth it.

The PTO and Memorialization

Since I've just shared some of my personal insights with you as to memorialization and documenting your idea, I thought it would be helpful for you to see where the PTO stands on the on the subject. It would also be beneficial to give you a bit of background and show you how the PTO has arrived at its present day system for both memorializing and granting patents.

Up until February 1st of 2007, for a fee of $10, an inventor could file a *disclosure document* for the sole purpose of registering an idea with the PTO. The inventor's idea would be retained in confidence for a period of *two years* and then the document would be destroyed. Under present day procedures, that program has been done away with.

It's important to note that the disclosure document was never intended to be filed in lieu of a patent, and the accompanying two-year *grace period* was never intended to give the inventor the luxury of taking his sweet time to file his application without jeopardizing the loss of patent benefits either. In addition to that, the recording date *was not* to be viewed as the initial filing date for a patent application. Nor did the PTO grant the marking of any item with the patent pending designation, based upon the submission of this form.

- Keep in mind this was the PTO's system for an inventor to document an idea. It had nothing to do with filing a patent. It was strictly a procedure for an inventor to memorialize his idea.

It's also important to note that up until February 1st 2007 USPTO used to operate under an entirely different set of rules as well. It used to be that patents were granted on the basis of who was the first person to invent. This was based upon who could *demonstrate through documentation that he/she thought of the idea first.*

As of June 8th of 1995, the PTO changed the way in which they awarded patents. Here is what you should know; a patent's primacy is now based upon *who has filed their patent application first and not who can document that they had the idea first.*

In order to facilitate this, they introduced the *provisional patent.* This new option affords the inventor two things:

- A recognized means for an inventor to document his idea.
- A recognized means for an inventor to establish an earlier filing date.

So we are clear, in order to do this properly, the provisional application *must* be followed up with a non-provisional patent application covering the same invention within 12 months or less, so that the earlier filing date for the idea can be established.

As you might expect, this new method will cost you more than the ten dollars it used to cost for filing the old disclosure document. The cost for a *micro entity* to file a provisional patent, which would include most of you backyard inventors, and non-profit organizations, is anywhere from $65.00 to $125.00 providing that you sign an affidavit that your gross income does not exceed $155,817 dollars. These fees are in a constant state of flux so just go the PTO's website, where it's all spelled out.

So, beginning in June of 1995, the USPTO began to offer inventors the option of filing a provisional application. According to the PTO, this concept was introduced to do a few things:

- First. It was designed to give the inventor a lower cost option for filing a first patent.
- Second. It was designed to give U.S. applicants parity with foreign applicants, because they already had a similar process in place.
- Third. It granted the individual permission to mark the item with the patent pending designation.
- Fourth. It was designed to give an inventor an opportunity to document his invention *without* having to specify the inventions claims and without the inventor filling out an oath or declaration.

- Fifth. A provisional patent gives the applicant an earlier filing date; so long as the applicant follows up with a non-provisional patent application within 12 months.
- Sixth. A provisional patent application *never gets issued,* because it never gets examined.

It's this last aspect of the provisional application that most seems to have filled the void of the abandoned disclosure document program, with two major exceptions:

- The two-year time frame has been reduced to one year.
- The provisional application can establish an earlier filing date so long as a non-provisional application for the same idea is filed within a 12-month period.

Here is what the PTO has to say with regard to provisional patents.

- Provisional applications provide the means to establish an early effective filing date in a patent application and permits the term "Patent Pending" to be applied in connection with the invention. Provisional applications may not be filed for design inventions. The applicant would then have up to 12 months to file a non-provisional application for patent. Provisional applications are NOT examined on their merits. A provisional application will become abandoned by the operation of law 12 months from its filing date.
- Inventors are also reminded that any public use or sale in the United States or publication of the invention anywhere in the world more than one year prior to the filing of a patent application on that invention will prohibit the granting of an U. S. patent on it. Foreign patent laws in this regard may be much more restrictive than U.S. laws.

So, before you run out and file for a provisional patent I want you to be aware of something. The PTO as thorough and helpful as they may be, they still *are not* in the business of instructing inventors on how to avoid intellectual property lawsuits. Their primary function is to officially clock-in invention submissions in the form of both provisional patent applications and non-provisional applications. They then subject the non-provisional applications to their examination process.

- Here again is what you must keep in mind; a patent's primacy is now based upon *who has filed their patent application first and not who can document that they had the idea first.*

In the event that you get into a dispute with another party over your patent rights, the extent of the PTO's assistance is going to be limited as to their participation. The PTO does have a Patent Trial and Review Board that are available to clarify certain matters, but there are specific criteria that have to be met in order to appear before them.

Should you appear before them, just know that there are going to be lawyers involved for both sides. This process will be both expensive and time consuming. Claim construction will more than likely be involved and complex patent law will rule the day.

So in the face of something called *patent interference,* or a *"priority contest,"* strong documentation will prove to be an inventor's best friend.

- An interference is a contest under 35 U.S.C. 135(a) between an application and either another application or a patent. An interference is declared to assist the Director of the United States

Patent and Trademark Office in determining priority, that is, which party first invented the commonly claimed invention within the meaning of 35 U.S.C. 102(g)(1). See MPEP § 2301.03. Once interference has been suggested under 37 CFR 41.202, the examiner refers the suggested interference to the Board of Patent Appeals and Interferences (Board). An administrative patent judge declares the interference, which is then administered at the Board. A panel of Board members enters final judgment on questions of priority and patentability arising in interference. Once the interference is declared, the examiner generally will not see the application again until the interference has been terminated.

Though the PTO will mediate in some matters such as interference, this is *generally not* the place where inventors go to get their patent problems straightened out. The Federal Court system is generally the venue where complainants must go in order to seek resolution for most patent conflicts that involve another party. The Federal Court system is the place where patent infringement, misappropriation of trade secrets and related disputes are resolved, not the Patent Office.

Should any kind of dispute relating to your patent arise, it's still going to come down to the same common denominator. It's going to be heartache no matter where you end up pleading your case, and it's definitely going to cost you both lots of time and money to have this dispute settled.

Now to recap. Provisional patents are patterned after the European model, and patent primacy is awarded to the party who files first. So to be perfectly clear, whoever files the application first wins the day, not the person who thought of the idea first.

So if you should find yourself motivated to file a *provisional patent* to save money, or if you intend on testing the waters for your new idea for several months, you must be prepared to file a *non-provisional* application no later than 12 months from the date in which you filed your provisional application or you will lose your place in line.

So here is my advice. For the time being and until we finish this teaching, be intent on memorializing your idea by employing an inventor's notebook and by getting your formalized idea notarized. And it certainly wouldn't hurt to mail a notarized copy to yourself using certified mail, return receipt requested. Save everything!

As we proceed, some of the potential benefits and possible dangers of placing your complete trust in filing a *provisional application* will come to light. But for now, you are a long ways off from doing that.

Patent Pending?

Here is the PTO's definition of what *patent pending* is.

- The phrase that often appears on manufactured items. It means that someone has applied for a patent on an invention that is contained in the manufactured item. It serves as a warning that a patent may issue that would cover the item and that copiers should be careful because they might infringe if the patent issues. Once the patent issues, the patent owner will stop using the phrase "patent pending" and start using a phrase such as "covered by U.S. Patent Number XXXXXXX." Applying the patent pending phrase to an item when no patent application has been made can result in a fine.

Based upon my personal experience and the case law that I've studied, I have developed a rather different point of view of what the term *patent pending* means. Here is why,

- Fact. Up until several years ago, your patent application, and what was contained in it, had remained a secret until such time that it was it was granted.

The PTO has since changed that practice to be:

- Most patent applications filed on or after November 29, 2000, will be published 18 months after the filing date of the application, or any earlier filing date relied upon under Title 35, United States Code. Otherwise, all patent applications are maintained in the strictest confidence until the patent is issued or the application is published. After the application has been published, however, a member of the public may request a copy of the application file. After the patent is issued, the Office file containing the application and all correspondence leading up to issuance of the patent is made available in the Files Information Unit for inspection by anyone, and copies of these files may be purchased from the Office.

Up until November 2000, nobody could view another person's patent application except those people working inside of the PTO. Hence, it was a rather even playing field, because what was contained in any given patent application was kept a secret until such time that the application was either granted or denied.

Of course that's all changed as of November 2000. Patent applications that are filed today become available to the public after 18 months and the clock begins from the earliest filing date. See 35 USC §122. That is something to consider since I have already shown you that the average application takes on average 24 months to be processed. In many instances, this change in the law can expose your idea to the public before your patent has been either officially granted or denied.

This new twist in the law makes it all the more imperative that what you do *before* you file, and what you do *during* the patent application process is so much more critical. Unfortunately, this also means that under the new law, your patent application can be pulled and studied by the competition at any time after the 18-month *quite period* has expired. So attention to both form and function regarding your application is extremely critical!

The point is, if your application remains in the hands of the PTO long enough, it will get published and become public knowledge before your patent ever gets granted. Prior to November 29, 2000 this was not the case, and your application remained a secret until such point that it was granted or denied.

Let's address what benefits an inventor might expect to gain under the patent pending designation.

- First of all, it signifies that the USPTO has received and recognized that you have filed a US patent application for an original invention.
- Secondly, your invention, for the time being, is afforded *some* degree of protection as noted by the PTO's definition of patent pending.

The patent pending designation *can* be placed on a product to signify that the particular product is covered by a specific patent application. However, the PTO *does not require* that the patent pending designation be placed on the item. It's strictly the inventor's prerogative as to whether he/she chooses to display the patent pending designation or not.

If the inventor *chooses to mark* his product with a patent pending designation; it affords him the opportunity to officially warn any party that the product is covered or protected by a pending patent application.

The act of *marking* a product with the patent pending designation is referred to as *constructive notice*. The placement of the patent pending designation on a product puts everyone on notice, that the inventor has the ability to enforce his rights as the *potential patentee* of that particular item.

The proper marking of a product, streamlines the inventor's or a manufacturer's ability to notify the offending party a *cease and desist* letter and warn them to stop producing the item. Usually such a letter can also state that should there be a refusal to comply; there is the possibility of a lawsuit being served.

Now you know why marking a product with the patent pending designation can be important. It's similar to a miner physically driving stakes into the ground around his claim.

- The PTO does not mandate that product brandish the patent pending designation. The option to mark a product with the patent pending designation is strictly left up to the discretion of the inventor or the manufacturer.

If the inventor chooses *not* to mark his product with a patent pending designation, it will complicate the inventor's efforts to ward off any party who might be infringing on his product, because his product lacks the constructive notice marking.

Here is a key to be mindful of. The patent pending claim only has teeth:

- So long as the patent application is still active.
- So long as the inventor chooses to mark his product.
- So long as the inventor possesses the necessary funds needed to enforce any cease and desist requests or the enforcement of any legal action.

It must be noted, that any protection afforded under the patent pending status will cease, should the application expire due to either the passing of time, inactivity regarding the file, or a final rejection by the PTO.

After it's all said and done, the act of affixing *patent pending* to an item gives you the right to send the offending party a cease and desist letter and enables the inventor to *begin* the process of calculating *damages* for an *alleged infringement*. Whether the offending party decides to stop producing or copying any aspect of the patent pending product is strictly up to them. The only true remedy to stop them is to file an *injunction* with the court or to file a formal lawsuit that claims patent infringement.

In either case, the offending party's general response might go something like this, "We believe that we are within our rights to produce this product. After seeking the advice of our legal counsel, we have concluded that your patent is *invalid as anticipated.* As a result of our investigation, we are fully prepared to defend ourselves *vigorously* in this matter. So sue us…"

Just so you know, I am not a fan of any backyard inventor marking an invention with the patent pending mark. Here are a few reasons,

- A smalltime inventor isn't capitalized enough to enforce his patent rights under the patent pending scenario.
- Patent pending doesn't mean all that much since 50% of all patent applications don't get granted anyway.
- In the case of a provisional patent that lacks any specific claims, by what grounds are you going to ask a potential infringer to cease and desist?
- Most importantly, since you are small and undercapitalized, why announce anything to the world until you receive your official grant. Because at this time, you'll just be defending your application and not the actual claims granted to you by the PTO.

Walk Tall and Carry Two Big Sticks

The individual or entity, who's best suited to play the patent game, should *ideally* have access to either one of two big sticks. I say this rather euphemistically, because chances are, you don't own the first stick.

- The first big stick is money. Tons of money. You need to have pockets deep enough to withstand the onslaught of enormous legal bills should any sort of intellectual property conflict arise.
- The second big stick is having solid documentation.

Again, if you have deep pockets that would be great, but in all likelihood most backyard inventors won't.

Just so you know, when I played this game, I didn't own the first big stick either. Despite the fact that I was miserably underfunded to mount a legal campaign against them, I was relentless in my search to find a law firm to represent me. Since my quest proved unsuccessful, I was left no other choice, but to sue them Pro Se. In a nutshell here's why,

- It will be nearly impossible for you to find a law firm that will take on your IP lawsuit on a contingency fee basis.
- The overwhelming majority of law firms want to be paid as you go. So be mindful that it takes a minimum of one to two million dollars in cash to take on a major IP infringer such as a Honeywell.

As for me, I was newly married, had two babies and I was cutting my teeth as a straight commissioned real-estate agent at a time when 10% mortgage rates were considered a bargain. You get the picture; we were just making ends meet and my wife wasn't killing it either as a first grade teacher. Now you know why I had to sue the bastards Pro Se.

So let me ask you a question. Is having a detailed inventor's notebook and strong documentation starting to make some sense? It's certainly within the realm of any backyard inventor's capabilities, and anyone with discipline can do this.

What you may not have realized until just a few moments ago, is that the patent pending designation only provides that you have the right to defend your invention. In reality, whether the designation reads *patent pending* or whether it reads *patent number 5,209,842* you are only granted the right to defend your patent.

It is important for you to understand that as an inventor, you bear the full *responsibility* of defending as well as enforcing your patent rights. So please, do not expect any government agency to come to your aid and help you enforce your rights under either of these two designations.

It may be rather a harsh reality, but the government agencies that will mediate over your intellectual property rights will not get involved until *you* have filed either a formal lawsuit or an injunction with the court. Then and only then, are they going to be compelled to act.

Simply put, this means that you are responsible for the enforcement of your intellectual property rights that may have been violated by someone else. This means that *you* must pay for all of the legal bills generated to do this. It requires large sums of money to defend your intellectual property. As a consequence, a huge and very powerful legal industry has developed over the course of the last fifty years to take part in this intellectual property gold rush.

However, there is a bit of good news on this score. The IP landscape is beginning to change. In response to the exorbitantly high priced legal representation and the correspondingly high values placed upon certain Intellectual Property, a blossoming cottage industry has developed. It's simply referred to as IP legal funding. I'll spare you all the details, but I will tell you I would have considered it, if I had known about its existence way back when. So there is now an avenue of hope for an inventor with a *very valuable* idea who's been attacked to receive both legal funding and representation.

I realize that the *Voices* out there promoting their free inventor's kits and their free idea appraisals aren't telling you about all of this, but I am.

Yet despite what I've just described, you can still become an inventor capable of making lots of money off of your intellectual property if that's your desire. Actually, you still have a better than fighting chance should some big company make a play for your invention. Here's how you should go about it.

First. You must internalize the fact that you are smarter than your opponent. I firmly believe that the one who dreams up the invention first, is more often than not, smarter than his opponent. The simple proof is that you have already exhibited a deep insight into the marketplace. And if my line of reasoning isn't correct, then please explain to me how a typical backyard inventor with a good idea can often times out-envision a company that is already engaged in that particular business?

Second. Since this idea originated with you, it tells me that *you* should take this more personally than the next guy. Therefore, *you should* be willing to outwork your competition, which by the way, in most cases really isn't that difficult, since now we are talking about being motivated by your dream.

Finally. The backbone of your second big stick is going to be made up of the following three areas:

- Strong documentation.
- Strong understanding of the inventing process.
- Strong patent claims.

Unfortunately, of late, the inventing game has been overshadowed by the hype of instant marketing, and the allure of making big money fast.

There is no such thing, especially when it comes to inventing.

As a consequence, the principals of the second big stick have more or less been cast aside. The most important concept of preserving one's intellectual property through rigorous documentation has been cast off, as if it were a bastard stepchild. Well it's not.

- It's so easy for an inventor to *unknowingly* put himself at risk and *forfeit his IP rights.*

And once lost, there's a very real possibility that you will lose the ownership of your idea forever and there certainly won't be any money left for you to claim.

Here's a key.

We as backyard inventors file patents in order to document our ideas in keeping with the Federal Statues. We keep our trade secrets very closely held and we authenticate our ownership by owning a nuclear grade inventor's notebook. We do all this so that one day under the right conditions we may approach an entity more powerful than ourselves in order to market our idea and come away with a fair and equitable licensing deal. We can do this in confidence knowing that if they should attempt to say that this information originated with them, we will have the undisputed facts of ownership on our side and we will be able to defeat them handedly.

It is the preparation of this second big stick that this book is really all about. For with this second big stick, you can play the inventing game. And you can play it to win.

I certainly did. And as I've already shared, there was no big *money stick* backing me up either. And as already noted, my second big *documentation stick* was not nearly as well constructed, as it should have been, but thank God it was sufficient enough to get the job done. Despite my shortcomings I still made millions off of my patents and I even made it through an IP lawsuit and forced a company the size of Honeywell to settle with me.

What really lies ahead, is your opportunity to become a much better prepared inventor than I ever was. Let's see if we can help you develop a second big stick with nuclear capabilities.

Chapter 4

SOME IMPORTANT THINGS

Market Trends are Very Important

Once again, I want you to be mindful of the marketing trends that will affect your invention. At this time, I would like to revisit timing the market trends for your invention in some greater detail. When we come up with an invention we must consider *what is hot and what is not.*

In great measure, the proliferation of information in conjunction with the speed of the Internet will affect the marketing trend that you're trying to capitalize on. In the long run, the abundance of information and how it dominates any given time span will affect whether your marketing trend will ever materialize or whether it won't. In the event that your marketing trend does come along, be mindful that the tremendous speed in which information now travels will have a direct bearing on how long your marketing trend might last.

Like it or not, information is growing at an astounding rate and so is the spread of that information. Consequently, product trend cycles are shortening as well.

For illustration purposes, let's compare two trends; the cell phone industry and the hand tool industry. Cell phone innovations have been changing at the speed of light over the last decade and haven't shown any signs of nearing a plateau. There's one thing for sure, none of us in the general population knows where this technology is going to end up.

So unless you're already a force to be reckoned in that field, you could never hope to catch that *trend wave*.

The field of electronics is so technologically advanced, and the rate of innovation is moving at such a tremendous speed, that only industry icons with massive amounts of capital, technological know-how and marketing capabilities could ever hope to succeed in this space. The point is, the trend wave in the cell phone industry is moving so fast, that only a few established players could ever hope to ride that particular trend wave.

On the other hand, let's take hand tools for instance. And specifically, let's take a close look at the hand-held nailing hammer. When we examine the hammer industry, we see that the technology is moving at a glacial pace as compared to the cell phone industry. That of course is due to the fact that the hammer industry has its own set of parameters, which are unique to that particular industry. Consider the fact that hammers have been around for thousands of years and the average person only tends to pull one out when needed.

On the other hand, cell phones have only been around for only a couple of decades, and now we're totally dependent on them. So much so, that most people consider it unthinkable to be separated from their phone for any length of time.

Here's my point. If you could come up with a significant improvement to a hammer, the hammer market will be there waiting for you long after you come up with your improvement and receive your patent. And if your idea happens to be good enough, you could even see your new hammer introduced into the marketplace and purchased by the masses.

One of the main factors why you could achieve this, is because the trend wave in the hammer business is moving at such a slow pace as compared to the cell phone business. Therefore, anybody with a significant improvement for a hand-held hammer is capable of jumping in and catching that wave. The result being, that you could foreseeably make a fortune if you came up with a significant improvement for a hammer.

Riding the trend wave is subject to the following:

- The inventing process requires time.
- Some trend waves are moving so rapidly that it would be impossible for a backyard inventor to even consider catching it.
- Understand that some areas of innovation and invention are much less time-sensitive than others.
- Some inventions will be a welcomed addition at *any* particular time and others won't.
- Keep your eye on your intended market and the trend wave that corresponds with your invention.

Be very mindful that every invention will have its own particular trend wave. Therefore, to be able to maximize the inventions value, its launch must run in tandem with the corresponding market trend. What I am really trying to say here is this, be vigilant as to how fast your particular trend wave is moving before you decide to jump in with both feet. If you can catch the trend wave early, well that's great! *Go for it*!

On the other hand, if you're not so lucky, and you get that feeling in your gut that you're going miss the trend wave, it's far better to just let it go and wait for the next idea to surface.

Reading a particular trend wave is a lot like looking at a little brook in the spring. It flows along at barely a trickle and takes little effort to walk alongside it. However, after a good spring rain, that same little brook can become a torrent and could carry you away in a flash.

Ideally, you want to enter your trend wave while the volume is low and building. You don't want to enter into a market when it's flowing at warp speed. I'm sure you see my point.

Claims

At this juncture you're still journaling in your inventor's notebook and your idea is beginning to take shape. Now would be a good time to begin thinking about *drafting* or writing your patent. The Patent Office, patent lawyers and patent agents, refer to drafting and the subsequent submission of a patent as *prosecuting a patent*. Or they will often times refer to it as *prosecuting a patent application*.

I want to draw your attention to the patent's claims, because the claims contained in your patent will become the heart and soul of your patent. In fact, the claims are the heart and soul of *every* patent.

- The claims define the inventor's *discovery*.
- The claims define what the invention *is*.
- The claims define what the invention *does*.
- The claims define the *legal scope* of a patent.
- The claims are *legally enforceable* under patent law.

That being the case, let's take a closer look at exactly what the term *claim* means. A claim is a written statement. It is a statement of fact that applies to the *inventor's discovery* and it must be able to clearly relate back to what has been put forth in the *description.* The claims section of the patent is where the inventor specifically states what their invention is.

The following is the PTO's definition of a claim.

- Claims define the invention and are what aspects are legally enforceable. The specification must conclude with a claim particularly pointing out and distinctly claiming the subject matter which the applicant regards as his invention or discovery. The claim or claims must conform to the invention as set forth in the remainder of the specification and the terms and phrases used in the claims must find clear support or antecedent basis in the description so that the meaning of the terms in the claims may be ascertainable *(clearly understood)* by reference to the description. See 37 CFR § 1.58(a).

Now that you're familiar with the term and the concept, pull up some patents on the PTO's website that are as closely related to your proposed inventions as you can find. Read the whole patent, but be especially mindful of how the claims are written or *constructed.*

Patents that are closely related to your invention and that are used for comparison are referred to as *the prior art.*

- A patented invention can be summed up as a new discovery that is useful, purposeful and novel *over* what already exists in the *prior art.*

Allow me to share a bit of personal experience with regard to pulling patents or searching the *prior art.* At the time in which I was working on my first two patents, an individual could only obtain copies of patents by either contacting the Patent Office directly, or by visiting certain major cities where a *patent depository* was located. As you can imagine, it was quite an expenditure of time and effort for me to do that, since the closest library was nearly a two-hour drive.

Today they are called *Patent and Trademark Resource Centers* and yes, they still exist.

Should you want to take advantage of this resource, the PTO provides a list of *PTRC's* on their web site. Once there, a qualified librarian will assist you with your research.

Practically speaking, you shouldn't ever have to leave your computer to do your research or to pull a patent. But in the event that you can't locate what you are looking for, the PTO is most helpful. They will of course for a fee, send you what you're looking for, either by email or by a delivery service.

So there are no excuses for not doing your research now that everything that you might need is accessible via the Internet:

- USPTO.
- US Code.
- Inventor and patent sites.
- Industrial references, raw materials and manufactures sites.
- Wholesaler and retailer's sites.
- Legal sites.
- Case law.

The point is, you have so much information at your fingertips, therefore you should immerse yourself in this process. The information that used to be so closely held is now available for the masses to educate themselves. The Internet has sped things up to the speed of light and in the process, has leveled out the playing field.

By the same token, *you* have to work faster as well. As a result, this incredible free flow of information is also available to every single creative thinker who's looking to hatch an invention as well. So remember, you are now about to embark in a race to the Patent Office, *where it's first to file is now first served.*

Framing Your Claims

Briefly; this is how to approach framing your claims. My best advice is for you to try and search out the patents that seem to be as closely related to your invention as possible. Take the time to study the whole patent. It's not necessary for you to reinvent the wheel, so follow the basic format that these patents have already disclosed.

Listed below are the main sections that make up the patent:

- Abstract
- Description
- Description of the Prior Art
- Objects of the Invention
- Summary of the Invention.
- Brief Description of the Drawings
- Detailed Description.
- The Claims

Begin the process by drafting a *brief description* of your invention. This is helpful, because it gives you an overall description of what your invention is *going to be*. If you happen to be artsy or capable of drafting, a simple sketch of your invention will do nicely toward describing what your invention may look like. You may sketch out specific parts and even some of the critical manufacturing steps. These are generally *simple drawings*.

If you have taken into consideration the history of your invention, and how it has evolved over time, it wouldn't hurt to cite some of the prior art that you feel is most relevant to your invention. You see, an invention's history and evolutionary progression can be mapped out by researching the prior art. This is something that you should do and not something that should get glossed over.

The next thing that you must consider, is what's the *object* of your invention? Because the object of your invention will addresses what your invention is *going to do*. And of course, you should be capable of explaining what your invention is going to do. This is the section where you would include any special material that you may be employing in your device. Examples are such things as raw materials, specific parts and sources. By sources, it could include anything from information, types of materials and who manufactures them.

Your completed thought will be contained in the *summary*. This is where your invention is going to demonstrate how it proposes *to do it*. How will it work? You need to clearly be able to communicate this.

The proper time to develop your claims will be:

- After you have developed a solid picture of what your patent is all about.
- After you have considered how it compares to the other patents in your inventions' category.
- After you have identified those items or processes that you have discovered that sets your invention apart.

The claims are essentially what *makes* your patent different or more advantageous as compared to the other patents that are already in existence. To be more specific, your claims must be different or *novel* as compared to what is already is contained in the prior art.

For the most part, the claims are written in a bullet point fashion. Constructing your claims in a concise manner is the name of the game here.

Now a word of encouragement. If you plan on taking my future advice, you are not going to be the only one responsible for drafting the final version of your patent or its claims. When the time comes, you are going to rely on someone who is highly skilled in this *art* to prosecute your patent application and we will explore who should assist you in much greater detail in the up-coming chapters.

Just so you know, at the time in that I was filing for either of my patents, I was rather blind as to the incredible value that is locked up in a set of properly constructed patent claims. I was unaware that patent claims needed to be carefully crafted and not just something put together in order to slip past the patent examiners critical eye.

Don't misunderstand me! Your claims as set forth must be good enough to get by the examiner, because if you fail there, you won't be getting a patent at all. But the examiner really isn't the final audience that you are preparing for. The really big picture is that your claims must capable of warding off the potential marauders who might one day come against your patents claims. The blatant infringer who has the unmitigated gall to tell you that your patent's claims are invalid. Now that's who you must have in mind when you're in the process of defining your claims.

The Castle and Your Claims

Now that we've begun to develop your patent claims, I'd like to draw a quick mental image as to what your patent claims should actually do. To do this, let's travel way back in time and land somewhere in mid-evil Europe. Now take a close look at how a well-constructed castle is designed. The castle as we know was the king's residence and it was carefully crafted to protect the king and all of his possessions. It was also designed on a grand scale to declare to everyone who passed by, that the king's presence was in the land.

The site was purposely chosen with both security and defense in mind. Most of the time, it was located either on a bend of river or upon a steep hill. Oftentimes, it included a moat and draw bridge for added security. The walls were always made of stone and were very thick and high.

In a nutshell, your patent claims should resemble a mid-evil castle. Like a castle, the first objective is that your patent clearly puts a stake in the ground and declares to the world, "Hey, this is my ground, I got here first!" The second purpose is to shout out to the world, "If you want a piece of this, be prepared to come and try and conqueror my defenses!"

There are two schools of thought when writing, or constructing your patents claims. One school is that the claims should be as broad or as encompassing as possible, so as to cast the largest net and cover everything remotely related to your invention. If this tactic is chosen, the claims stand a chance of becoming rather vague. In my opinion, by choosing that approach it can lessen the impact of what your patent is all about.

The other school of thought is that your patent's claims should be as precise as possible and cover exactly what the invention is about. Based on my personal experience, I favor this approach and I'll tell you why. My reasoning is as follows; if your claims are precise, well written, and easy to understand, you will have presented to the examiner a clear-cut reason to either allow or to disallow your application. Should he or she reject your claims for any reason, you will be in a better position to hopefully revise them and earn their final approval.

Secondly, and just as important, if your claims are precise, well written, and easy to understand, you will have a much greater weapon in your hand when it comes time to make a potential interloper see what they're up against. If your patent has a stop sign with flashing lights and a siren that goes off, there is a good chance that the interloper might think twice before he attempts to run his big truck through your stop sign.

On the other hand, if your claims are vague, the offending party just might want to drive his big truck through your *stop sign* and see what the company's stockholders' money might buy him.

Let's consider this example. Say you've invented a remote sensing device that can be attached to any mailbox. The purpose of your invention is to signal via radio waves when the mail has been delivered. You claim that your device has a trigger mechanism that is spring-loaded and will be activated after 5 grams of pressure is applied. The spring then supplies 5 millivolts of current from a cadmium battery for 1.5 milliseconds to 3μ capacitor, which in turn will trigger the actuator that will send a signal to a remote buzzer located within the house.

Well, you get the idea.

Now let's take this example one step further. Say you've recently been granted a patent for this device. Then one day while strolling through the Chicago Hardware Trade Show, you happen to come upon a widget being displayed at one of the booths owned by the Massive Mailbox Company. Low and behold, you notice that their device performs exactly as yours. Upon careful examination, you come to find out that they are employing same technology that your patent claims! The point of this illustration is that your chances of enforcing your patent rights will be much better if your claims are as explicit as possible.

- Concise patent claims will make up the tip of the spear should it be necessary to defend your patent.

For arguments sake, let's just assume that the manufacturer *didn't* know of your patents existence before they launched this product. But regardless of whether they had the foreknowledge of your patent's existence or not, you opt to send them a *cease and desist letter*. You inform them that their product is infringing on your patent and that you want them to stop immediately with the manufacture and sale of that item.

Typically, the company's next move is to seek the advice of *outside* legal counsel. They do this, because most large companies have any number of powerful IP firms on a perpetual retainer. They also avail themselves of this service in order to get a more substantial evaluation of their position with regard to your patent's claims. The law firm that they will call upon will no doubt give them a detailed evaluation of both your patents strengths and its weaknesses.

If it turns out that your claims are sufficiently strong enough to bar them from manufacturing your product and offering it in the marketplace, their outside counsel *should* advise them that they will face an uphill battle litigating against the *invalidity* of your patent. At that point, the company should cease and desist, thereby halting the further sale and production of their *infringing* item. At this point, it's *not inconceivable* that they might consider taking a license from you. That of course is the best-case scenario of what might happen.

I must tell you this; only honorable companies that actually believe and operate in accordance to their vision and values statements will do this. So don't be shocked if a company disregards your patent as if it were an old fish wrapped in newspaper, because honesty and reason do not necessarily prevail in the money grab.

The reality driving this entire game is simple; great ideas that possess the potential to earn significant profits are indeed very rare, so people are willing to fight over them. So when an offending party with deep pockets gives a powerful IP firm carte blanche to run the meter in a protracted patent battle, the hands on the billable clock are going to spin like an electric meter during a Christmas light show.

In my view, your only hope is that your claims are as strong and as mighty as the castle that I've just previously described. So strong that even a powerful defense firm doesn't want to get their reputation tarnished by losing to you in court. That again, is yet another best-case scenario.

But be strong and trust me on this one, at some point you *will* prevail, because of three things:

- How well you've documented your invention.
- How well your inventor's notebook stands up to scrutiny.
- How well your claims were constructed.

For now, it's best for you to think long and hard about your claims, and how to best organize their impact on your invention.

Here's what inventing boils down to for each one of us, who has been blessed to encounter a *Flash of Genius*:

First. How many great ideas are you expecting to receive in your lifetime capable of generating a significant financial return for you? In truth, you might only get one great patentable idea in a lifetime.

Second. Do you realize that this patent odyssey could take you anywhere from three years to only God knows how long to accomplish?

My point is this. Great patentable ideas may come only once in a lifetime and in the process may take a significant part of your precious life to make it happen. So this is not the area in which to get sloppy.

Your Claims and the Examiner

This is how it works. When your application is finally plucked from the examiner's stack, the first thing that he or she is probably going to do, is to glance over your drawings and give a quick read through your application. Then undoubtedly, the examiner is going to study your claims. He's then going to pull from the massive patent archives as many patents as he/she can find that might contain claims that are similar to yours.

As previously mentioned, the other patents that your patent is going to be compared against are referred to as the *prior art*. The way in which your patent essentially gets the patent examiner's *initial approval* is that your claims must be found to be different, novel or new as compared to the known *art* that your application is being evaluated against.

If your patent's claims are not found or *cited* in the patents that the examiner has pulled, then for the time being, you've passed the first test.

It doesn't matter whether the patents that have been selected have long since expired, or whether they were granted just the day before. All that matters is that the patent being cited against your application had been granted at some point in time.

Here's the key; patent rights for a specific claim can only be granted once. Once a claim has been granted it can never be granted again. As a result, once a patent expires, its claims automatically enter the *public domain* and they are up for grabs, which simply means that anybody can use them for his/her own profit or gain.

- Once a patent expires, its claims enter the *public domain* and become public property. At that point, anybody can use that information for any purpose.

Take the pharmaceutical business for example. Valium® *comes off patent.* The very next day the same formulation is available to any number of competitors, making the same exact drug, but under a different trade name. The pharmaceutical business refers to these drugs as generic drugs. The same exact chemical formula can be used, but of course the name can't, because that specific name has been *trademarked* and is protected. Trademarks unlike patents can be renewed; therefore, they do *not* have final expiration dates attached to them like patents do.

The second test that your patent must undergo is something that is referred to as *anticipated claims*. It works something like this. During this phase of the examination, the examiner will now determine whether the other patents that have already been granted could have anticipated your claims. That simply means, did the other inventor's patent's claims already presuppose or *anticipate* what your patent application is now proposing as something new? Is it possible that your claims as put forth, were already foreseen or anticipated as something *obvious* to the previous inventors who were cited in the prior art?

- The claims in your patent will get rejected based upon whether your claims are redundant to what already exists in the *prior art*, or whether they were *anticipated as obvious* in the prior art.

This process pretty much sums up the most important aspect of the examiner's job. This in effect lays out what you need to mindful of, if you intend on getting your claims put through.

Although I made this process seem rather simplistic, in actuality, it's a fairly tall order. And as a matter of procedure, the examiner will initially tend to reject your claims on any number of grounds more times than he will allow them. Upon the rejection of your claims, you will be given a few more opportunities to revise them. The hope being that you will be able to put them in a form that will finally be acceptable to the patent examiner.

As I've been telling you, just because you went through the trouble of filing a patent, that in *no way* guarantees that the examiner will grant you your claims. If the patent examiner should refuse to grant you your claims, the PTO will not be issuing you a patent for your invention.

So, focus on your inventions claims! In many ways this is like baseball. You are allowed a few times at bat to fix things, but when the examiner says it's over; it's pretty much over.

Yes, under certain conditions, you can appeal an examiner's call. But I can tell you that it's pretty much over, unless you can prove to his supervisor's satisfaction that he made a really obvious mistake. The patent examiner is the gatekeeper for the PTO.

And yes, should you decide to file an appeal, this process will cost you additional time and money for the privilege of appealing the examiner's decision.

One can always go back and fix the drawings, the specifications, or the summary and that's relatively simple. Those issues can be looked upon as minor roadblocks, but as I will say throughout…

- It's all in the claims.
- It's all dependent upon how the examiner will allow the exact *form* of those claims to be granted.

It is important to note, the examiner not only wields the power to allow your claims, but he or she has the authority to dictate the final form of your claims. He or she will determine what is going to be allowable. This will be based upon what the prior art has taught, in light of what the examiner believes what should have been *obvious to the prior inventors*.

Yes, there are rules involved for the examiners to follow. But when you boil it down, this claims business is much more of a subjective process then you might expect.

When your claims are finally in an acceptable form and everything else is in place, the PTO will send off a *Notice of Allowance* to you. This is their way of notifying you that your patent will be granted once you pay all of your required fees.

A Tale of Two Examiners

You're due for yet another snapshot taken from my patent odyssey. Allow me to present to you a brief picture of two patent examiners. I want to make you aware of what can happen to you and your patent's application while dealing with an examiner. Everything that I'm about to share with you has to do with the claims.

You bright-eyed inventors don't have clue what can happen until I show you.

Just so you know, a registered patent agent represented me on my first patent. Upon receiving the '901 my first patent, I was so jubilant that I could barely contain myself! And if can recall, my claims got approved pretty much as they were presented. So I did what came natural to me, I rather innocently picked up the phone and called the patent examiner, wanting to thank her for granting my application. Unbeknownst to me at the time, this was a violation of PTO protocol.

I think it is important to point out, that the PTO regulations do not permit direct communications between the inventor and the patent examiner. That is unless; the inventor is prosecuting his/her own application and is therefore representing himself.

On the other hand, if a registered agent or an attorney is representing the inventor, only those individuals are permitted to communicate directly with the examiner. Not the Inventor.

Nonetheless, I remember her as being an angel. To this day I *still* hold fond memories of her kind words, as she said to me, "Mr. Moor, you've really got a great patent here. In all my many years of being an examiner in this art group, I've never come across an oil filter patent quite like yours. Your idea is truly novel for this category and I certainly hope that you make a lot of money with it." Examiner E. Rollins Cross not only knew her job, but she was a visionary. I'm sure that she would be pleased to know that her predictions about this grant had come true!

Just so you know, a registered patent attorney prosecuted my second patent application. The patent examiner on '842 my second patent, was in plain English a stubborn bastard, actually I'm being nice, because he was very incompetent. So much so, that I went through the trouble to temporarily discharged my attorney so that I could represent myself and have a personal dialog with the examiner regarding my patent's claims.

The crux of the matter was that the examiner wasn't allowing my claims in their *original condition* as submitted. His official response was that my claims were *anticipated as obvious*.

Now on the surface that's a typical examiner's response and I can almost guarantee that you could be reading those very same words after your first application gets submitted.

But here's the rub. No matter what argument my attorney made on my behalf, the examiner wouldn't budge. So I decided to have a go at him myself.

The prior art that he was citing, *taught* about one particular invention that was limited to micro fine Teflon particles held in a colloidal suspension in a specific carrier oil *that was contained in a bottle.*

On the other hand, my invention proposed to treat *the media of an oil filter* with a colloidal suspension of Teflon that would be spayed or pumped onto the filter media of an oil filter and that my filter would be treated at the manufacturing facility and the colloidal Teflon would be become part of the oil filter media.

So, where hell was the bottle?

At that time, treating an oil filter with a liquid material was totally novel and I already held that patent for treating an oil filter with a beneficial liquid compound. Prior to my application, there had never been a patent granted for a Teflon treated oil filter. So where was the obviousness? How did the previous inventor anticipate my claims? His invention was in a bottle; did he anticipate putting this mixture into an oil filter? Obviously the answer in my mind was a big no.

The examiner was dead wrong, but he wouldn't budge. So in the end a few things happened. The examiner insisted that I accept *his version of my patents claims*. My claims were being rejected based upon the stuff that pours out of bottles into engines. Instead of properly being reviewed against the prior art that specifically dealt with oil filters. And more specifically my first patent dealt with additives being applied to oil filters in a liquid form and I was the first one to ever establish that category! So why didn't he grant me another patent for a liquid additive treated oil filter using a totally different additive for a totally different purpose?

I'm still baffled!

The examiners terms were quite simple. Either I agree to a much lesser set of claims, which bore no resemblance to what I had first proposed, or there wouldn't be any patent grant for my invention. Period.

Make no mistake; this is not some figment of my imagination, this could happen to you. And how you will deal with it will only depend on how it occurs and who you might have on your team to represent you.

So keep in mind that patent examiners are people. Like any other walk of life there are good ones, bad ones, smart ones and the occasional incompetent one.

With regard to my choice of representation, as mentioned, I employed a patent agent on my first application and a patent lawyer for my second application. Though both practitioners did an adequate job, that's not the level of performance that you are looking for. Looking back in the rear view mirror, I could have picked better team members, but I didn't. The answer for this one is simple; I was limited by two things:

First. My own ignorance of the process and my underestimation of the expertise that was required to file a proper patent application. For this, I have no one to blame but myself.

Second. I lacked the sufficient cash to get either of these jobs done properly. Again, there is no one to blame but myself. So make sure that you have adequate funds set aside to file a proper patent application.

Loose Lips Sink Ships

I have yet another real-life lesson for you to consider. What I am about to share has everything to do with patent claims and trade secrets, and how an inventor can get into serious trouble by not adequately protecting them; *even when you think are protected.* With this snapshot, we are going to momentarily jump way ahead. In so doing, it will not only set the tone for the rest of our adventure, but it will show you how inventing for big money can be a dangerous game for the uninformed.

After I had signed both a *proprietary information agreement* as well as a *test marketing agreement* [both of which contained confidentiality clauses] with Fram / AlliedSignal / Honeywell, I found myself in white-hot marketing mode. As I worked my way deeper inside of the Fram Filter Division, I couldn't help but notice that the fear of failure dominated their corporate culture. I knew right then and there, that if I didn't regurgitate my storehouse of knowledge like a mother stork force-feeding her baby chicks, there'd be no license agreement for me at the end of this rainbow. So in due course, I divulged all of my trade secrets and IP… every bit of it.

During this time, I shared with both the marketing and the engineering departments how the patent examiner forced me to accept a set of watered down claims in order for me to be granted my '842 Teflon treated oil filter patent. I shared this in great detail, because the '842 along with my trade secrets was after all, the platform for the Fram Double Guard Teflon treated oil filter.

It is paramount that you understand that early in my relationship with Fram, the filter giant was *only contemplating* the possibility of producing my Teflon treated oil filter. As the world leader in oil filtration, they were far from committed to my idea. The reason that they put forth, "Was that something like this had never had been done before in the field of oil filtration." To say that they were overwrought by the fear of failure would be a gross understatement. To say that I sold my butt off, would be a gross understatement as well.

My first book, *The Greed of a Dime,* chronicles these various episodes as I experienced them. If you really want get a behind the scenes look at how this all went down, the story of my complete journey inside Fram / Honeywell has been accurately portrayed in vivid detail.

At this juncture, I feel that it's important that I refresh your thinking, so allow me the courtesy to set the stage. When I first called on Fram, none of their engineers held a single patent for an oil filter, and there were at least a dozen engineers in that department, and that included the lead engineer who I personally mentored regarding the production of this filter. The lead engineer and I had a close working relationship and it was nothing for us to call each other at home.

I'd like to remind you that when I called on Fram I owned the '901 and the '842 patents, both of which were benchmark patent grants even at that time. Besides owning these two patents, I had compiled a boatload of trade secrets, all of which was my IP.

So here's what I did.

While under the protection of two separate confidentiality agreements I shared my trade secrets in excruciating detail. I did this in an effort to prove to them that I had a super-viable idea. And by the way, they encouraged me to do so. Now on the surface, my course of action appears to be quite proper and in keeping with the documents that I had signed. Surely my IP was protected. Right? Simple enough.

This is what Fram / AlliedSignal / Honeywell did.

On August 1, 1996 Fram filed a patent application for the exact same patent that I had been intimately schooling the lead engineer, Gary Bilski on. I can unequivocally tell you that Fram incorporated both my trade secret materials and my proprietary manufacturing protocols in order to obtain the patent grant for the Fram Double Guard oil filter.

Just so you know, in the case there may be any doubters amongst this audience, I just want you to be aware of one minor detail. I personally took Gary Bilski's deposition at Fram's engineering headquarters in Perrysburg, Ohio. At the time, Honeywell provided Bilski a lawyer from a 30-man intellectual property law firm from NYC to defend this deposition against my line of questions. His name is David Braffman, he had graduated first in his class from Columbia University and Magna Cum Laude from Harvard law school.

Just so you know, I got everything that I needed from Bilski on the record proving this. After Braffman defended against my seven depositions, and after deposing me twice on video; totaling 12 hours of testimony, he found himself no longer employed by that New York law firm.

So getting back...

The timing for their actions couldn't have been more obvious. They filed their first patent application less than 10 months after we had signed a licensing agreement. The facts are, they had the gall to file this application while I was under a license agreement that did not extinguish my confidentiality agreements. I'll fill you in on those details later as your understanding of the process grows.

And of course they filed this first patent application without my knowledge nor my consent. As I previously mentioned, they violated US patent law 35 USC §115&116, contract law, The Uniform

Trade Secret Act and our licensing agreement and our test marketing agreement amongst other wrongdoings.

On March 10, 1998 Fram / AlliedSignal / Honeywell was awarded US patent 5,725,031, for the very same technology I had so artfully taught them about. At the time this patent was issued, our license agreement at that time was only 2 ½ years young.

Now here's the kicker, I didn't have the slightest clue that this was happening behind my back! They never mentioned a word to me as to what they were doing, and they never invited me to be the co-inventor, since 35 USC §115&116 clearly states that this is not an option, but it is mandatory.

Just so you know, during that timeframe there certainly wasn't an Internet that I could use to monitor their filings at the PTO either. And here's another yet little wrinkle. USPTO's protocol at the time dictated that all patent applications prior to November 2000 were to be kept a total secret until the application was either accepted or rejected! So the contents of this application was kept secret under the law.

Besides that, Fram / Honeywell were my business partners and they were sending me some fairly respectable royalty checks. So who knew what they were up to? I certainly didn't. Yet somehow I have a sneaking suspicion that they may have known what was going on.

Lesson One

So you may ask, "How did the PTO grant another entity a set of claims that you had previously of filed for?" In a word Perception. Remember what I had mentioned to you in the beginning about the power of perception. Well it is my firm belief that the USPTO *will always* be way more inclined to grant a large entity a patent over a sole individual who files for the same thing. Why? The answer is simple, "Who are you… and who am I compared to an esteemed and powerful corporation?" If you're being honest you should be able to answer that without my help.

Secondly, large entities like Honeywell have been granted tens and tens of thousands of patents. Fact. All of these patent applications and their maintenance fees cost multiple millions of dollars a year to support. So figure it out, who's going to get preferred treatment, a company who's doing business with the PTO on a daily basis paying them bushels of cash every day in fees, or a one timer like you or I. As you can well imagine, this is a much different relationship than the one you will be establishing with the PTO.

Lesson Two

Never trust your licensing partner. Never heroically market your product in an unguarded fashion! *Just so you know,* this information should have never have been disclosed by me in the manner in which I had! Even though I was protected under the law!

Lesson Three

Never put your complete faith in the legal documents that you sign. Make the documents protect you, by being proactive and vigilant. At face value these documents are designed to protect you, but in reality, in order to enforce these documents, you must file either an injunction or a law suit! There is much more to come on this topic.

Moral

Yes, you can divulge your trade secrets and yes you can trust these documents with the following caveat; you shouldn't do so until I teach you how to properly protect yourself! As we proceed further on down the road I am going to systematically provide you the ways in which you can avoid this very situation. That said, at various points throughout this teaching I'm also going to expose how my licensing partner carried out their deliberate plan to illegally acquire my IP in an all-out effort to cut me out.

In order to keep good on my promise, I'm going to teach you how protect yourself in these situations and avoid making those same mistakes. Most importantly, I'm going to show you how to anticipate these various scenarios before you could become ensnared.

I'm compelled to wrap this segment up with a bit of irony and a tinge of humor. Honeywell's patent 5,725,031 had three inventors credited for its authorship. As you might have expected, the lead engineer Gary Bilski [who had never earned an oil filter patent prior to working with me] was named as the first inventor on this patent. No surprise there.

But here's where I get a chuckle. I can vividly recall my encounter with the individual that was cited as the third inventor on the '031. As I questioned him, he politely informed me that he was confused as to why he had been named as a co-inventor on the '031 patent in the first place. Turns out, that he was a janitor at the oil filter manufacturing plant in Ohio and that the plant engineer Charlie Probasco [the 2nd inventor named on the '031] put him on the patent as a parting gift for retiring! True story. His name is Franklyn Voight and I took his deposition.

Memorializing Your Idea

Now that we've dispatched with that real-life snapshot, it's now time for you to begin thinking about your first public disclosure. That said, I want you to summarize your invention and write down your claims as accurately as possible.

If you are able to include a conceptual drawing of what your invention looks like, or if you are capable of illustrating how you envision the process by which your widget is manufactured, so much the better. Keep in mind that you must express yourself as clearly and as simply as possible. The illustrations are an added level of protection, but they're not absolutely critical for what we want to accomplish here. What we're essentially going to do at this point is to put an irrefutable time stamp on your invention in its current state.

This by no means etches your invention in stone. Proceeding forward from this juncture doesn't prevent you from improving upon your widget at a later date either. Nor does it preclude you from filing a *non-provisional patent application* with a different set of claims to the PTO. I realize that at this point, you may not have formulated *the final version* of your invention, and that's quite okay. Nevertheless, I want you to go ahead and begin this process anyway.

The intended purpose of this exercise is to concisely establish a launching point for your invention's conception date. Remember…

- As with all documentation, you must begin somewhere.
- The United States operates under the principal that it is now the first person who files the patent owns the invention.
- The European system operates under the principal that it is the first person who files the patent owns the invention.
- Yet your conception date is extremely important as to how it relates to your inventor's notebook and how you can demonstrate the ownership of your idea should an unforeseen conflict ever arise.

Keeping that fact in mind, it's still very important that after you have completed your summary/claims, seal this in an envelope and mail it to yourself certified mail, return receipt requested. Make a couple of original copies for yourself prior to mailing, so that when the envelope arrives, *you won't open it*, but rather, you'll put it away for safekeeping. That's your proof of timeline.

I know that this seems like it doesn't carry the same weight, as it would have under our prior system of WHO WAS THE FIRST PERSON TO INVENT. But nonetheless, as far as your documentation and establishing that you invented this first, *it will count if you ever find yourself embroiled in a legal confrontation regarding either the priority of inventorship, the validity of your patent claims or the origin of your trade secrets.* Reread this paragraph again.

I personally didn't do this, but there is no question that I should have. Right about now some legal geniuses might be given to saying that this is a wasted exercise and that it doesn't count. Believe me, it's admissible and it *does* count.

Let me drop a little experience on you. There is an entire guidebook called the *Federal Rules of Evidence*, and suffice it to say, it states many things regarding what qualifies as evidence. If you should suddenly find yourself in the vortex of litigation, I want to make something very clear to you, *everything that is properly written down can be introduced as evidence and it will count!*

The second method is for you to present a notary public with the same document and written statement declaring that you are the first and true inventor of this idea, having the identified summary/claims in hand you are hereby memorializing your invention on that particular date.

However, keep in mind that this notary is a living breathing person, and though he/she is bound by her office to notarize a document's authenticity, they may also get a chance to read your document. Remember at this time you never know what someone else will do with your idea, so paranoia should still reign supreme, because "loose lips sink ships."

Just so you know, I personally opted for this second method and *it counted so heavily* that I incorporated it as an exhibit in my legal complaint. That said, it is imperative that you carry through with this exercise. I suggest that if you have a lawyer, visit his or her office and have him/her or someone trusted in his employ notarize your idea. Remember…

- The PTO specifies that it is proper procedure for you to get your idea notarized.

In any case, you must choose the proper means to document your idea. Here's the variable. During the product development stage, oftentimes you can't project how long that it's going to take for you to perfect your idea. In order to file a non-provisional patent application, you need product that is in its finalized state of development and that takes time! Authenticating your inventor's notebook will go a long way towards documenting your idea's conception date, your original idea, and memorializing that you are indeed the first and true inventor of this idea.

If you should come up with additional improvements during the inventing process that you believe are either patentable or crucial for the success of your product, it is important that you memorialize them again by using the same means. Don't be lazy… do it!

As an aside, when your *non-provisional* patent application is being prosecuted, you will be required to swear an official inventor's oath. At that time, you will then have an opportunity to *officially swear under penalties of perjury* that you are the first true inventor.

Prototypes

At this juncture, we have more or less covered the bases with regard to both the formation and the preservation of your IP. Of course there's still more to come about that stuff, but I'd like to switch gears for a moment and discuss *prototypes* with you.

- The PTO does not require a working prototype to demonstrate the practicality of an invention, but I do.

For our discussion, a prototype is going to be a working model of your invention. The first thing to know, is that it doesn't have to be in its final form.

Just so you know, nobody in manufacturing can pull off building a final prototype on the first try, so I certainly don't expect you to be able to do that either. Let's just begin by simply trying to envision what a working model of your invention is going to look like.

I know that may sound like a tall order for some of you, but nonetheless it's something that you must deal with. Here's how I want you to handle it.

During your research, I instructed you to gather the materials that would apply to your invention. I realize that those efforts were mainly aimed at gathering information in the form of documents. Now consider this, if your invention employs a special material or a certain part that happens to be already available, now would be an appropriate time for you to try and secure it.

But, this is still not a safe time to share your idea with anyone, *especially not* with any of the parts and material suppliers that you might be dealing with!

Remember, paranoia still rules! So don't get cocky, because at this point your memorialization document does not carry the same legal weight that your patent application will. As already pointed out, it's one thing to register your idea with yourself. Yet it's quite another to officially register your idea with the United States Patent and Trademark Office in the form of a *non-provisional patent application.*

The point is this; if you can build a working prototype without divulging your idea, then by all means, begin to do so. But if you can't build a prototype, because either you can't obtain your materials without divulging your idea, or you need someone in a specialized manufacturing business to do it for you, then without hesitation - I'm going to tell you to wait! That said, I don't want you worrying about putting this off, because for the moment, you still have lots of time.

Here's the bottom line. There will come a point when it's going to be very important that you or someone else produce a working prototype of your invention. Remember that this inventing stuff is foundational. Hopefully you can recall what I told you early on. If your invention can't be realistically made or produced in a cost effective manner, then you're just spinning your wheels. This principal is never going to change.

Just so you know, here's a ridiculous oversimplification of what I did. My invention took a standard spin-on oil filter, which by the way was a *pre-existing device* as a means to deliver various combinations of beneficial chemical compounds into an internal combustion engine's oil system.

My vision was to develop an oil filter that would have a superior edge over the 500,000,000 oil filters that were presently being sold in the US on an annual basis.

My vision was to invent an oil filter with a dual function. It would not only perform its standard job of keeping the oil clean, but it would also perform an entirely new function of adding a beneficial additive to an engines oil supply. After much research and soul searching I *discovered* how to introduce various performance-enhancing materials into an engine's lubricating system through the means of treating the oil filter or its filter media at the point of manufacture.

The primary ingredients that I selected was, Alkyl-zinc-dithiophosphate for my '901 patent which was granted in 1988, and micro fine mixture of Teflon in a carrier oil for my '842 patent, which was granted in 1993.

I'm duty bound to give you a brief snapshot as to how I came upon the key materials for my two filters and how I set the stage to come up with two viable prototypes. This illustration will open your eyes as to how important it is to immerse yourself in your idea. Good things will happen and fruitful opportunities will prevent themselves if only you apply yourself… I promise.

As the owner of a tractor rig, I was very sensitive to the health of my engine, so I would periodically send an oil sample out for analysis. Engine oil much like our blood, is the heart and soul for maintaining the health of one's engine. When properly analyzed, it can tell a lot about the engines wear patterns and as well as its performance.

I used to get my oil analyzed by a South Jersey lab known as Ana Laboratories. I was referred to this facility by Mr. Bill Ashton, who was the VP of maintenance of Holmes Trucking, then a prominent east coast trucking company. Through Bill, I got friendly with the director of the lab, Sadiq Ali. As our relationship grew Mr. Ali taught me more and more about the scope of oil analysis. Over time, I told him about my idea for an additive treated oil filter and he schooled me on how additive packages in motor oils worked. At some point, I needed more information, so he referred me to his longtime friend who was a retired research chemist for Chevron oil, his name is Ben Certo. Ben had long been retired from the company and was living in a retirement village near me. So one day I was fortunate enough to have breakfast with him, and I told him of my plan to make an additive treated oil filter. Before long I was at a Chevron facility on the banks of the Raritan Bay in Jersey. I met with a wonderful field salesman who at Ben's request supplied me with a sample of Alkyl-zinc-dithiophosphate the named ingredient in in my '901 patent. The rest is history.

Just so you know, during my trucking days, Chevron's Delo® was the world leader in both the sales and technology as it related to diesel engine lubricating oil. Shell Oil's, Rotella T® had a much smaller percentage of the market and at that time was mainly specified for CAT® engines.

For my second patent I was able to come upon its key ingredients and knowhow this way. My first course of action was to manually scourer the various libraries for material sources and uses for PTFE or its chemical name Polytetrafluoroethylene. I was hot on the trail of Slick-50 since it had created a market where the combined sales for that category was worth tens of millions of dollars annually.

As you take in what I'm sharing, I encourage you to analyze your products trend wave, your products market as well as your upcoming assignment to develop a realistic prototype.

Anyway, I called DuPont since they were the inventors of this material. And during my course of interaction with this world leader, I accomplished some very important things…

- I had various samples of micro fine Teflon samples sent to me.
- I had literature and Material Data Handling Sheets sent to me.
- I developed a personal relationship with my very knowledgeable sales rep.

- I was afforded the opportunity to have her share with me what she knew about the product etc.
- I was educated as to how DuPont wanted its product used and in what quantities, in order to be incompliance with the use of their Teflon trade mark.
- I signed a product licensing agreement with them for the use of their product and the proper display of their trademarks.

My trademark license with DuPont in conjunction with my understanding of its branding strength was the fuel that was going to launch this rocket.

As an aside, I asked my contact at DuPont for any formulators that made a colloidal suspension of micro fine Teflon and carrier oil, but she was at a loss to guide me. She just reinforced the fact that DuPont didn't make such a product and that the company was unaware of what their end users were using their product for.

It was during this research mission that I came to know that AlliedSignal's chemical division made Polytetrafluoroethylene, but I was not interested in their product nor any other chemical makers' product. Really now, what marketer would have been stupid enough to put PTFE on the side of a revolutionary oil filter. Not I, but I can tell you who fought me tooth and nail as to whether PTFE or Teflon would appear on the side of filter. You really owe it to yourself to read *The Greed of a Dime*, if you have any plans of licensing you patent and IP.

So there you have it. My search to find this elixir was launched. And I tell you that I didn't spare any horses to uncover the source.

- I searched the major engineering universities located in my state.
- I contacted the National Laboratory Consortium of the United States of America.
- I communicated with several resident PhD's regarding the use of Teflon as an oil additive.
- I sought to understand how Teflon could increase lubricity by reducing the drag co-efficient of oil.
- During this foray, I corresponded with laboratories such as Los Alamos and several others within that group.
- I contacted the Society of Automotive Engineers, SAE. I contacted The American Society of Petroleum Engineers, AIME. I did so that I could comb through their library catalogs and order various papers and scientific studies that might help me in my quest.
- I even picked the brains of the ex-senior VP of Purolator Oil filters. Over time, Richard Dye would become an oil filter mentor to me. As a matter of fact, we grew close, and I even hired him as my oil filter expert during my lawsuit.

As you can see, I was teaching myself to become well versed on these various topics. Before it was over I would become very knowledgeable about oil filters, lubricating oil, additive packages, the properties of Teflon, trademarks and a rather long list of other things that were crucial for the lasting success for either of my products. This is exactly what you need to do where your invention is concerned. This is how you are eventually going to fill the shoes of becoming visionary, master salesman, marketer and eventual expert where your invention or new product is concerned.

- Here's the key. Through all of this information gathering, I was prepping myself on how to realistically manufacture an economically feasible prototype of my invention.

So let's get back, because I really want to share with you how I found my key ingredient regarding my trade secret information pertaining to my '842.

I love to fish. And I've been known to watch a fishing show from time to time. Anyway I was watching "The Orlando Wilson Fishin' Show," and Slick-50 happened to be one of the shows sponsors. During the show, a certain Slick-50 commercial came on where they actually showed a copy of an SAE report on Slick-50! I knew immediately that I had to get my hands on this report, but the image of the cover came and went in a flash. I was devastated. Well, I had to wait all week for this program to come on again and I prayed that this same commercial was going to air. And it did! Bingo! This time I was ready, my VCR was running and I caught the elusive cover of that study on tape. I was able to pause the tape and I got the study's number as clear as day. I immediately purchased a couple of copies of that study from the SAE's library.

Now it was this very study that led me to the Holy Grail of trade secrets with regard to my '842. It was this chance opportunity that gave me the key that I was looking for. Notice what I'm sharing. I was constantly looking and so should you. Remember, you must be armed to the teeth in order to do a powerful marketing presentation when a licensing agreement for your invention is on the line.

This test study led me to Acheson Colloids, located in Port Huon, Michigan. It was that crucial bit of information that led me to discover the material called Acheson Colloids SLA 1612. It was this material that became the cornerstone for the creation of the Fram Double Guard oil filter. It was this information that I shared in detail with Fram's lead engineer, Gary Bilski under two separate confidentiality agreements. By the way, I personally gave an original copy of this SAE report to Bilski.

This is an excellent opportunity to illustrate in practical terms what a trade secret actually looks like. Notice, the oil filter itself was not my trade secret, nor were the additives that I was experimenting with. That's because both the oil filter and the additives were already in the public domain. As previously shared, if something is in the public domain, it cannot in of itself be claimed as a trade secret or a patentable claim.

Here's the key: *Should the inventor [you] come up with either a new product, an application or a process that has an advantage over what is presently known in the public domain, that information can be treated as either a trade secret, or at the discretion of the inventor; can be filed as claim for a new invention with the PTO.*

As always, a closing snapshot. As I waded tirelessly through the multiple thousands of meaningless discovery documents, a certain document trail started coming together. It just so happened that Mr. Bilski took a trip to Port Huron, Michigan shortly after I had shared my technology with him. As the rightful inventor, I should have been invited to attend, but true to form I was totally unaware of this junket. As the paper trail began to tell its story, I was able to string together correspondence records, phone records, and a purchase agreement for SLA 1612. These documents proved beyond doubt, that prior to my relationship Honeywell, they never had purchased Acheson Colloids SLA 1612 to put inside of an oil filter.

Getting back…

When I arrived on the scene in the late '80's, the science of oil filtration was a *very mature* business model. The mere thought of introducing anything, other than dirty oil, into an oil filter was thought to be crazy! With all due candor let me just say this, the filter engineers were nearly

100% opposed to my idea! The long and short of it was this; "Oil filters were designed to take stuff out and they were never intended under any circumstances to put stuff in, even if that stuff was found to be beneficial to an engines lubricating system."

In anticipation of this nearly inflexible mindset, my key objective was to have my invention work without altering in any way, the mechanical design of the *industry's standard* oil filter. This design had been in place for over a generation and it was looked upon as being a sacred cow in the filtration industry.

As an industry outsider, if I had made even the tiniest change to the mechanical design of the standard oil filter, my marvelous concept would *never* have seen the light of day. And of course I was right, any alteration to the mechanical design would have sent the industry insiders over the edge, and my invention would never have been produced.

In the final analysis, I was able to take something complex and reduce it down to something quite simple. Often times I compared what I did to be something akin to putting peanut butter inside chocolate, much like a Reese's® peanut butter cup.

Here's my point. I made prototypes and I tested them in various ways. I made prototypes in my garage and they worked. I made prototypes and in the end, they were capable of being manufactured on a large-scale basis and in a cost effective manner.

Here's the key. So must you!

Understand this about building prototypes. Most prototypes that an inventor will build will *always* cost more than the finished product that rolls off of a production line. This is due to the fact that it is so much more expensive to make a single copy or a limited production run of a widget than it is to make a production run for thousands, and hopefully millions of units! Yet that shouldn't stop you, since you're not going to be building a rocket engine.

Over time, and with some adjustments, the manufacturer that you may team up with will change their means of production and make your product even more efficiently than even you might have envisioned, thereby significantly lowering the production costs to manufacture your invention.

In any case, if you can build a prototype at this point it will go a long way towards refining and clarifying your claims and will help you write a better patent. If a picture is worth a thousand words, a working prototype is worth so much more.

Just so you know, the Patent Office no longer requires a working prototype in order to consider your patent application. They have long since done away with that requirement. But that doesn't mean that you should! If there is one thing that I know for sure, both your licensing partner and the buying public *will certainly* require that your widget perform exactly the way that you have envisioned it.

Never lose site of the fact that the patenting process is not just about going through the rigorous process of documentation.

It's not just about secrecy and paranoia. And it is certainly not just about adhering to the protocol foisted upon you by the Patent Office either.

I can't stress this enough. Inventing is the process of creating something novel and something that works, and works well. If you should be so blessed to achieve that, then your invention merits the protection under the patent laws of the United States. To me, this is where the true value of inventing lies, because anything less than that is just a pipedream.

Chapter 5

CONSIDER YOUR OPTIONS

Your Options

Up to this point you have done some very important things - great things! You have worked hard and you've gone through a truly unique process. By now your precious idea has morphed into a glorious widget. And by the same token, I hope that the inventing process has now become your dream. You certainly should be feeling more empowered than you did at the start of this journey!

Hopefully the inventing process has become much clearer to you and you've come to realize that the way in which you go about the process will greatly influence your future success.

Do you recall the list of options that I put forth in the introduction concerning which path you might choose for your inventing journey? Well now is the appropriate time for us to review your options once again and consider which path is the best one for you to choose. Allow me to once again to summarize those options before you.

- There are numerous postings on the internet for you to consider.
- You could contact a patent lawyer and pay him a minimum of $300 per hour and let the meter run for a good 15 hours or so.
- You could go to one of those invention services and pay them several thousand dollars and in many cases more, before it's all over.
- You could spend hundreds of dollars for a professional to conduct a patent search for you.
- You could consider enlisting the services of a registered patent agent, who by the way is not a lawyer.
- You could file an inexpensive *provisional patent* application, but you *do not have to make any claims or adhere to the same criteria as a non-provisional patent.*
- Finally, you could go it alone. Today with the aid of the Internet, that's a very real possibility as well.

Consider the Internet

The first option I put forth was the notion of searching the Internet, with its numerous related postings.

This first option simply points out that there is far more information on the Internet than you could ever hope to digest regarding the inventing process and patents.

When an aspiring inventor types in relevant keywords such as "inventor" or "patent," he or she is bombarded with an immense amount of information. Unfortunately, your query *will not* produce a comprehensive site that will provide you with all of the necessary real-world information that you'll need.

One of the many things that I found in abundance on the Internet; is that there seems to be no shortage of individuals who are offering their services to *help you with your idea.* As you're now aware, getting help with your idea is just the very tip of the iceberg. And speaking of icebergs, wasn't it the ice that was hidden *below* the waterline and not the tip of the iceberg that ripped open the side of the Titanic?

Conclusion. The Internet is a great source of information for inventing and patents. However, in my opinion, it's *not* the place where you can learn how to become a successful inventor all by yourself.

Consider a Patent Lawyer or Agent

"You could contact a *patent lawyer* for a minimum of $300 dollars per hour and let him run the meter for a good 15 hours or so. And let me assure you; after he or she files your patent application you won't be any closer to becoming a successful inventor."

"You could go to a *patent agent*, who is not a lawyer at all, in the hopes of saving yourself lots of money for his services - as compared to a lawyer. The result? Often times you get what you pay for."

I am going to handle both of these options in tandem, simply because patent attorneys and patent agents are both qualified to prosecute patent applications before the PTO.

Note. From this point forward, I'm going to lump them together by referring to either one of them as *practitioners*. When it's proper for me to address either one of them specifically, I will make it clear by referring to their respective titles.

At this time, I'd like to explain why I didn't advise that you choose either one of these options at the very beginning. Again from my standpoint, you simply weren't ready to do so. And you certainly weren't ready to do so on any number of levels. In all practicality, their ability to take nothing more than your embryonic idea and then prosecute a proper patent application is really quite farfetched. That's why if you had contacted them right out of the gate, it would have been a terrible waste of both your time and money.

That's right! Their ability to perform a proper job for you, in great measure, is going to be determined by how much *you* know about *your* widget and how well you comprehend the inventing and the patenting process beforehand.

In essence, the more prepared you are to file your own patent, the better off you'll be. So to a large degree, *you* are the limiting factor in the patent equation. Since this is the most expensive and delicate part of the process, you would have been wasting your resources if you had prematurely engaged either practitioner. The reality of it is this, you can't realistically expect another person that hasn't a clue about what your invention really is, to figure it out for you. Likewise, if that person doesn't have a full understanding of what your invention is, then he/she certainly won't be able to get your claims right either. This path will simply not result in a good patent application or a strong set of claims.

In light of what I've just said, let's take a moment here and reflect back to where we began this process.

Humor me for a moment. Before we got acquainted, were you ready to call upon either practitioner to file a patent application for you?

If you're being honest, your answer should be no. The fact is; the inventor bears the major responsibility for the successful outcome of his or her patent quest. Ultimately, you're the one who's going to be responsible for a successful outcome, not the practitioner. Assuming that you do find a capable practitioner, the equation works exactly like it does with computers, "garbage in, and garbage out."

Here's one more thing that I'd like you to consider. Do you really believe in your wildest dreams, that an attorney would have volunteered what I've taught you thus far about inventing?

By chance if you just answered yes, you'd better run outside, because there's a herd of pigs flying over your house!

Consider an Invention Service

"You could go to one of those invention services and pay them several thousand dollars or more, and they will produce a pretty binder with the expectations of a patent that will secure a lucrative licensing deal with big industry for you…"

Here's what I was counseling against when I first presented you this option. I didn't think it was wise for you to entrust your embryonic idea to any invention service without at least having the benefit of what I'm going to teach you.

I still remain a very firm believer that if you're going to be successful in this patent odyssey, you're absolutely required to be the lead sled dog, and I certainly don't see your role in this scenario as being that.

So let me ask you a couple of basic questions…

- Who's going to keep your secret safe?
- Does the patent service have a patent agent or a patent attorney directly on staff? And if they don't, whom are they going to refer you to, because after all, someone is going to file your application?
- Who are you going to trust to prosecute your patent application and properly construct your claims?
- How much input will you have in the patent application process?
- Are their practitioner's qualifications going to meet all of your standards?

If you end up receiving your patent, and I hope that you will, then looming off on the distant horizon is the next set of mountains that you must scale. Marketing and Licensing.

- Who's going to do that for you?
- Is the inventing service?
- How capable are they at performing this one shot deal?
- How can you play the role of the master salesman if you are letting someone else represent your idea?

Think about this one.

- Who's more capable of protecting your dream and your future better than you? Especially in light of the information that I've presented thus far?

My answer is simple; *no one can, but you*! For obvious reasons, an inventor's service is not the avenue that I am advising you to follow. To be absolutely clear, I am no fan of inventor's services. Period.

Conclusion. If what I've presented to you thus far seems like a heck of a lot of work and responsibility - you'd be right. Likewise, if you're not up for this task, that's quite all right too.

Upon the completion of this teaching, should you find that the inventing process is more than what you have bargained for, then perhaps you should just pick the best inventor service you can find and go with them.

Consider a Patent Search

"You could spend hundreds of dollars on a patent search. Or you could do it yourself for free. In either case, the results may or may not tell you a darn thing as to whether your idea is patentable or not. Chances are, the outcome of that search would only serve to confuse you."

The first thing that most patent lawyers or agents might say with regard to a patent search is something along these lines. "You can order a patent search, but the reality is, it may or may not tell 'us' in black and white whether your idea is patentable or not."

So if that's what a "patent expert" is going to tell you right out of the box regarding a patent search, then how could you be expected to interpret the results any better on your own?

My answer is - you can't.

Do you recall that I previously pointed out that in all likelihood you may not have come up with a stand-alone idea and that it's more probable that you've come up with an improvement for an existing product that already exists?

Chances are, the results of that search if performed too early would have discouraged you from moving forward, and perhaps it could have discouraged you from filing at all. As an inexperienced inventor with a terrific new idea, that's not the result that you're looking for.

Be honest. When we first met, was your idea as concrete as it needed to be? Simply put, if you had run out and ordered a patent search based upon sheer impulse, it would have resulted in a waste of your precious resources.

Another big question yet to be answered is this. Who's going to compare the claims of the prior art against the new set of claims that you intend on proposing? The search service only pulls patents that are related to your general idea. They don't perform claim construction. That means that they don't evaluate the various claims; they just pull relevant patents.

I'm willing to bet that before we started, you didn't even know what patent claims were. And if you did, I bet you weren't aware of their great importance. So in my mind you were *never* going to be the individual who was going to bear the responsibility of reviewing your claims. I hope you can agree that you would have been woefully unprepared, in light of all you've learned thus far.

In conclusion, it's still not a wise move for you to order a patent search at this *particular* time. You still don't know enough about the patent process and you aren't deep enough into this teaching yet. So at this juncture, you'd just be wasting your time and money.

Provisional Patents

"You could file an inexpensive *provisional patent application*, but what will that really get you, since you do not have to make any claims or adhere to the same criteria as a *non-provisional patent*."

Let's look at the downside. This instrument will expire in one year's time and then the application lapses. The provisional application must be followed up by a *non-provisional* application in one year's time from the initial filing date or you will lose any prior filing date.

You are permitted to mark your product, but in my estimation that just puts you in the dangerous position of having your device reverse engineered by your competition before you ever receive the *full benefits* of real patent protection.

You see, provisional patents lack two of the critical elements that put the teeth into a patent instrument. Chiefly, a provisional patent doesn't require the inventor to specify his patents claims nor does it provide for the inventor's oath that swears that you are the first true inventor as specified under 35 USC §115 & 116.

The upside is that if you want to officially document your idea, it *could* be worth the rather inexpensive filing fee. If you want to establish an early filing date it *certainly* would be worth it, *but only if you're positive* that you'll be able to follow it up with a non-provisional application in one year's time or less.

One more important thing to bring to your attention. What if your idea significantly changes over the course of that year? You know during the creative phase of the inventing process that's a very real possibility. And if your idea does in fact change, the provisional patent application that you had already filed will not cover your new idea. So at the very least, you'll be required to file yet another provisional application to protect the newer version of your idea.

If you think that you need more than year to fine-tune your patentable idea, then a *provisional application* is not a smart thing to do either. And as you can see, to prefect your idea and boil it down into the form of a patent application, in many cases this *will* exceed one year's time. This option like all the rest we've considered so far has both pros, but in my opinion, some very serious cons. As you can see, if you ran out and filed a provisional application based on sheer impulse, without the benefit of what I've been sharing with you thus far, I believe that you'd just be putting the cart before the horse.

Just so you know, I am not a big fan of provisional patent applications. I will concede that in some cases that option will work out just fine. However, I much favor the route of fine tuning one's idea and fleshing out all of the particulars that we're going to cover in this teaching before filing for any patent. Regardless of what path you may choose, *only a non-provisional application will matriculate into a patent grant.*

Consider Going it Alone

"You could go it alone you know…"

I'm sure that by now, you've already caught my drift. I have already disqualified you from filing your own patent application. And I believe that I have already put forth a fairly good argument as to why I feel that you are not qualified to perform that task.

Simply put, prosecuting your own patent application is well beyond most individual's ability to get it right. The scary thing is that this process has been masqueraded as something that's within the grasp of anyone who might possess some intelligence and common sense. In my mind, that is the furthest thing from reality.

Although the PTO's website doesn't have any disclaimers such as what you'd find on a pack of cigarettes or a bottle of whisky, that still doesn't discount the fact that going it alone could one day cost you the farm. However, if you do check out their FAQ section, the PTO does recommend that you use a registered patent attorney or a registered patent agent to prosecute your application. In addition to that, the PTO does warn first time inventors to exercise caution when considering inventor's services.

As an aside, there are innumerable websites that encourage you to buy their books and offer to teach you the ins and outs of filing a patent. And on the surface that notion appears very scholarly. Yet the filing of a proper application has more twists and turns to it than the average scholar could ever hope to handle.

Before doing so, I heartily suggest that you carefully study the PTO's website and see if you're in that league. If it makes you feel any better I'm definitely not capable of filing my own patent and I wouldn't, and that goes doubly after what I've already been through!

In addition to that, study the U.S. Code, particularly 35 USC where it specifically applies to patent law. Then after you're done, pull up the patent examiner's manual and take it for a spin. It's at least four inches thick. If you come away feeling confident, then I truly tip my hat to you.

In the event that you absolutely insist on filing your own patent, I'll be the first to admit that it certainly can be done, and I'm sure many individuals are doing it every day. Between the PTO's website and the information that you could glean from the Internet and other sources, it could go a long way towards accomplishing that enterprise. But before you launch out and file your own patent, I think it's only fair to pose a few simple questions that you may want to consider.

- In the end, what would you have gained by forgoing the experienced and expert advice you sorely needed when it came time to prosecute your patent application? And more importantly, what advantages would you have lost?
- Can you trust yourself to do an expert job on your claims construction?
- Can you handle the examiner's rejections to your claims and the other various deficiencies that are going to be cited in your application? Remember, claim rejection and application deficiencies are the norm and not the exception.
- Are you up to date with all the new rules and regulations, as well as the old ones?
- Are you aware that even the most seasoned intellectual property lawyer must be at the top of his/her game during claim construction?
- Don't forget, 50% of all patent applications receive final rejections.
- Are you comfortable dealing with patent law?

If you are, and you can trust yourself to do an expert job on your *claim construction*, and if you can handle the examiner's inevitable rejections to your claims as submitted in your application, then go ahead.

Conclusion. If you want to file a patent just for the sake of receiving an official copy suitable for framing, then by all means go ahead and file your own patent. But on the other hand, if you're convinced that your idea is *valuable*, and that you stand a chance of making a significant amount of money on your idea, *then don't!*

Who are You Going to Choose?

After all, that we've discussed so far, isn't it rather amazing that the general public has been led to believe that the invention process is such a casual affair; left to the likes of tinkerers and dreamers?

I don't know whether you have considered this before, but do you realize that there are only three entities that are permitted to prosecute patent applications before the PTO?

Just so that we are perfectly clear, here is the definitive list of individuals that are allowed to prosecute a patent application before the PTO. I am going to list them in the order of their qualifications, beginning first with the individuals who are the *least* qualified.

- First of all, there is you. Any individual, regardless of national citizenship can submit a patent application for a new invention to the USPTO.
- The next individual that is permitted to do so is a registered patent agent. This person doesn't have to be a college graduate or a licensed engineer. All that's required is that this person has taken a test administered by the PTO and has passed it. This agent is afforded the privilege to prosecute patents and interact with the PTO based upon obtaining this certification.
- The last individual permitted to do so is a licensed patent attorney. These attorneys have also taken a test administered by the PTO and have passed it. In addition to that, they are licensed by their respective state[s] bar associations and are allowed to practice law before the courts.

Just in case you may not have noticed, invention services are *not* listed among these qualified groups of individuals.

I've shared all of this with you for a reason. It's time! You are now going to begin the process of picking your team, and you'd better know what you're doing. From now on, I want you to consider yourself to be the team captain. It's now time to begin shopping for your star fielder. So let's consider both the lawyer and the patent agent.

Chapter 6

CHOOSING YOUR TEAM

Part I

The Good, the Bad and the Ugly

As we all know, in every walk of life there are both good practitioners and there are bad practitioners. So why should we expect the field of patent practitioners to be any different? The answer to that question is... we shouldn't.

Allow me to conjure up a picture for you. Do you remember the guy whose truck was emblazoned with "professional so and so" all over it? Complete with professional license and registration numbers? And can you recall what your house looked like after he got finished?

My point here is this. When considering a patent practitioner, we are seeking an individual with the best possible credentials and qualifications to help us in the patent prosecution process.

During the selection process it's important that you remain focused on your goals. Don't just expect to find someone to run with your patent application and perform flawlessly, as you sit on the sidelines not paying attention to the game in front of you. This is a critical juncture in the patent odyssey, and it's where some of the most serious errors in judgment can be made.

Here's a key. Ask pointed questions of your practitioner and let your expectations be made known from the very beginning, as to how you want this collaboration to work. Let that person know what you hope to accomplish during this relationship. Don't be shy.

Everything about this game is about to ratchet up exponentially. In my opinion, there are really only two choices left. That being said, let's delve into some of the respective qualifications of both the patent attorney and the patent agent.

General Qualifications of Patent Practitioners

The first order of business is to highlight the differences between a patent agent and a patent attorney. So let's get that out of the way.

As previously pointed out, patent agents are not required to meet any specialized education requirements to practice before the PTO, other than passing the test. A patent agent's practice is limited to practicing before the PTO, such as prosecuting patent applications and other related dealings. A patent agent is not an attorney; therefore, they *cannot* give you legal advice like a lawyer can. A patent agent *cannot* litigate patent matters in a court of law. Simply put, a patent agent is not a lawyer and is not allowed to practice law.

On the other hand, an attorney is not only a college graduate, but he or he has attended law school for three years. Only after passing the bar exam is an attorney permitted to practice law. Even after all of that, an attorney's ability to practice law is by and large limited to the particular state[s] in which he's been licensed. To become a patent attorney, a lawyer must also pass a separate test administered by the PTO in order to practice before them.

The world of patents is the only field of law where such a designation is required. This is an important distinction and I don't want to gloss over it. I want to make this perfectly clear; *not* every attorney can practice before the PTO. In my opinion, that is a very important qualifier.

As I've been telling you all along, this patent stuff can be a complicated matter. Apparently both the Bar Association and the Patent Office believe this as well. As such, patent lawyers will fall into two general categories:

- Prosecution. Some patent attorneys specialize in prosecuting patent applications only, and do not litigate patent matters in court.
- Litigation. Some patent attorneys specialize in litigating patent matters in court and do not prosecute patent applications.

Of course there are exceptions to this generalization, because some attorneys might do both. But for the most part, they will either *specialize* in filing patent applications or specialize in fighting over patents in court.

What you're going to actually find is that patent attorneys will either litigate patent matters, or they will prosecute patent applications. In this day and age of specialized services, that aspect should be easy to understand. From what I've experienced, the field of intellectual property litigation is so intensive; I don't know where an attorney engaged in litigation would ever find the time to prosecute a patent application effectively.

So please don't get fixated on trying to find an attorney that does both litigation and patent prosecution, just because you might think that the attorney might know the process from both vantage points. That said, the litigator will understand the processes from both sides, but that won't necessarily make him better at prosecuting patent applications.

More often than not, I'd be *against* picking an attorney that is engaged in dual practices, because each area of patent law has its own demands. In my opinion, it's best to stick with a specialist who does the same thing day in and day out. So my advice would be to seek out an attorney that specializes in prosecuting patents for a living. Remember, it's all in the claims!

So there you have it. By the looks of things, a lawyer is certainly more highly qualified to prosecute a patent application than a patent agent. And in my opinion, that is generally going to be the case. So, who are *you* going to pick?

There's still more for us to consider, so let's see if I can fill in some more of the blanks and help you make an educated decision.

Some Important Qualifications

If we could make a wish, our dream practitioner whether it's an agent or a lawyer, would look something like this. He or she would be an excellent patent writer. So skilled that they would get the majority of their patents approved by the PTO, and suffer a minimum amount of rejections. They would also play an integral part in their clients going forth in securing lucrative licensing deals. Their work would be so thorough and so precise that the patents that they've helped to craft, seldom if ever get challenged. And as a bonus, they are both personable and affordable!

Almost sounds dreamy, doesn't it? It's a fantasy for sure, but nonetheless you're going to make it your quest to find such a practitioner.

The search to locate your star fielder has officially begun, but before you do so...

- You must be convinced that your idea is highly prized and capable of making you a significant amount of money.

- You must try to make sense of this specialized field of practitioners.

What I'm telling you, is that you can't expect to do very well in the patent odyssey without considering the guidance of a skilled practitioner who has a working knowledge of the PTO's myriad of procedures and a working knowledge of patent law.

Go on the PTO's website and see if you can make heads or tails out of their pension for creating new rules, forms and procedures every time you turn around. Remember the voluminous patent examiner's manual I told you about? These individuals should not only own one, but they should be fluent with it.

Like it or not, you are about to embark on a legalistic journey and you'd better have the proper guidance, or two things could happen:

- First. You will not get your patent application through the process and therefore, you won't end up with a patent.
- Second. You might end up with a patent that has so many holes and defects in it, that it won't even be suitable for wrapping dead fish in.

Patent Agents

I must be blunt; patent agents are my second choice for this job. It all comes down to the fact that they are not licensed to practice patent law. Patent law is an extremely complex endeavor and agents are not permitted to counsel you regarding matters that are based upon the workings of the law. With that said, I still cannot completely discount a qualified patent agent, because there are some very skilled ones. Here are some reasons why you might consider choosing one to help you file your application.

Some patent agents may be as competent to prosecute patent applications as an attorney, minus the law degree.

Some may have been professional engineers or highly trained in a specific field before they became an agent.

Many patent agents were formerly employed by the PTO as patent examiners. As it stands, the majority of examiners employed by the PTO are patent agents, and not licensed patent attorneys.

You should find out if the agent that you are interviewing has worked as a former examiner. This real world experience is as valuable as having an accountant or a tax specialist who has worked for the IRS.

Here is something that you may not be aware of. Many law firms employ patent agents in their patent prosecution departments. That in of itself should speak volumes as to some agent's qualifications and abilities.

If you should consider a patent agent, his professional credentials and qualifications are an extremely important consideration. Take the same care to examine his background and track record is as you would any lawyers. Whatever you do, don't pick a patent agent solely on cost.

So my advice is this, don't discount a well-seasoned patent agent. Plain and simple, you want to align yourself with an expert in your respective field that you feel confident about. Second, your practitioner must have verifiable qualifications and a demonstrable track record.

When looking for a patent agent, you will not find their bio's listed on the *legal search engines*, simply because they are not licensed attorneys. You will be able to locate them if they have either a website or if they are employed by a law firm.

Again, use the Internet and locate a qualified patent agent in the area of your invention and see how it works out to your overall satisfaction.

Qualifications and Abilities are Two Different Things

As discussed, the individual practitioner's qualifications and credentials come to mind, but what is most important, is each individual's *ability.* And yes, there *is* a difference. In life, a lot of people stack up awards and trophies, but they don't always live up to all the accolades, now do they?

Here's how I want you to go about the selection process. I'm specifically referring to lawyers here. At first blush, a Harvard-trained attorney more times than not, is going to lift an eyebrow or two, just because of where he or she has attended law school. That's fine, but if you allow yourself to look beyond the lawyer's pedigree, you'll see what really matters. I'm saying all this, because many of the lawyers that you're going to be researching will have some very impressive bios, beginning with where they attended college and what law school they graduated from. However, in my opinion, it's more about what you've done with your schooling after graduation that really counts.

Yes, indeed, these people are all going to be book smart, there's no denying that. But there is an equally important second ingredient, it's called common sense and it's very important. This prized attribute is oftentimes overlooked when it comes to these genius types, but our search requires that we find a practitioner who has got more going for him than just book smarts.

Here's why. Regardless of how smart these attorneys may appear; the patent game is so complex that…

- Attorneys *can,* attorneys *do,* and attorneys *will* make mistakes while handling your file.

Ultimately, any of their mistakes made while prosecuting your application will become your responsibility and you will have to live with the aftermath.

That should give you just an inkling as to how finely hairs can be split in the patent game. It's worth repeating.

- The mistakes that *any practitioner* makes while prosecuting your application could cost *you* in the end.

So how do we limit that?

Hopefully, we can limit any potential mishaps by scrutinizing that person's ability, by being involved, and by asking questions. You're going to be on the meter now, so you'd better begin to ask *why* if you don't understand something. Better yet, make it your policy to ask *why* often, so that you will better understand the prosecution process. Don't let the rudiments of filing a patent application be something mysterious to you. If you get involved in the application process, much of the mystery will fade.

The Right Specialist for the Job

When deciding on an attorney, your first major consideration would be this; what field does this particular practitioner specialize in?

As already mentioned, the PTO and the practitioners in the field refer to these filing groups as *art groups*. These art groups are further divided into patent *classifications* and according to the PTO there are approximately 450 separate patent classifications. For example, they are divided into apparel, bridges, cutlery, firearms etc., etc. Now that's something to consider since an attorney who specializes in plant genetics isn't going to be any help to you when it comes time to file a patent on an electrical circuit. For one thing, the classifications are too wildly diverse and he/she will lack the necessary expertise to understand your invention like he should. To pursue such an attorney would be a waste of energy, regardless of how impressive their credentials might be.

Your job is to find an attorney who is both fluent and successful in prosecuting patents in the particular field that your patent falls under. An honest attorney *should* tell you that there is a world of difference from field to field, and that specialized knowledge is required when filing a patent application in a particular field.

Think with me for a moment. Consider how complex the field of chemistry is. There is organic and inorganic chemistry. There is qualitative and quantitative analysis. There is stereochemistry, and the list goes on. By the same token, think for a moment just how complex the electronics field is, or consider the complex mathematics and the applied physics that are involved in engineering a special part for an airplane.

I certainly don't know what your invention is about, but I can tell you that the person prosecuting your patent *must* be well versed in your specific field. The very first rule when picking a practitioner is this; don't consider a practitioner who does not specialize in the field in which your widget belongs. The second rule, is don't pick someone who's too inexperienced, because he or she will just be learning on your file.

So when you go shopping for an attorney, it's important to pay careful attention to their bio, and it is imperative to make sure it's in a field related to your invention. Once you get past their bio, do yourself a favor and begin to zero in on their track record of achievements. Hopefully, you'll find that their achievements will be commensurate with their bio. If their achievements are lacking, then you might have picked an individual who might be smarter than his capabilities. And that's what you *don't* want. You're looking for a capable practitioner here.

- A lawyer who is skilled in the related field of your invention.
- A lawyer who gets their patent applications approved.
- A lawyer who has a respectable amount of clients that go on to get their inventions licensed.
- A lawyer whose patents aren't successfully challenged by outside parties.
- A lawyer who may have some relevant licensing connections.
- Not some book smart genius that doesn't accomplish the job at hand.

With regard to clients obtaining licenses, a well-seasoned lawyer or an agent may have connections in his respective field due to years of practice in that particular field. However, you must exercise some common sense here as to your expectations. Be mindful that the overwhelming responsibility for obtaining a license will always be squarely placed on the inventor's shoulders, and never on the lawyer's or the agent's.

Just to be perfectly clear, your prosecuting attorney or agent may have an *in* or some possible connections in your field, but that holds no guarantee of your future success in this area. This added benefit should only be viewed as a potential opportunity that a connection might be made on your behalf, but nothing more. Yet at the same time, I don't want you to overlook this potential benefit either, because networking is a beautiful thing. And you just never know.

Steady as You Go

This may be the first time that you've ever had to hire an attorney, especially one that's so sophisticated. Many patent attorneys were once engineers in their respective fields and some of them will have either their Master's or Ph.D.'s in their respective fields of expertise as well.

I realize that I just got done advising you not to get bowled over by their qualifications, yet sometimes it's hard not to. It just so happens that the brainpower of these individuals is near the very top of the food chain.

Just so you know, to this day even as a college graduate and a successful inventor, I still have to remind myself that these folks have to get up in the morning and brush their teeth, just like I do. My only advice to you is that you need to rein in any of your insecurities and just go for it.

Remind yourself that they won't eat as well at the end of the week if you don't hire them. Don't lose sight of the fact that you also won't be using them if they simply aren't up to the task of producing the desired result for you either.

As you can see, the field of patents and the world of practitioners aren't filled with lightweights. In many ways, patents and all of the attendant rules and regulations that govern their existence are near the pinnacles of human thought. The point here is this. You don't want to experience that pinnacle going up your backside in a patent lawsuit, because you were either too *cheap*, or too *sloppy*, or too *uninvolved* at this stage. So please, make it your mission to try and identify the best possible practitioner you can find.

Ah, Law Firms

Just like the attorney, a law firm's pedigree might get us to stop and take notice, but achievement in the field is still the horse that we want to ride in this race.

Some of the oldest established businesses in America are law firms. Often times, they are steeped in history, a sort of nobility that goes back to the founding of this country. So when the time comes to decide which law firm to pick, I strongly recommend that you go with a firm that either specializes in patent prosecutions, or at the very least, is a firm that does a significant portion of their business with the PTO.

It's okay to be impressed, but be careful, because so much of *lawyering* is window dressing. Lawyers and law firms can be likened to watching a bevy of male peacocks in full plumage, squaring off over a single kernel of corn. These guys live in a different world from what most of us are accustomed to. It's a world where you have a bunch of men acting like little boys playing with marbles, forever trying to outsmart one another. As a result of having plenty of time to practice, they are darn good at it.

Just in case you might need a gentle reminder, President Bill Clinton, who is said to be a smart lawyer himself, once tried to worm his way out of a Monaca Lewinski question by responding, "It depends on what the definition of '*is*' is."

In the case of investigating a law firm, consider whether they prosecute patents as a sideline to pay the light bill, or if it's one of their core specialties. In most cases, you will begin your attorney search by first shopping for the firm, and that's just what I would recommend. Posted on their homepage they will clearly let you know if they engage in the practice of intellectual property. The field of intellectual property covers patents, trademarks, trade secrets, and often times licensing and *anti-trust* matters. If you find a firm that has a significant intellectual property department conducting those types of practices, then chances are they will have a patent prosecution department as well.

The law firms that tend to specialize in prosecuting patent applications are often times the ones with the best track records. In addition to that, the firms that specialize in patent prosecution and not litigation might tend to be more affordable as well.

From a common sense standpoint, keep in mind that it's a good practice to focus on firms that have an assortment of like minds, filled with professionals that are doing the same kind of work day in and day out. Lawyers do brainstorm, and I've seen it. So I want you to consider selecting a firm that has several patent attorneys in it. Simply put, the more brains meeting around the water cooler, the better.

This is where the Internet is going to be a great help to you. Naturally, you're going to type in any number of key words such as *patent law firms* to begin your search. It's going to be hunt and peck at first, but eventually you'll be pulling up listings of firms and attorneys that practice patent prosecution in the area of your invention.

There are also legal search engines such as LexisNexis, Westlaw or FindLaw. My advice is to try and find a firm that is located within a reasonable driving distance from your home and preferably within your state. That way you can personally meet with the particular practitioner of your choosing.

I've always felt that it was best to see the firm and its lawyers firsthand. I am also the type of person that prefers to meet someone personally, even if it means driving a couple of hundred miles in order to do so.

However, I also realize that sometimes this is not always possible or practical. With all of the communication options available to us, the job can still get done properly without having to meet face to face.

In all due candor, personal contact is no guarantee of picking the right attorney anyway, so don't obsess over that aspect if you can't make it happen.

The Pecking Order

There is no doubt in my mind that while searching the Internet, you're going find an attorney's bio that's really going to grab your interest. The first thing to be mindful of is that there is going to be a little designation listed after the attorney's name that will identify his or her rank within the firm.

Listed below is the ranking order, going from the top to the bottom.

- Senior partner
- Partner
- Junior partner
- Associate

In the legal business rank and experience goes hand in hand, and so does the corresponding *billable hour rate*. The hierarchy found within the legal profession is the same as you might expect in many specialized service professions, such as accounting or medicine.

The attorney with the *least* amount of experience and the *lowest* billable hour rate is going to be the associate. You don't want this person to prosecute your application due to his or her lack of experience.

On the other end of the spectrum is the senior partner. Just the same, you might not want this person prosecuting your application either, because he will command the *highest* billable hour rate. Or, because he's too preoccupied servicing his larger clients and will pass you off to that new associate fresh out of law school and again, that's exactly what you don't want.

The trick, is that you want to choose someone within the firm who has the proper mix of experience and expertise that won't be costing you the family jewels. You also want to pick an individual that will be *personally* working on your file. Your goal is to find out the following:

- What's his or her experience in your field?
- What's his or her billable hour rate?
- Approximately how much will the job cost?
- Approximately how much time will the job take?
- Will that individual be personally working on your file?

Don't hesitate to put these, and any other questions that you might come up with to the attorney. Whatever you do, put your questions down on paper so that you have them in front of you. Don't trust your memory when it comes to either asking questions or remembering any of the answers. Write everything down, because you will forget it!

Here are some other good questions to ask:

- Are the graphic artist(s) used for the application in-house?
- If not, how much does the graphic service charge for their drawings?
- Other than the PTO's fees, will there be any other outside related charges?

Again, it has been my experience that attorneys are not nearly as sensitive to expenses as their clients are. Attorneys when they are in the midst of working on your case can tend to get caught up in performing the job at hand, and the cost of doing so, is just the cost of getting the job done. You should let it be known that you want your money spent wisely during the prosecution of your application. I highly suggest that you should shop around and ask plenty of questions and be sure to get everything in writing.

Some Good Questions

Before we launch into this section, I want to impress something upon your thinking by providing an illustration for you to consider.

Let's just say that you had to call in a plumber to replace a toilet in your home that recently cracked at the base and has begun to leak.

After the plumber finished the job, did he bother to explain how he went about his business as you handed him the check? Did he explain to you the nuances of his craft? Did he describe to you in detail how he had to first carefully drain the broken toilet without getting the dirty toilet water all over your clean bathroom floor? Or how he had to disconnect the supply line from a seized up cold water supply valve that hadn't been used in the past ten years? Or how he had to fight with the rusted Johnny bolts, which he had to cut off with a cordless reciprocating saw, because the knucklehead before him neglected to use brass bolts? Or how he deftly applied an additional wax ring, because the previous plumber neglected to raise the toilet flange for the tile setter who replaced the floor sometime back? Which by the way, was the root cause why the toilet cracked in the first place, due to the excessive rocking?

Did he explain to you that he has an automatic policy of changing out the fill valve with a modern state of the art model? Since the fill valve that comes as original equipment with nearly every new toilet was designed over forty years ago and is subject to premature failure in hard water conditions.

No, your plumber didn't volunteer any of this. He just pulled out your old toilet and made it look easy. What you don't realize is that he charged you for not only his expertise, but for his ability to think ahead and his ability to overcome the obstacles that were placed in his way.

So when he finished, he just politely handed you the bill and took your check.

By the same token, did you care enough to ask your plumber how he went about performing his job? Chances are you didn't ask him anything, because as a homeowner, you don't have any interest in the intimate details of a toilet extraction. Most of the people that I run into don't.

So here's my point, regardless of what craft is being performed, whether it's pulling a toilet or pulling a patent, most practitioners don't generally elaborate on the nuances of their craft. Perhaps keeping that specialized knowledge close to their vest perpetuates the need for their services in the first place.

But whatever the case, most people seem satisfied in leaving the details up to the experts. After all, they are paying a qualified individual to perform a task of which they know little or nothing about and generally they can't be bothered, so they just end up paying the bill and move on with their lives.

I want to destroy that mindset when it comes to dealing with lawyers! There is absolutely no room for it in the inventing game where your questions regarding *anything* in this process are concerned. If you're inclined to take my advice, lawyers are going to be an integral part of this process, so you had better be prepared to deal with them.

It's going to be *your* job to not only frame out the questions that you would like to have answered, but it is also your job to ask them. I want to be fair about this; if you don't ask your attorney questions, chances are good that he is not going to volunteer what he's doing and why. It's just not in his professional makeup to volunteer information any more than it's your plumber's. Consider carefully the track record for each individual that you interview:

- How long have they been prosecuting patents?
- What is their success rate?
- On what basis do their patent applications get rejected?
- How busy are they?
- Can their present workload accommodate your timetable?
- What is their fee?
- Do they charge by the hour, or by the job?
- Have them break down their fees.
- Are their fees all-inclusive?

This is an excellent opportunity for you to find out, from the attorney's mouth, basic things such as patent coverage, protection and enforcement. Let *him* tell you the facts; don't just rely upon what I've said. Go over the concepts that I've brought to your attention and let him explain it to you firsthand.

All I have to say is that both of our explanations had better mesh!

Your first meeting is about getting informed, as well as informing him about your invention. Don't lose sight of the fact that you are someone who's doing this for the first time and that you are a private citizen and not some engineer working for a big company who's been sent over to get the company's patent filed. This is *your* patent application, so it's up to you to get all of your questions answered.

Keep in mind, as in most trades and services, you can't just waltz in and have someone say; "I'll get on it right away for you." Since these people are qualified and successful, they'll tend to be busy and a patent application isn't something that just gets slapped together. As I've already covered, the average application takes over two years to work its way through the PTO.

Ask the prospective attorney about how long might it take him or her to complete and file your patent application?

Provided that you did all of your homework beforehand, now would be a good opportunity for you to ask how *you* might be of assistance.

I know that I've already mentioned it, but now would be the best time to find out what the particular backlog is for your art group?

The attorney or agent that you are interviewing can surely give you an idea of what you can expect as far as time frames are concerned, since he or she is doing this every day for a living.

Foreign Protection

Though I told you that I wouldn't spend much time on this aspect, that doesn't mean that you shouldn't find out from your attorney what advantages there are to having foreign patent coverage. Now would be the appropriate time to discuss this subject, because it's a very good question.

This is a subject that I'm strictly leaving up for both you and your attorney to discuss.

Just so you know, I never filed for foreign protection for two reasons. First, I couldn't afford it. Second, according to my research, I didn't believe that over three billion people riding around on bicycles were going to be needing a Teflon treated oil filter anytime soon. In my particular case, I was right.

Again, that doesn't mean that you shouldn't be considering foreign patent protection for your idea. You need to consider foreign patent coverage with all of its potential costs, as well as its potential advantages. Therefore, you need to be able to analyze the foreign markets just like you would for any U.S. based market and make your own determination of how you plan on protecting your idea.

In practical terms, this conversation cannot take place until your patent is in its finished form and you are very confident that one day you'll be receiving *a notice of allowance.* At that time, both you and your attorney can examine your patent and intelligently evaluate the potential market value of your invention. In particular, you need to address:

- Foreign coverage as it applies to both *protection* and the *enforcement* of your *foreign rights.*
- How much it will cost and when you should strategically file any foreign applications.
- Keep in mind that all of Europe as well as the International Community operate under the guidelines that the first to file is the inventor of the patent.
- Keep in mind as of November of 2000, the USPTO now discloses its patent applications after 18 months. So after that period of time, your application becomes public knowledge for all the world to see.

Chapter 7

CHOOSING YOUR TEAM

Part II

It's all in the Claims

Who you are about to choose is a very important consideration. So before you make up your mind, it's only fair that I fill you in on few key areas.

It's all in the claims, remember? How many times have you heard me say that?

Of course there are other parts of the patent, and yes they are important in their own right, yet nothing is as important as the claims. It's time that we stop here for just a moment and put this claims business into the proper perspective once and for all.

Just so you know, in a patent lawsuit there is a legal exercise that is referred to as *claim construction*, but it could just as easily be called *claim deconstruction.* It is a legal exercise that takes place during patent litigation and it's a process that's conducted before a judge. I want you to be mindful that it's also a legal exercise that will involve patent attorneys.

Now here's some food for thought. Most judges who preside over IP litigation were *never* practicing patent attorneys before they got appointed to their posts.

Anyway, during claim construction, the opposing sides literally wage war over the *agreed upon meaning* of each and every word contained in the claims of the disputed patent! Their intention is to first agree upon the exact meaning of each and every word in the claims, so that they can fight like hell whether the claims are valid or not.

The lawyers don't fight over the drawings, the summary or the body of the patent, heck that rarely comes up. What they wage war over is the claims!

Just for kicks, pull up a patent and think about the exact meaning of every word that is found in the claims. Now attach a billable hour to the process and the prospect of this exercise is truly frightening. When big firms bring out their big guns, billable hour rates can eclipse a thousand dollars an hour depending upon the battle being waged.

In simplistic terms, this is an exercise of pure haggling over the *agreed upon meaning* of the words contained in the claims. All in front of a judge that doesn't necessarily understand what the fighting is all about in the first place. I dare say, you probably don't possess enough money to play at this table.

- The ability of a patent attorney is measured by the achievement of what he or she has accomplished in the field of patent prosecution.
- Claim construction is the pinnacle of the patenting process.

So what we are searching for is a verifiable track record of the individual's performance and it's going to be your job to ask for it. Likewise, it's the attorney's job to produce it, that's if they want to work with you and earn their fee.

In the final analysis, schooling and pedigree might get us to stop and take notice, but as you can see, achievement in the field is the horse that we want to ride in this race.

As far as patent prosecution is concerned, you're buying the individual attorney and his ability - more than you are buying his firm.

The Patent Search

Remember the patent search? Allow me just a moment, because I'm about to tie this in with the examiner, your practitioner and you.

Just so you know, a search of the prior art is going to be conducted once your patent application is submitted to the PTO. The patent examiner is going to perform a very thorough search and that search is going to form the basis as to whether or not he grants your application. That's why it's so important to conduct a proper search of your own, before submitting your patent application.

- The object of conducting a search, is so that you may obtain in advance many of the same patents that the examiner will be citing whether in support of, or against your application.

By conducting your own search, you'll be in a much better position to evaluate the claims cited in the prior art before submitting your own set of claims to the examiner.

This is will also afford a great opportunity for both you and your attorney to engage in some meaningful claim construction. The point of this exercise is to enable your *team* to really focus in on your claims and protect the important aspects of your invention.

Although a search is an added expense, in my opinion it's worth it. A proper search may cost you hundred dollars, and that's just for the search. In addition to that, you're going to have to pay your patent attorney to summarize exactly what that search means. This research and summary is usually presented to the client in the form of a *legal opinion*.

Searches today are done at lightning speed, as compared to when I was filing my patent. It wasn't that long ago when trained researchers had to manually search through the patent archives and perform this task one book at a time. Of course with the advent of high speed computers, the patent database can be explored much faster and more accurately than it was in years gone by.

Have your attorney send you a copy of each and every patent cited in the search, because I want you to go through each patent and highlight the claims cited in the prior art.

The key is, don't be intimidated here, you can handle this!

You are certainly far enough along in the process to know exactly what your invention is and what it's supposed to do. Now is the time to compare your invention to the ones that have previously been granted. Be sure to notice both the similarities and the distinctions between what the prior art has established and what you intend to claim.

Now would also be an appropriate time to take a good look at your invention in the light of day. I encourage you to judge for yourself both your patent's strengths and weaknesses.

This is also the best opportunity for you to adjust your claims. Not *after* the examiner has rejected them. In the final analysis, a patent search is a necessary exercise. It will be both time and money well spent. It's also an opportunity for you to find out first-hand just how knowledgeable your practitioner really is.

The PTO's Job

If you think about it, the patent examiner is the gatekeeper for the PTO. Keep in mind that the patent examiner for all intended purposes has the last word as to whether your patent application gets approved or not. Simply put, if the examiner at the PTO approves your application, then you will be issued a patent. On the other hand, if he or she denies your application and you've exercised all of your appeal options, then you won't be issued one.

In the final analysis it's just that cut and dry, so don't expect to receive a patent simply because you've gone through the patent filing process.

Somewhere along the line, you may have been under the impression that the primary purpose of the PTO's was to issue patents so that the formulation of new ideas might spur business along. That's a noble thought, but you'd be wrong.

Do you realize that PTO receives on average over 500 thousand applications each and every year? Actually, the PTO's job is more akin to thinning out the herd and culling through the onslaught of applications that flood their dockets. These applications hale from nearly every corner of the planet. It's truly a Herculean task for the staff of the PTO to research each and every idea submitted and then pass judgment as to whether each application merits patent protection or not.

The truth of the matter is that *nearly half* of the patent applications submitted to the PTO suffer final rejections. Although there are any number of reasons that an examiner can put forth as grounds for rejection, some of the most serious grounds are based upon *deficient claims*. Deficient claims can be attributed to the following:

- First. The claims as put forth are *insufficient and therefore lack merit.*
- Second. The claims as put forth have *previously been granted and are already contained in the prior art.*
- Third. The claims as put forth have been deemed to be *obvious and could have been anticipated by somebody already skilled in the art.*

Up until now, what you may not have realized is that there is a common thread that runs through each and every patent application. The PTO is not only acutely aware of it, but they're prepared for it. Every submission, whether it be from the largest corporations or the most obscure backyard inventors share in the universal quest for an *exclusive right* which only the U.S. PTO can offer. That exclusive right is embodied in an instrument called a United States Patent and it gives anyone who might earn one, the right to have a monopoly on a very specific idea for a lengthy period of time. Twenty years in the case of utility patents and plant patents. Fourteen years in the case of design patents.

It is therefore the PTO's mandate to hand out these exclusive rights in a judicious and conservative manner. If you think about it, these very patents can act to restrict free commerce to the same degree in which they can act to promote it.

Let's take a look at an everyday hammer used for banging nails. We all know what one looks like, and at one point or another everybody has picked one up. Now for the sake of illustration, most handheld hammers are all rather similar in design. They all employ a handle of some sort and they have a striking head made of metal that is made to strike a blow to drive in a nail.

As a result, there are numerous hammer manufacturers and that's great. The proliferation of hammers manufacturers spurs competition and often results in better design and pricing for the consumer. Ultimately, it's this competition that will spawn the new advancements in hammer technology.

Now just think of all the confusion and chaos that would ensue if every hammer manufacturer were granted a patent for each and every hammer model that they manufacture. It would be ridiculous! Think of all the artificial barriers that would have to be dealt with, just to allow the manufacture and sale of something as utilitarian as a hammer.

Now expand that thought and put those same restrictions on each product that we touch and use every day. It's easy to see that the world as we know it, would come to a grinding halt if a patent had to be obtained every time an improvement of some kind entered the marketplace. The point is this…

- Patents are special and are only issued for exceptional improvements.

With that said, please allow me to explain what the fuss is all about. Inherent in every patent is the exclusive right, which *can* span up to 20 years in duration. The power behind the exclusive right grants the *patentee* the power to have, to hold, to sell or to license his patented item in any way that he sees fit. This exclusive right means that the patentee can compete in the free marketplace, absent of any competition for up to 20 years, which could very well enable the patentee to *get rich at the exclusion of others.*

It's kind of a contradiction if you really analyze it. Competing in the free marketplace for 20 years without any competition? How do you compete against something if you don't have something to compete against?

Anyway, that's the beauty of it. So if your idea is good enough, and you receive patent protection, you'll be able to compete in the free marketplace without any competition for up to 20 years. Honestly!

That's exactly why all potential patentees will subject themselves to the ordeal of obtaining patent protection.

- Remember, a US patent only protects your product within the confines of the United States. It does not afford the owner any protection outside of our borders.

With that said, patents are not that easy to get. Which is exactly why under certain circumstances one company will infringe on another company's patent. The root motivation for the infringing company is to gain market entry, where there previously hadn't been any, due to the protection afforded by the other guy's patent.

As a result, when one party deliberately muscles in on another party's patent, it is called *patent infringement* and it is a form of theft. Really, it's plain old stealing. During the course of this battle, the offending company will often times try and say that the patent in question is *invalid, w*hich is basically an argument that pleads that the patent shouldn't have been granted to the inventor in the first place. The party who has been accused of infringing will try to make the case that he should either be free to use the idea, or that he should be allowed to take possession of the idea for his own exclusive use! I realize that this sounds like a case for outright theft, but this argument forms the basis for *nearly every* patent litigation case!

As you can only imagine, patent fights bring the art form of "he said - she said" to an insane level. In the end it all boils down to money, and who has the right to profit from the patent. As you might expect, these attacks against one's patent are the result of a premeditated and cost-benefit analysis scenario driven by the offending company's greed.

Attorneys are My First Choice

As you've probably figured out by now, a patent attorney is my first choice to prosecute your patent application. To my way of thinking, this exercise is just too critical to entrust someone with lesser qualifications to handle it for you.

Look, I'm no particular fan of lawyers or their profession. Yet despite my tumultuous dealings with the whole legal thing, I can honestly say that I've had the privilege of knowing a select handful of wonderfully skilled attorneys. It is my sincere desire that you end up finding just such a person to work with.

The fact of the matter is that I highly recommend that you *do not* file a patent application without first considering the professional help of an attorney. As I stated previously, if you intend on filing a patent with the hopes of making a significant return on your invention, and you want to have the peace of mind that you stand a good chance of being able to defend your patent against all comers, then I strongly advise that you hire a licensed patent attorney that you can trust, handle this aspect of the job.

As you may recall, I stated that an attorney has attended law school and that a patent agent has not. Law school is three years in duration and is expensive. Not to mention the additional cost and effort that it takes to attain a four-year undergraduate degree. Understandably, the attorney wants a return for both his investment and specialized knowledge. And who can blame them for that?

Based upon that fact alone, an attorney's fee will be more than a patent agent's. Here is the reason why. An attorney is skilled in the general workings of the law, but a patent attorney will also be skilled in patent law as well. Therefore, if you combine these attributes with a working knowledge and practice of intellectual property law, then you really have quite an advantage by working with a registered patent attorney.

Then if you were to take it up another notch and add to that a strong track record for patent prosecutions, unchallenged patents, and his/her ability to enter into licensing deals; then at least in my mind, you'd have an outright winner. There's no doubt about it, an attorney with these qualifications is at the top of the patent prosecution business.

To compare. A patent agent is my second choice. It seems to me that the chief consideration why an inventor would opt for a patent agent is that their fees *should* be considerably lower than that of an attorney's. And as already put forth, this will be based upon the fact that a patent agent lacks a law degree.

Therefore, it's up to each individual inventor to determine what is going to be most expedient in his or her particular case. Since this is going to be your decision, it's best that I leave the fee comparison up for your personal consideration.

In the event that cost savings is your primary motivation for selection, just remember one thing..., over the long run it could wind up costing you more than you could possibly ever imagine.

The Attorney and You

At this juncture, I have to assume that you are very pregnant with your idea and that you are totally driven to give birth to your invention. The only thing that will satisfy you at this point is a United States patent.

In my opinion, a highly skilled attorney is one of the best tools that you might have in your arsenal to get past the obstacles that the examiner will invariably put in front of your application. I'm a realist, so my best advice to you is this; if you *can* find an attorney that you can trust, that you can work with, that you can like, and that you can afford - that attorney would be my first choice. That is assuming of course, that he or she has the proper qualifications and achievements. And to repeat, my second choice would be a well-qualified patent agent. In case you might be wondering, I don't have a third choice to offer you.

Your attorney-client relationship should be rooted and grounded in trust and respect. It should be built upon a foundation of give-and-take, not based merely upon the attorney's fee.

If you feel at any point that your attorney is not performing like an accomplished professional, then perhaps you should consider formally dismissing him/her.

This would also be an appropriate time for you to part ways with an attorney that you feel might not understand what your invention is all about, or simply because he or she happens to be someone that you just can't work with. It can happen you know, we're all just people and we all possess personality quirks.

If this should ever be the case, then you are in a bad marriage and you should bail out.

The patent search and the opinion are yours to keep, because you are paying for it. The fact remains that you possess the authority to discharge your attorney, if that's what you should decide. Keep in mind that after you pay your attorney whatever is owed, you must have your file delivered to you immediately. Don't be bashful, demand it and move on!

On a much more positive note, this should be the time where both you and your attorney can come together. It is also a time where you can both gel as a team and formulate some incredible claims. Claims that in the end, will land you a United States Patent accompanied by its exclusive right to do with it as you see fit within the confines of the United States.

It is also essential that your attorney return your calls in a timely fashion and he should keep you abreast of your file's progress whenever he is interacting with examiner.

Also, make sure that the attorney sends you a copy of *each* and *every* document that he/she sends to the PTO, as well as any responses he/she receives regarding your application. The point is, every paper and receipt that gets generated must be mailed to you in a timely fashion. As a result of proper communication, you should have a duplicate file that is up to date sitting in your home, with the official copy located in your lawyer's office.

Another key to a good relationship is to make certain that your attorney reaches out to you and obtains your approval every time he does something that could affect your patent application. Even though he's the expert, you need to know the rationale behind each and every tactical move. In addition to that, you need to be kept abreast how much each bit of work being performed is going to cost you. Preferably ahead of time!

It's your job to make sure that you understand what's going on, so ask questions constantly.

On the opposite end of the spectrum, your attorney shouldn't be the least bit threatened by either your intelligence or your knowledge of the patent process. He or she would do well to welcome your thoughts and your active participation with an open mind.

You on the other hand, you must trust your attorney and not badger him/her, *especially* if they are doing their job. Don't expect them to hold your hand; it's totally unnecessary during this undertaking. There are going to be weeks, and perhaps even months where a word won't be exchanged between the two of you, because your application is in the hands of the PTO and your input won't be required.

Work as a team to craft your patent, so that it can be the best it can be. Do this despite the fact that you are paying the attorney a sizable fee. In many ways, this will make their job go faster and easier. In the final analysis, you will wind up with a better product and in the end that is what you are looking for.

Don't ever entertain the thought that you're paying this guy a king's ransom and therefore he should be doing all the work. Not so! Whatever you do, don't lose your perspective; you are the inventor and you are the visionary of your invention. You are the one who is going to live with this patent for the next 20 years and you are the one who is going to reap the true financial rewards of its success. Not your attorney! So help them to be the best practitioner they can be!

By the same token, don't lose sight of the fact that your attorney is the one responsible for taking your non-legal words and concepts and putting them in the proper form and format that the PTO requires. Your attorney is also the one who will take your claims and structure them into a fortress that will stave off the marauders who will try to chip away at, or try and outright steal your 20-year exclusive rights.

Remember, patents are about the money and the protection that they afford to the one who owns the invention. Nothing less. The smart individual who can lockup a great idea and the 20-year exclusive right can feasibly get rich, if it's done correctly.

You're no doubt familiar with the pharmaceutical business. Did you ever hear the financial analysts tout that "so-and-so" was about to be granted a patent for "such-and-such" a drug and that it's going to be worth…, well Viagra®?

On the other hand, you've also heard those same analysts lament that "so-and-so's" stock is going to plummet this quarter, because two or three of their major drugs are *coming off patent*. What that actually means is that the company is going to lose its exclusive right in a specific market, for a specific drug, and now the competition is going to be allowed to compete with a generic equivalent form of that drug.

What that usually spells out is that the company's profits are going to drop precipitously, due to the loss of patent protection.

Surely, you must be getting it by now. Work with your patent practitioner as closely as you would with a brother or sister. If all goes according to plan, your attorney should be able to secure the patent that you've been dreaming about.

Retainer Agreements

Again, you need to get all the details of what exactly is going to frame out the working relationship between you and the practitioner. In any case, you should get the specifics spelled out in an employment or *retainer agreement*. In most cases you won't even have to ask for this contract, because nearly every lawyer will require that you sign a contract before entering into any business relationship with you.

Hint. Before signing this agreement, it certainly wouldn't hurt for you to have your personal attorney give it a quick once over, before you do sign it.

- Make sure that the retainer spells out that if you are being billed monthly, that all expenses are to be itemized.
- Make sure that the retainer spells out that you will be sent copies of each and every document that is generated on your file. This especially applies to all correspondence that is generated between the PTO and the attorney.
- Make sure that the retainer spells out that work product that has been produced and paid for by you, will become your property, in the event that you and your attorney part.
- In some cases, you may be told upfront what the entire job is going to cost. If so, the same rules apply with regard to correspondence and the like.

Of course you can expect to pay separately for the patent application, and any related costs and fees, in addition to what the attorney or the agent might charge. But make sure that this is all spelled out in the agreement.

For example, did you know that when you receive a rejection from the PTO, and you address those rejections in the form of a response, that there is a not only a corresponding time frame in which to do so, but there is also a corresponding fee.

You should be aware that the PTO has quite an elaborate fee schedule. As a rule, the PTO will charge you a fee every time that you interact with them. In the case that you want to speed things up, you can also do so for a fee. If you need to buy some extra time to address a specific issue, the PTO is very accommodating as well, provided you pony up the appropriate fee.

With regard to the PTO and their fees, you have no choice other than to pay them and move along. Once you stop paying your fees, the prosecution process on their end will come to an abrupt halt. Inaction on your part will cause your application to lapse.

Your practitioner should have the PTO's fee schedule handy and should be capable of informing you about any of the fees that you will be responsible for. Keep in mind that any time that you anticipate a new procedure, there will be a fee. Remember to ask your practitioner ahead of time what the PTO is going to be charging you.

- Just so that you are aware, the PTO has a fee schedule posted on their website for you to consult as well.

Here are another few good questions to ask.

- Has any of the practitioner's clients ever *sold* or *licensed* their patents to industry?
- Find out what these inventions were.
- Find out if you can, how much revenue that invention has generated for that particular client.

Keep in mind that there is a vast difference between *selling* and the *licensing* of a patent. So far, I have been talking in terms of obtaining of a license; which is more the norm than an outright sale of a patent. At any rate, we will be discussing both options and the related details when we arrive at the section that deals with licensing and royalty rates.

How Much is this Going to Cost?

If I could read your mind, I'll bet a primary concern of yours is the cost of hiring a qualified practitioner to file your patent application. I'm certain that particular concern has got to be right up there, along with getting things right. To be honest with you…, it should.

For many individuals, this could very well be one of the biggest financial gambles of your life. I can truly relate to any resistance you might be feeling on the subject of spending money to obtain a patent, because when I got involved in the process, my bank account was anything but flush. As a consequence, I did my very best to cut costs and I succeeded at doing so, but the end result was that those cost cutting measures *could have* come back and bitten me hard as I traveled further on down the road.

So, here's my advice. Do not prepare a patent application on a penny-pinching budget. There is absolutely no way around the money issue and you need to accept that fact *before* you ever begin your patent odyssey. Patents and the people that are going to help you properly file them are not cheap. The baseline cost of filing a patent starts at around $3,000 and the costs can escalate depending on the number of required *office actions* as well as complexity of your invention an. So my advice is that you should prepare to deal with those facts now, and not later.

Here's, how you must play it. Let your attorney know that you must be informed in advance of the approximate cost of each task that the practitioner intends to perform for you. If his fee is going to exceed what he initially told you, then he knows that it's his obligation to communicate that fact to you.

If you're on a budget, let the attorney know that from the beginning. Don't be too prideful or embarrassed, because not everybody is blessed to earn what a successful lawyer earns. Tell your attorney that open billing is not something that you're comfortable with. Advise him/her that you need an itemized statement sent to you each month with a breakdown of what his/her hourly fees were, plus whatever costs that your file has incurred for maintenance.

My advice to you is as follows. Be prepared to file your patent with an attorney and spend what is reasonable and necessary in order to make this happen. As previously mentioned, these costs will vary based upon the lawyer, your billing arrangements, and the complexity of your invention. If your idea is valuable, it will be money well spent!

Chapter 8

MOUNTAIN CLIMBING

Things You Should Know

Right about at this point in the journey you might be taking a breather. And I might add, a well-deserved one at that. I trust that you found the right attorney or the right patent agent to file your patent application for you. I also trust that after much waiting and some serious hard work, the United States Patent Office has granted you an official United States Patent. Therefore, I'd like to wish you my heartfelt congratulations! The invention process has successfully concluded and you've reached the summit of Mount Patent!

Careful now. This is only the first peak to be conquered in the great mountain range that I can only refer to as World Class Inventing. There are at least two more daunting peaks yet to be scaled before we can begin to bestow upon you the title of *world class inventor*.

Ah… The world talks about inventing, yet in reality they know precious little about the odyssey. Just like Mount Everest, unless you've paid the price to sit upon its summit, you'll just never know.

As you sit upon your perch high atop Mount Patent, you can't help but see off into the distance, rises yet another gigantic mountain peak that beckons to be scaled. I refer to this next peak in the mountain range as Mount Marketing. This mountain is rumored to be even more treacherous than the previous mountain that you've just scaled, and there's no straightforward path to this summit either.

As you sit atop Mount Patent lost in your thoughts, you must be wondering to yourself, what's it going to take to summit this next great obstacle?

At least that's how I remember it.

All I knew was that I had never scaled anything like this before in my entire life and nobody was there to show me how to do it. Understandably I was a bit scared, as this new mountain appeared out of the clouds, even bigger and more menacing than Mount Patent. Once I began the climb, this mountain would soon teach me that even my best-laid plans were no match compared to having a seasoned guide.

So come along with me, I've already made the climb. I tell you that Mount Marketing beckons to be conquered by someone just like you! I know that with some hard work, diligent planning and a good measure of brass, you're going to dominate this mountain too!

Inventor's Waivers

As promised, I included a section for those aspiring inventors who might already be working for a company. There is something called an *inventor's waiver* and we should spend some time going over it before we move on. As you will soon find out, this agreement will apply to many would-be inventors. This wavier is often times standard operating procedure for many employers with regard to their respective employees.

- This waiver can be utilized regardless of whether company publicly traded or privately held.
- This waiver could be presented as a separate document along with an employment agreement, or it simply might appear as an addendum to such an agreement under a heading labeled *"confidentiality…"*

Anyway, depending upon your particular affiliation with your employer, chances are it could be in there.

For those of you who already find yourself working for such an employer, you should already be familiar with this contract, because you've already signed one as a condition for employment. However, in the case that either you don't recall signing one, or you didn't pay much attention to it at the time that you were hired, now would be an appropriate time to bring you up to speed as to its ramifications regarding your future inventing pursuits.

For those of you who are contemplating working for one of those entities requiring such a document, please pay very close attention to what I'm about to say here. This is a topic of critical importance to you, and there is much for you to consider before you sign such a contract.

Here's how it works. This is the type of waiver that potential employees of many companies must sign as a provision for employment. As such, an individual that works for a company in the capacity of an employee, often times must first sign an *inventor's waiver* as one of the very first conditions for employment.

Simply put, a waiver is a legal and binding contract. A contract that specifically states that in the event that the employee comes up with an invention, or anything that is perceived as being an invention while on company business; that employee will automatically surrender his intellectual property rights to the company. In this particular instance, an invention could be considered an entirely new concept or an improvement to an existing device. Or it could be related to specific devices manufacture and production as well.

- The transfer of an individual's IP rights can occur as a condition of employment.

It's pretty cut and dry, and I've read considerable case law along the way that proves at least to my satisfaction, that these inventor's waivers are very serious business. Now here is where you have to be really careful. In certain instances, it doesn't seem to matter whether you get the idea before you hire on, or if you get the idea after you leave. And in certain instances, it doesn't seem to matter whether your idea is even remotely capable of competing against what your employer is producing.

- As an employee bound under such a contract, be mindful that chances are very good that a red flag is going to be raised if your employer gets wind that you are personally involved with any invention that even remotely has anything to do with your work related activities.

The actions that might be taken against you by the employer are stated in your contract. The remedies could range from the termination of your employment, to the seizing of your intellectual property and or a legal action filed against you such as a lawsuit. The sky is the limit where these contracts are concerned. In the event you were found liable, you could even be responsible for any legal costs incurred by your employer on top of any damages awarded by the court!

Here's the dilemma and it's quite simple. The lines are blurry as to what circumstances might have spawned the invention. It's a gray area as to who was doing what and when, first. Now that we've studied the inventing process, you should be able to better relate to this.

In this particular situation, due to the manner in which this waiver is crafted, the employer is going to win nearly all the time.

Look at the facts. As an employee, you spend a considerable amount of time in your work environment every week. And it's quite understandable that your employer will view his facility as the incubator for any of the inventing activities that you might be engaged in. Especially if it's part of your job description.

Hence, your free time is basically viewed as company time, at least where the invention of related widgets are concerned. As you might expect, it would be rather impossible to separate what you did on the clock as an employee as opposed to what you are doing off the clock as a private citizen in your garage.

The scope of the waiver will invariably claim that as an employee of the company, you must relinquish any ownership of your intellectual property rights while working for that specific company. In most cases, that agreement shall be enforced for a specific time period even after your departure from the company as well.

This is very similar to a *non-compete clause* commonly found in commercial real estate. The following illustration provides a good example as to what an inventor's waiver is all about.

In this example, Joey is going to sell his building to Sammy for a considerable sum of money.

Joey has been selling pizzas at this same location for twenty years. After two decades of selling great pizza, Joey needs to relocate to a newer and larger building in order to accommodate his growing customer base. The new building is located only a quarter of a mile down the road.

The sales contract will contain a restriction that will plainly state that *any* new buyer, cannot operate a pizza business at this location for the next five years. Furthermore, the contract will also contain a provision that will state that the new owner of this building cannot sell pizza within a five-mile radius of Joey's new location for at least the next three years.

Joey's lawyer introduced these clauses into the sales contract in order to protect him against any future competition that could arise as a result of him selling the building. This type of restriction is known as a "non-compete clause." An inventor's waiver is basically going to do the same thing on the company's behalf. It is designed to prevent any competition between the company and their workforce where the formation and ownership of IP is concerned.

As demonstrated, these inventor's waivers can make up the backbone of many manufacturing businesses. As I've already presented, you are dealing with two very powerful forces here, money and the twenty-year exclusive right that covers a protected invention. These companies feel that they are paying you adequately and in addition to that, they are providing you an atmosphere to be creative in order *for them to profit from you*, and not for you to profit from them. So who can blame them?

Here's the dilemma for those of you are in this position. This is a readily enforceable contract and you've already signed it! So in my opinion, you are pretty much done. If you have any doubt about what I've just said, then please finish the rest of the book. I'll soon be proving out that reality when we get to topic of signing contracts.

If you truly believe that you've come up with an invention that is *not going to compete* with your employer, your first step is that you must find a highly qualified contract attorney who can interpret what your employment contract actually says. In the case that the attorney advises you that you seem to be all right pursuing your invention, I would then go through the entire documenting process as I've already presented. That means you are going to memorialize your invention and begin to document your activities in your inventor's notebook.

Despite obtaining legal counsel, I still believe that your circumstances are still somewhat tenuous at best. So I wouldn't invest any more time and energy outside of documenting your idea.

This I what I suggest. I would go to your employer and tell him about your invention and wait for their reaction. In my opinion, your inventing career independent from your employer rests squarely in their hands.

In my opinion, how your employer views the matter is really what counts. You *only* consulted a lawyer to get an interpretation of the employment contract and to get his opinion as to your situation. In the final analysis, it will be your employer who will in effect govern over the contract the both of you have signed, and not the lawyer I just advised you to consult. Remember, should you decide to forge ahead against the company's wishes; they have the power to sue you and you certainly don't want to be on the receiving end of that.

On the flipside, should your company give you permission to proceed independently without them, it would be most wise for them to sign a *non-compete waiver* and a confidentiality agreement regarding your invention. And that's if they will even consider doing that.

Have a qualified patent/contract attorney draw this up and make sure that the company signs it!

Don't disregard what we've already gone over concerning the inventing process. Document every single communication that you have with your company in writing via certified mail.

As a result of your employment arrangement, you now have an uninvited guest that got an early peak under the tent. Due to these special circumstances, you especially have to guard yourself about what future actions this could spawn. In the simplest terms, your company could wind up being your biggest competitor one day. Therefore, it's critical that you compile the proper documentation to bolster the fact that you were the first and true inventor, should you find it necessary to file an action against them.

As you might expect, I don't like this situation at all, but it's really all you have to work with. How you choose to handle this situation is truly predicated on how driven you are in the pursuit of your idea and how bad you want to become an independent inventor.

If you are successful in obtaining your company's permission for you to pursue your invention, all I can advise is what I've already laid out thus far, which is to go about the inventing process in earnest, and follow the blueprint that this book lays out for you to follow.

On the other hand, if the company should turn you down and says *no*, at least I already warned you upfront that they might.

As an aside, if you are contemplating taking this matter above your employer's jurisdiction, that's a call that only you can make. In my opinion, it's a long shot at best and be prepared for a heck of a battle. Their first stock response to you is going to be as follows, "We offered you a job and you accepted it by signing this waiver."

My point is this. You should deal with your employer upfront even if you stand a chance of losing your idea. Being a dishonest inventor can get you into deep trouble and this is a perfect scenario for this to happen.

Whether it was a good thing or a bad thing, you signed the waiver. You did in fact sign a contract. So, now as a paid employee of a company, you have the highest duty to abide by that company's rules, because they are paying your salary.

In my opinion, quitting your job and waiting out your employer's contract to expire because of your idea, isn't a good idea either. Let's face it, the chances are very good that you signed a fairly ironclad contract and the last thing you need in your life is some Goliath chasing after you. So let's face it, unless something special and creative allows you to become an inventor, your independent inventing opportunities are going to be severely limited because of this waiver. Sorry as it might seem, you still need to eat.

One final consideration. Maybe both you and the company can form a recognized partnership regarding this specific invention. You won't know unless you ask.

Here is my disclaimer. For those of you who have already signed an inventor's waiver you must pull it out and carefully read it. If there is the slightest chance that you don't understand it, go to the human resources department and have them clarify it for you. If their explanation isn't palatable, then I would certainly get a qualified attorney involved to give you the lay of the land.

Obviously I don't know what you signed, and I'm betting that you may not either. As far as I'm concerned, playing by the rules and being honest is by far the best policy.

As for those of you who haven't signed one of these contracts yet, consider all of the ramifications. At the very least, if you have inventing on the horizon, I'd have this sort of contract reviewed by a qualified lawyer before ever signing it.

A Honey Do List

Before we launch into the aspect of licensing, I want to make doubly sure that during your relationship with your practitioner you've covered all of the bases, so a brief recap is due. It is imperative that you have a crystal clear understanding of what the lay of the land is. This is a time when you are making the bed that you'll be lying down in for a very long time.

Just so you know, after I was granted my second patent I came up with some significant improvements that were not originally covered by the claims as put forth in my '842 patent. So instead of listening to that little voice inside my head…, I decided to pass on filing a new patent application for my improvements and treat them as my trade secrets.

I chose not to file a *new patent application* and document those possible *new claims* with the PTO, because I was already under both a trade secret and technology sharing agreement with Fram.

Keep this in mind, my newly formulated improvements *were legally disclosed and communicated to Honeywell under 2 separate NDA's and were mandated to be handled as my trade secrets.*

And that's ok. But here is the variable, and it's a rather big variable. Should you ever find yourself in this position, it depends on who your licensing partner turns out to be. So unless you are some sort of a soothsayer, you won't know exactly who you might be dealing with either.

Just so you know, although I did handle my trade secrets properly, both from a contractual and legalistic standpoint, in my particular case that still wasn't enough! Looking back, I still could have done things with a much-greater sense of security, *but I didn't know*. In the final analysis, I never dreamt that Honeywell would have crossed the legal and moral lines like they did. *In the end I was too damn trusting that the agreements would protect my valuable IP.* In the final analysis, I was dead wrong, so you better take a lesson here.

I will have much more to say about this type of situation as we move further along. Just know that my game plan is to arm you to the teeth, so in the event that this stunt should be pulled on you, you'll wind up having the offending party by the short hairs. Anyway, getting back…

- Did you go over the aftermath of getting your claims put through? Meaning, did you and your practitioner actually discuss how your patent claims came out?
- Were your claims strengthened or weakened by the examination process?
- In his or her professional opinion, how strong are your claims as they now stand?
- Have you made any significant improvements to your invention that could increase the scope of your claims?
- Have you come up with any additional claims that should be put forth in a new patent application?

Here are some other key areas that you should revisit with your attorney as well.

- Did you discuss foreign patent coverage with all of its potential costs as well as its potential advantages?
- Did you and your practitioner explore whether he or she had any possible contacts with regard to licensing your invention?
- Did you and your practitioner discuss any *trade dress* issues such as either *trademark* or *copyright* protection?

Another thing, I hope you found out when your *anniversary maintenance fees* will be coming due. Don't panic, because the first maintenance fee installment of isn't due for another three years. But take care of this housekeeping issue now, while the thought is still fresh in your mind. Maintenance fees are required to be paid every third, seventh and eleventh year to keep your patent active and enforced. The counting of the time begins from the date of your patent grant.

As of now, there is a half-year grace period for each anniversary date, and you will not incur a late fee if you pay within that six-month window.

In any case, if your fees are not paid within the proper timeframe as defined by the USPTO, your patent will lapse. In the case that you let more than 12 months lapse from your anniversary date, your patent will not be resurrectable!

I warned you from the very beginning of a couple of things:

First. Patents are not play toys.

Second. The Patent Office has a strict set of rules that govern their operation.

The micro entity fees are as follows:

- As per the PTO, the first anniversary fee is due at the 3 to 3 ½ year mark and are presently $400. The 7 to 7 ½ year anniversary fee is going to run $900. The 11 to 11 ½ year anniversary fee is going to clock in at $1,850. That is what the fee schedule is as of January 1st, 2014. A late fee is due and payable if you are late within the last six months' window and that fee is presently $40. SEE 37 CFR 1.362(d), (e) & 35 USC 41(b) and 35 USC 21

In any case, your drop-dead date for your patent to lapse is 4 years, 8 years and 12 years from the date of your grant date. My advice is simple. You should never allow yourself to get into this bind if you plan on holding onto your patent. I feel that this is important enough that I refer you to USPTO patent section, 2506 Times for Submitting Maintenance Fee Payments [R-08.2012].

Disclaimer. You are the one responsible for going to the PTO's web site and looking up the maintenance fee schedules. This includes any of the other things that I have been telling you about regarding the USPTO. That is why this excellent website exists and that's why I'm telling you to use it.

That said, I suggest that your first order of business is to create a patent folder. This is a folder that will hold any and all correspondence between you and the PTO. On this folder, I want you to copy down the PTO's maintenance fee department's phone number and right alongside of it, copy down your due dates noting any extensions and the appropriate fees that are to come due. From my experience by the time you get to the next anniversary date, the fee may have gone up or the date schedule could have even possibly changed. As a matter of habit, please check the PTO website from time to time. Keep in mind that the USPTO is like any gigantic bureaucracy, therefore its rules and regulations are constantly changing.

Pay your fees on time, because it's your responsibility to do so!

Just so you know, I was vigilant in this area and I made absolutely sure that my patents wouldn't lapse due to something as innocent as not paying my rent to the government. It can certainly happen, so don't get sloppy!

The Right Negotiator is Critical

I realize that during your relationship with your practitioner, the both of you may have grown close. Perhaps you may have even developed a personal relationship during the prosecution of your patent application. If that is the case, that's what I wanted for your outcome.

With this great accomplishment behind you, it's time once again for you to be looking ahead. Now is the time for you to decide whether your practitioner is the proper individual to represent you during your upcoming licensing negotiations. I must warn you ahead of time, don't let your past history and any warm feelings that you may hold toward this individual cloud your judgment. If you feel that he/she isn't absolutely qualified to handle your license negotiations, then you must begin to think about shopping for someone who is. This next step is every bit as critical as the patent application process.

Remember don't skimp on the practitioner's qualifications or achievements, even if the referral should come directly from your practitioner. I would much prefer that the person at the helm of your licensing negotiations be a qualified and seasoned *trial attorney* that has an active trial practice in intellectual property law. My experience has taught me that contract law is one thing, but contract matters framed around intellectual property law are yet, quite another. Don't even consider your local attorney that does real estate and wills. Big mistake.

Let me just say this. During license negotiations, or any other financially based negotiations, things can pop up out of left field; things that neither you, nor even the best lawyer can foresee happening.

Reaction time and fierce bravery on the part of your negotiator is critical! Negotiations of this sort, aren't something where you can call a time out while your negotiator can go to the gym and develop his courage. This is something more akin to raw horsepower and brass and either your practitioner already has it, or he/she doesn't.

If my past experiences are any predictor of what you may face in the future, it is this; you need a hired gun to do your licensing negotiations for you. And you need to make deadly sure that he or she is qualified to do so.

Here's a key. Have your licensing negotiator in place and ready to go before you place your first marketing call. Enough said!

Inventor or Entrepreneur

You're about to get weaned, as you prepare to venture out beyond the security of the academic side of inventing process. Up until now, you have been engaged in a more of an intellectual pursuit. But I can assure you; at this juncture the business aspects of the process are going to take center stage. You must begin to look at the inventor's odyssey in a new light, because you're about to embark on the most important sale of your life!

Author's note. The only thing that should alter this new course would be if you find it necessary to put an entirely new set of claims through. If that's the case, it's most advisable for you to properly attend to this before proceeding forward.

Aside from that, you now know what it feels like to make the hard and important decisions and you definitely know what it feels like to be pulling the sled. In case it hasn't already dawned on you, being an inventor and being an entrepreneur are very closely related. As such, I purposely chose not to make a big deal of it earlier, lest you take your eye off of the patenting process.

Remember we are inventors first, and there is a notable difference. The inventing odyssey requires that you must become a disciplined inventor who attains a patent worth the paper it's written on, long before you can begin to contemplate becoming an entrepreneur.

On the other hand, it is quite the norm to become an entrepreneur without ever achieving inventorship status. For example, the individual that you buy your pizza from is an entrepreneur and quite probably, a successful one at that. He derives his competitive edge based on three things; quality, price and how long he's been occupying his corner spot making pizzas. Obviously, he doesn't need a patent to sell you a good pizza.

In our case, we chose to become inventors first. Simply because we believed that it was to our advantage to protect our intellectual property with a patent and attain all the rights and privileges associated with that achievement. That's our edge, and it is very similar to us owning the corner spot.

The next step that lies before you is marketing. Your goal is to dominate it, just like the other processes you've already been through. Your future awaits, you are going to become a master salesman as you begin your climb towards becoming an entrepreneur.

So without any further ado, let's begin our climb.

Are You Ready?

Everything's in place now, your patent, your negotiator, the market… so what's next?

You've already identified who's going to represent you during your license negotiations, because one thing is for darn sure, you're not.

You've already methodically complied the list of companies that you are about to contact, and you've gone over every detail of your patent inside and out. Your sales presentation is prepared and you've gone over every possible negative objection that might be hurled your way. Your invention and your patent are viable and you know it!

In addition to that, you're absolutely convinced that you can slay the great dragon that goes by the name of *Not Invented Here*, the great beast that's been rumored to have a lair high atop Mount Marketing. Surely, you're more committed to your dream now than ever before.

At this time, you're at peace with your decision as to whether it was necessary to file for patent protection outside of the Unites States or not.

Notwithstanding, every loose item regarding this process has been carefully attended to and dealt with, except one thing, *'what's this invention of mine really worth?'*

So before we make any sales calls, let's begin the evaluation process and take a realistic look at what you've invented. This is a critical exercise and it must be done well in advance of making any sales presentations. You need to know the value of what you're selling. And you need to be able to justify your financial compensation for your contribution long before you find yourself sitting across the contract table with a license agreement staring up at you.

Before can we begin to evaluate your patented invention from a monetary standpoint, I feel that it's essential to first go through the logical process of the *how's and why's* that will dictate your *royalty rate*. Chances are, nobody is going to do this for you ahead of time. Furthermore, even if you should ask, there are precious few people that are even capable of providing you with a satisfactory explanation as to how to actually arrive upon your royalty rate.

Just so you know, well in advance how serious this matter is I'd like to paint a couple of scenes for you. And just so you know, I had done my homework on this matter and I went into this aspect of the deal with open eyes and an educated mind. I knew what my share was, because I had done my homework, but there was a little wrinkle. The company I was about to deal with hadn't done theirs. So here we go…

Scene I. I negotiated my own licensing agreement. When I arrived for our meeting to discuss my royalty rate as well as my other compensation, I don't recall having "Idiot" tattooed across my forehead. Well, maybe I did. I'll let you be the judge of that.

My licensing counterpart at Honeywell, was the Head of Strategic Planning and Worldwide Development. During my first meeting with her, this high ranking official offered me a penny per filter for my product. You've heard the expression, "a penny for your thoughts," well they wanted to pay me a penny for a patented product that over time, as mismanaged as it was, would fatten their bottom line by some 100 million dollars. Again, *The Greed of a Dime*, captures these details in HD.

Just so you know, I wanted a quarter per filter and that figure was still very lite.

Scene II. Honeywell over the course of our legal battle spent several hundred thousand dollars in forensic accounting and expert witness fees in an all-out effort to downplay what their financial obligations were to me as the inventor.

The lion's share of those fees were paid to one of the top accounting teams in the world, KPMG. Honeywell hired KPMG along with other financial experts in a nuclear attempt to *minimize what their reasonable royalty to the inventor should be*!

I can recall this as if it was yesterday. My lawyer and I were both seated next to each other at this huge conference table perched high atop the Citi Corp building. We were invited guests for the day at the law firm of Kirkland and Ellis.

From time to time I would gaze out at the East River and watch the barge traffic passing by. The view of the Manhattan skyline was straight out of a movie and I tied to forget why I was even there. The law firm's décor was cold and commanding. I figured some sort of Scandinavian motif, with all white walls and lots of brushed stainless steel framing. The use of exotic and rare woods for the furnishings and built-ins made for an opulent and rarefied setting.

I couldn't help but be awestruck, as I tried to calculate what their monthly rent might have been. The law firm occupied 15 floors. They had fully equipped kitchens capable of creating the finest fare, suitable for any hostile takeover celebration.

The banter exchanged between the experts and attorneys was boring and I was glued to my watch, grateful that I wasn't paying for this by the hour, or I would have stroked out. The exchanges had little to do with what I had brought to Honeywell, and everyone seemed to ignore the giant cattle prod that was sticking out of my backside.

Wow! What a bonanza for the Kirkland lawyers billing out at over a grand an hour, and their experts that were raking in a king's ransom for making this stuff up. I had to chuckle as I took it all in, fully aware of the part that I played in this game. You see, I was just fodder. I was the one providing the sustenance for everyone who was feasting on this humble little lawsuit. Everyone gathered around me, from the videographer to the gal who brought in the tray of sandwiches would be moving on to the next feeding frenzy once my case was dispatched with. I couldn't help but realize that the entire exercise was a total contrivance, from the fake politeness and platitudes, to the veiled barbs.

I noticed that a private meeting was about to get underway in the glass conference room across the way from ours. A young attorney in a crisply starched shirt with a thread count I couldn't afford had just walked in, leading his group. As he did so, he flicked a switch and the clear glass conference room instantly turned opaque, as if filled with smoke. "What a magic trick," I recall telling myself, marveling how they were able to make these rooms so soundproof, despite the fact that they were made of glass.

Then out of left field came this lunacy. It was hurled directly at me by the woman in the neatly tailored navy blue business suit. As I struggled to reign in my emotions, I can remember trying not to get ill. Without a tinge of emotion, nor a hint of self–incrimination, she addressed both me and the group in one fluid motion. I didn't catch all of the mumbo jumbo that came spewing out, but I did catch the tail end of what she was saying. She unabashedly told me to my face that according to her analysis, my contribution to this whole financial affair that earned over 100 million dollars for Honeywell wasn't actually worth anything…, and that it all just happened as a result of their day to day business activities.

In the simplest of terms, Honeywell spent hundreds of thousands of dollars in an attempt to justify what would have been the lowest royalty rate for me to have received for my contribution to the development of the Double Guard oil filter. As a result of their accounting gymnastics, they concluded that my contribution for the development of the Double Guard oil filter was initially estimated to be zero cents per filter!

Now this wasn't a dream, and I didn't just teleport in from an asylum, I was there in the flesh. Honeywell had a fleet of accounting experts conjure up *opinions* that stated that the basis of a reasonable royalty rate for my contribution to the Double Guard oil filter began at zero cents per unit!

Try and wrap your brain around that madness in light of everything that I've shared with you thus far. Now I want you to consider your role as being the first and true inventor. I want you to picture yourself being the one who not only held all of the patent claims, but the one who gave birth to the trade secrets and devised the marketing plans.

Just so you can understand the magnitude of the game, I want to make it clear that Honeywell spent an exorbitant amount of their shareholder's funds in order to justify the royalty rate for *only one* of the inventions that they took of mine! And… This dog and pony show did not include a second invention of mine that I would soon stumble upon... the TRT oil filter.

As noted earlier, the TRT was another oil filter of mine that was also available on a nationwide basis. It was a product that had earned them many additional millions of dollars in untold profits and a few versions of this filter are still available today. In you guessed it…, Walmart.

Should you be wondering, the TRT was an oil filter that was genisised from my first patent, the '901, and its trade secrets. The very same patent that I had presented to Fram's senior engineering department more than a decade earlier during my first sales campaign. Fram's TRT filter embodied the very same technology that the VP of engineering sent me packing on, after we had concluded our luncheon at the Rustler Steak House. It embodied the very same technology that the chief engineer declared that I didn't have a patent on…, my Alkyl-zinc-dithiophosphate additive treated oil filter. Yes, that one.

I'm not quite done here yet, and as such I'd like to draw your attention to something else. This scenario as crazy as it was, did not take into account the other fifteen or so additional patents that were eventually going to be granted to Honeywell after the conclusion of my law suit. It didn't take into account all of the patents and the products that were born out of my trade secrets and what I had taught them regarding the inner workings of my two benchmark patents under the protection of the 2 NDA's and the licensing agreement that we had signed.

In the event that curiosity may have gotten the better of you, allow me to fill in the remaining blanks.

I came upon the TRT late one night, while strolling through Walmart. At the time of my discovery, I was nearly four years into this lawsuit and I was staring down the barrel of pre-trial preparation. Under the conditions that I was battling, it would have been totally impossible for me to get any additional causes of action introduced into my lawsuit. To do so would have required that I have a fleet of lawyers and accountants at my beckoned call and I had no such army. It would have also required that I owned a bank large enough to fund such a massive undertaking, since I was already way too deep into my home equity line of credit to consider escalating the enormity of the battle any further.

You see, at the time, my legal team was a bit undermanned. Just the prospect of engaging in another battle of this magnitude was unthinkable, since my legal team consisted of one gutsy young attorney, myself and his newly acquired copy machine that had already logged a few million copies. Unlike the lawyers that we were battling, our base of operation was a refurbished hundred-year-old horse stable in south Jersey. As you might well imagine, we were stretched fairly thin trying to hold off a hoard of lawyers the size of the Red Army. Consequently, I had to let those newly discovered transgressions pass.

Case in point. Upon the settlement of a lawsuit, neither party is allowed to ever bring forth another lawsuit related to the same matter. The execution of justice is based on a simple premise; bring in the whole kitchen sink while you're able, because the court won't allow you fight over the same thing twice. So obviously, I am forever barred from ever enjoining them in another court battle despite what time has uncovered.

Needless to say, the upcoming sections on royalty rate evaluation are going to be quite important for you to take in.

What's a Royalty?

Whether you realize it or not, you've done most of the evaluation work already. To begin with, you've already identified the market and its scope. By this time, you've surely figured out the demographics. Accordingly, by this time, you're acutely aware of where you see your market going and whether the trend for your invention is either picking up steam or dying. As to the future and your particular trend wave, it's about as fine-tuned as it's ever going to be. That's unless you can get your hands on some inside information.

So with that said, it's time to begin thinking about your royalty and what the term *royalty* actually means.

As an inventor, chances are, you're going to be receiving a royalty for your invention and as such, you are *not* going to be involved in an *outright sale* of your patent. I will explain the difference between an outright sale of your patent as compared to receiving a royalty rate as we progress. But first, let's examine what a royalty is.

- A royalty is simply any fee an inventor might receive for licensing his invention.
- A royalty rate is a percentage of the products *pre-tax gross profits*.
- A royalty rate is a percentage that an inventor receives for any product or device that is made under the *scope* of any one or more of his patents claims and or trade secrets.

A royalty rate by definition is the fee that is based on a percentage that is tied to a specific product that is actually being *made* or *sold* under the *scope* of any one or more of the claims as put forth in an inventor's patent. This can also include an inventor's trade secrets so long as they've been properly disclosed and documented under a proper non-disclosure agreement[s].

A flat rate per piece may be the basis for this payment. Or payments may be made based on a sliding scale and calculated on the volume of pieces made. There are any number of formats that can be employed to structure a royalty rate. As such, we'll explore some of the nuances of how royalty rates can be arrived at as we begin to move along.

- The scope of a patent refers to the boundaries or the limitations of the invention as defined by the patents claims.

That leads me to remind you of something that I've been rather unrelenting about. Remember claim construction and how important it was to have your claims put forth as succinctly as possible?

Remember how I kept admonishing, that it was all in the claims?

Well now that you are about to license your patent to a manufacturer, you are in effect going to be renting your patents claims to them. Through the granting of a license:

- You are agreeing to rent your patents claims to them under certain specific conditions, for an agreed upon period of time, and for an agreed upon price.

You can license your patent to just one manufacturer, which is referred to as an *exclusive license or exclusive right*. Or you can license your patent to more than one manufacturer at the same time. This is referred to as a *non-exclusive license or non-exclusive right.*

- License agreements can run for the life of the patent, or sometimes license agreements can run for a *pre-agreed upon* part thereof.
- License agreements can be *exclusive* or *non-exclusive* in nature.

The difference between licensing a patent and patent infringement is that as the inventor *knowingly and willingly* allows someone other than himself to profit from his invention. In exchange for that right, the manufacturer is going to pay the inventor an agreed upon amount of money referred to as a royalty. For the inventor's part, he is going to grant the manufacturer permission to make a specific product or device and offer it for sale *under* one or more of his patent's claims. In exchange, the inventor expects to receive a percentage of the manufacturer's *gross pretax profits*.

In its simplest terms, this is a symbiotic relationship that takes place between the inventor and the manufacturer where the net result is a win-win for each party. The inventor doesn't gouge the manufacturer with an overly burdensome royalty rate and allows his host to earn a healthy profit.

On the other hand, the manufacture doesn't try to steal the invention from the inventor and pays him a fair fee in the form of a royalty. This relationship is the culmination of all the inventors' hard work. And if you think about it, it's only fair, since the inventor has already performed the lion's share of the Research and Development burden and has discovered an entirely new business platform that the manufacturer didn't have to go out and create. It is a relationship that is under girded by the exclusive right afforded by the inventor's patent and governed by an enforceable contract.

Just so you know, if the inventor [you] brings a manufacturer a *valuable idea* for *a valuable new untapped market,* you could potentially be saving the manufacturer a vast amount of R&D capital as the result of your efforts. As such, do not underestimate what your contribution to this entire process is truly worth.

In the final analysis, it will be the patent that will then enable both the manufacturer and the inventor to produce a product and profit from it without any competition for the duration of the license agreement.

In my mind, there is no other way to view it. This is should be an *arm's length* a business partnership where both parties have pledged to help one another profit.

The Reason Why You Would License

Before we delve into the methodology behind calculating what a fair royalty rate should be, I'd first like to address why an inventor would contemplate entering into a licensing agreement in the first place.

To a large degree, pure economics is going to be the driving force behind why *most* inventors *would* enter into a licensing agreement.

Have you ever heard the expression, "that no man is an island?" Well I'm going to explain how that adage *applies* to the inventor who wants to profit from his patented invention.

Nearly without exception, most back yard inventors who just received a patent *will lack* the four essential elements necessary to become that independent *island.* They are the following:

- Capital. Gobs of it!
- Means of Production. Which means that the inventor already owns or has access to an operational manufacturing facility.
- Strong Market Penetration. Which means that the inventor already is a recognized and established player in the product's intended market.
- Strong ongoing product and brand recognition. Which means that the inventor has brand recognition that's capable of swaying a consumer to purchase a particular product based upon the strength of the brand's name.

Well, go ahead and take a good look at yourself. Only you can answer whether you possess the necessary means to be that island unto yourself. Chances are you're not that island, and that's just what I had expected.

Just so you know, I didn't have access to any of those valuable assets either. Yet I was able to climb this mountain all the way to the very top. Now it's my job to teach you.

Here's a key. You must come to grips with the reality that although you may own the patent, you're still far from being in the most advantageous position to dispose of your invention and make a profit from it. The sooner you grab hold of that reality, the sooner you can begin to formulate a plan to change things in your favor.

Here's another key. I realize that as the inventor who just gave birth to a patent, it's your heartfelt desire to be in control of your patent. Yet the greatest irony of all, is that you're really not in control!

- The cold hard reality is this. As an inventor with a valuable patent, you're never really in full control. This is precisely what makes marketing an invention such a dangerous game.

With that said, allow me to lay out your options.

The first question that will come to mind is the following: Should I attempt to raise the necessary capital through family, friends and private investors so that I can make and distribute this widget myself?

Just the thought of it, can keep you up for a month.

The second question that arises goes something like this: Should I approach a manufacturer and license my patent? By the looks of it, this manufacturer has an infrastructure already in place that's capable of making me successful. This option will have great appeal since you *perceive* that you will be able to place much of the responsibility of your products success on the manufacturer.

The third question is this: Should I just get on with my life and just sell my patent outright? I realize that this question will come up as well. It's a simple fact; you've been pushing this dream for a long time now, and you've been doing so without a breather. There's no doubt in my mind that you're probably mentally exhausted from the three or four-year odyssey to get this far.

On top of that, you've invested many precious thousands of dollars into this dream and so far you have nothing to show for it except a piece of paper and another mountain that's just been dropped at your doorstep. Understandably, you could have opted to invest both your time and your money in another endeavor that certainly could have been more concrete than inventing. And I certainly recognize the fact that you might be mentally exhausted and that you just might want to cash out. But for the moment, perish that thought!

I want to make something crystal clear to all of you back yard inventors. Other than *shelving* your idea or *quitting*, there are only three options that are available to you:

- Going it alone. Where you take full responsibility to manufacture and market your product.
- Licensing. Where you partner up with a manufacturer.
- Outright sale. Where you dispose of your invention for a onetime fee.

Once again, here's another example why you need to be the lead sled dog and personally conduct your own research. It's going to be your responsibility to determine which option is best for you to choose. In my opinion, only your intimate knowledge of the economics surrounding your patent's assets will determine how you go about profiting from your invention.

Monopoly, Oligopoly or Free Market

Let's take a look at three market forces that you could be facing. For instance, is the market that you are trying to enter a *monopoly*, where there is *no* freedom to entry? Or is it an *open market* with plenty of *freedom* of entry?

Or is it going to be an *oligopoly*? An oligopoly is market that is controlled by just a handful of specialized and powerful players. It is a market where the freedom of entry is possible for a new player to enter, but yet, not very probable.

These are certainly important considerations for the inventor whose about to turn salesman.

There are three types of economic forces that an inventor must evaluate when the appropriate time comes to dispose of his invention. They are the following:

- Monopoly. Characteristic of a *very tight* market with *no freedom of entry*.
- Open Market. Characteristic of a *very free* market with lots of opportunities of entry.
- Oligopoly. Characteristic of a *tight* market with *little or no* freedom of entry.

We are all familiar with the terms free competition. Likewise, we are all familiar with the term monopoly. Most of us know that each one of these markets exists at the opposite extremes of the business model. I'm also fairly certain, that unless you've taken some economics courses, you won't be familiar with the term *oligopoly*. So for now, let's just say that an oligopoly is a market condition that possesses more monopolistic tendencies than it does free market conditions.

If you could look at business as being a straight line, a monopoly would be on the extreme left side of the line and a totally free market place would be on the extreme right side of the line. An oligopoly would also be located on that line as well, somewhere to left of the center. That said, I'd like to illustrate how any one of these three economic forces could affect the marketing of your invention. So for illustration purposes, let's view yet another snapshot from my past experience and have a look at you might one day face. Let's start off by examining what an oligopoly/monopoly looks like.

The Automotive Original Equipment Manufacturers Market, such as the one that I broke into with my oil filter inventions comes to mind. The market forces driving this business could be categorized as an oligopoly, that borderlines on a monopoly.

Just so you know, there's only a small handful of tier-one Original Equipment Manufacturers; or *OEM's* that participate in the oil filter market for both cars and light trucks in the United States. As an OEM supplier, theses oil filter companies are recognized by the auto manufactures as producing an approved product that *will not* in any way jeopardize the function and the performance of their engines. This means that these oil filters will not be the root cause for any warranty related problems for them.

These select filter companies are Fram, Purolator, and AC Delco. They in turn produce the lion's share of the oil filters that come as original equipment on most new cars and trucks that are made in North America and Mexico.

Synonymous with the term Original Equipment Manufacture comes the responsibility of being recognized as having the highest quality standards and being universally accepted within a specific industry.

There are yet another small handful of other filter manufactures in this country and they also sell *OEM certified* replacement filters, but they do not come as the *original equipment* that's found on your new cars engine.

Now let me ask you a question. As a back yard inventor, how practical would it have been to round up a group of investors and form a company that makes and distributes oil filters under these conditions?

How would you go about gaining the certification standards required by the various agencies and the independent engineering laboratories that oversee and certify these oil filters?

And most importantly, how would you go about earning the *trust* of the automobile manufactures that your new oil filter wouldn't blow up their engines? The product liability factor alone is incomprehensible. Even the most trusted companies in the automotive business are not above getting things terribly, terribly wrong. Remember the Ford Pinto's exploding gas tanks? Firestone's tires that turned deadly do under inflation at highway speeds? And the latest OEM crisis'..., Takata's fatal airbag deployments and GM's fatal ignition switches.

The dynamics of the oil filter industry could be described as being somewhere between a monopoly and a very tight oligopoly. Therefore, an oligopoly is an established market with very little freedom of entry, bordering on a true monopoly.

Did you ever hear of Mr. Tucker, the maverick car manufacturer of the late 1940's that snubbed his nose at the Detroit automakers by daring to innovate? Do you recall what happened to his car company? He got pushed out of the business after selling only fifty cars. My point exactly.

Here's a key. If you are contemplating breaking into either a monopoly or an oligopoly where there is little or no freedom of entry, you have no other choice but to either sell your patent outright to one of the major players, or enter into a licensing agreement of some kind with one or all of them.

Just so you know, I was really hemmed in by the market forces and I was left only two choices; either the outright sale of my intellectual property or enter into a licensing agreement. The opportunity for me to independently attain OEM status for my oil filter invention was totally out of the realm of any possibility.

Therefore, knowing this ahead of time I chose the second option and channeled all of my energies into trying to license my patents to one of only six major oil filter companies that did business in the USA: Fram, Purolator, Wix, Hastings, Champion Labs and AC Delco.

Here's the risk that I faced. Had I failed to secure a license agreement with any one of these six players, I would have been out. The patents I had earned would have been rendered worthless and I would have squandered a priceless decade of my time, along with it the tens of thousands of dollars that I had invested down a dry hole.

So there you have it. If the business model that your invention fits into is either an oligopoly or a monopoly or any shade thereof, your only choice is to sell out completely or enter into a licensing agreement. It's a long shot at best and is definitely a hard row to hoe, but those are the facts. That said, only you can determine if you want to continue on, or climb back down the mountain.

The Outright Sale

The outright sale of an inventor's patent rights is a rather straightforward proposition, whereby an inventor would attempt to sell his or her patent rights to a manufacturer. Obviously any manufacture that would offer to buy an inventor's patent rights would do so based upon the rational that they could capitalize on the protection afforded by such a patent.

As such, you would hope to sell the company your patent outright for a one-time fee. Often times when this is done, it is referred to as an *assignment* of your patent. Accordingly, that assignment could also be recorded with the PTO after the transfer if that's what both parties had agreed upon to do.

This is exactly what happens when a company employee signs an inventor's waiver.

In this particular case the employee develops an idea for his employer, which eventually matures into a patent application. Upon acceptance by the PTO, the patent is granted naming that individual as the inventor and the company as the assignee. This occurs, because the application was initially filed as a joint application with the company being designated as the assignee of the patent. So in one fell swoop, the patent becomes the rightful property of the company and the issued patent would read Jimmy Jones inventor; assigned to the Ace Hammer Company.

In the case of the employee's compensation, he might receive a couple of shares of company stock and perhaps a windbreaker with the company's logo on it.

In the case of an outside inventor like yourself, when you're assigning your patent to a company through the means of an *outright sale*, you're hoping to receive a very sizable check for all your efforts and not just a monogrammed windbreaker. That's the big difference between being a freelance inventor like yourself and someone who's bound by a company's inventor's waiver.

Now that you are familiar with the basic mechanics of an outright sale and the assignment of your patent, I want to let you know that I wholeheartedly frown upon even the thought of the outright sale of your invention. In my estimation the chances of you receiving a sizable check by engaging in this type of situation is very slim indeed.

Allow me to explain.

Let's get back to hammer illustration and I'll dissect exactly why nine out of ten times you won't even come close to being fairly compensated for your great achievement.

There have been hammers around for thousands of years. Likewise, there are hammer manufacturers in virtually every country and on every continent. Though your improvement may be significant, chances are in all probability it's not earth shattering like the invention of the light bulb was. Your idea though great in its own right, probably lacks the cache and the marketing prowess as something revolutionary, like Apple's new Iphone® or Ipad®.

Chances are, you are not some genius that has been working in the medical field and has developed some newfangled heart catheterization stent that the biggest medical supply manufactures just have to have either, but then again you just might.

As an aside, though I didn't specifically target high level inventors to be the main audience of this book, in the rare case that you happen to find yourself turning these pages, *you more than anybody* should be taking heart to everything that I have to share.

Here's how it breaks down. You are a lone backyard inventor who's come out of obscurity with either a good idea or better yet, a great idea. You have absolutely no established track record of inventing and therefore nobody knows who you are. Quite possibly, this might be your first invention and most probably your last. Remember, both you and I are not on the same the level as an inventor like Dean Kamen, and we don't own an inventing facility capable of turning out a product such as the Segway®.

In a great sense, you're just a flash in the pan. After all, that's exactly how I viewed myself during the time that I was trying to unlock the power inside of my patents. And you want to know something; I was absolutely spot-on. So let me tell you about it.

Do you recall that in the beginning of this teaching that one of the very first requirements for inventing was that you had to be very honest with yourself concerning the relevance of your invention?

And didn't we also go over such areas as the practicality of your invention and how it would in turn dictate the public's level of motivation to purchase your new product?

What I am telling you, as an inventor about to make his or her mark; you're going to derive much of your clout from two sources:

- The first source of clout is going to come from the strength of your invention.
- The second source of clout is going to come from you.

Look at it this way; you don't become a Michael Jordan or Derek Jeter overnight. Therefore, you cannot expect any manufacture to fall over you like they would over one of those two guys for an endorsement.

These two guys haven't invented a thing that I know of, yet the world is beating a path to their doorsteps even while they sleep! They are both very famous and have generated negotiating power of a nuclear kind. That kind of respect can only be achieved over time and it is based upon *innumerable repeat* performances at the highest levels of their craft. If either one of these guys catches a cold, it becomes news!

That's how it works in a nutshell. At the very least, you'd have to be on your third or fourth *earth-shattering* invention before your credibility level would even begin to earn you an equitable payout for the outright sale of your intellectual property.

As a fledgling inventor, I was acutely aware of this reality way ahead of time where my personal clout was concerned, and that's precisely why I never pursued the outright sale of my patent.

Trust me, what Honeywell initially offered me for a total buyout of my patent rights was both laughable and insulting. As a matter of fact, their initial offer to me in the form of a royalty was a laughable at a penny apiece for each filter that they were going to make!

My only logical option, was to negotiate a license agreement with them based upon a royalty rate for my patent that *I* in fact calculated and not based solely upon what *they* wanted to pay me.

Likewise, that's how I suggest you begin to approach this process as well. You have to be realistic. Even if it hurts!

In all *practicality* licensing your patent is the way to go, that is unless you can have your widget manufactured for you by an independent source and you can take it upon yourself to market it yourself or through avenues such as the Internet, Walmart, QVC, HSN, Amazon or eBay.

So there you have it. A wise inventor is an individual who is well aware way in advance as to how the market forces can affect the potential value of his invention. From here on out, you can better begin to chart your course and pursue whatever option is best for your particular circumstance.

Make It and Market It Yourself

From my vantage point, the only circumstance that will allow you to raise both the necessary capital and to compete with your patent on a level playing field is the free and open marketplace. It is the only venue that is not susceptible to these various forms of competitive restrictions.

Please allow me to provide you with yet another simple example demonstrating what the free marketplace looks like.

You just received a patent for a revolutionary new hammer that you came up with, and it's far superior to any of the hammers already found on the market. Upon close evaluation of the hammer market you've concluded that this market is wide open with *plenty of freedom for entry*. That simply means that there is little or no restriction for any new player to enter the hammer market, and that there doesn't appear to be any monopolistic barriers blocking your entry.

As for your invention, a hammer is rather a simple device. So even with your new improvement it would be rather straightforward to engage any number of manufactures to produce this hammer exclusively for you.

Your most daunting task would be to raise the necessary capital and structure a suitable marketing strategy that would enable you to market your hammers. I have to tell you; this is quite another mountain in its own right. Just so we understand each other, the inventor who chooses to *go it alone* must be able to devote much more energy on this aspect as opposed to the inventor who is contemplating entering into a licensing agreement.

This is the point in the odyssey where you must weigh whether it's to your advantage to make it and market it yourself, or whether it's not. Should you decide to make it and market it yourself, you would be in the best position to own and control both your patent / product without having to relinquish any control to a licensing partner. Since there wouldn't be one.

But as I previously stated, even in this scenario, you cannot attain the island status of being in complete control. To a large extent, you would be beholden to your investors for both the trust and the money that they placed in you to perform.

Yet all in all, this is the only type of scenario that would afford you *highest degree* of control and flexibility. So let's take a closer look.

We've already established that the hammer that you just patented fits into the *free marketplace model* and it just so happens that you're the type of individual that can only be satisfied by having total control of your destiny. That being the case, it would certainly be in your best interest to investigate what it would require for you to manufacture and market your invention under your own control.

Whether you realize it or not, as we worked our way through the inventing process, we've already covered much of the plan for *going it alone*. For those of you who envision manufacturing and marketing your own invention, we're now going to take those same fundamentals and apply it towards the real world exercise of becoming an entrepreneur.

Let's go back and refer to the hammer patent to better illustrate what we're looking at.

There is no doubt, you've just invented the next great hammer of our generation and accordingly, you're totally convinced that you can have this hammer made to your specifications. You're also totally convinced that with a solid effort on your part, you would be very successful at marketing it.

On the surface, the premise appears rather straightforward: Invent, Patent, Manufacture and Market. In all reality, what lies beneath the surface yet to be accomplished is still quite complicated.

Let's take a look.

My first admonition to you at this point is to make absolutely sure that the market forces in place will allow you to both manufacture and market your hammer in an unimpeded fashion. In simple terms, make sure that you are about to compete in as free of a market place as reasonably possible. If you can compete in a free marketplace with a great invention and with a strong patent and *solid trade dress*, you stand to maximize your ability to capitalize upon all of your hard work.

As a matter of course, any business plan that you would institute would require that you secure the necessary capital to be able to institute your plans. In my opinion, that is the most vital element of going it alone. Only you can realistically answer how much money it's going to cost to produce and market your patented product. Furthermore, you are solely responsible as to how you propose to raise this rather large amount of capital necessary to institute your plan. This one exercise alone, will pretty much dictate the outcome of your future success.

Since I've never raised any investment capital for any of my projects, I can only recommend that you conduct your own research as to how you propose to raise this funding.

As for the means of production and market penetration we've already covered those aspects in some detail in the prior sections, where we focused on market trends and becoming a visionary. You would approach this aspect of going it alone as an advanced exercise of producing prototypes and shopping for a suitable manufacturer and distribution partners. Again, hopefully you've already done most of the legwork required here as you went through the prototype and patenting process.

But there's more for you to consider. In addition to prototypes, you'll be exploring boxing, packaging, graphics, printing, inventory control, drop shipping and *just in time* manufacturing principles; *JIT*.

JIT means that little or no inventory is warehoused and the product that is being sold almost as quickly as it is produced. Then it is shipped according to the products demand. As such, there is little to no warehousing of inventory involved. The advent of modern computer driven inventory systems in conjunction with our super-efficient transportation network has made this method of inventory control possible. In any event, that's just to mention the basics for even getting started in the going it alone venue.

The next key area to consider is the aspect of product recognition and product protection. Unlike the license agreement with a manufacturer you are going to be the one personally responsible for the enforcement of your own intellectual property. And with that additional responsibility comes the aspect of enforcement of what is often time referred to as *trade dress*. I will touch upon what constitutes trade dress protection momentarily and I will explain what those various *marks* such as ™ *for trademark or* © *for copyright* are.

In addition to that, I will also be discussing how this added layer of protection will fit into the plans of both the inventor who plans on going it alone as well as how it may apply to the inventor seeking to license his patent to a company as well.

Accordingly, if you choose the path of *going it alone*, then I would definitely expect you to go through the necessary steps to attain any additional trade dress registration needed to further protect your intellectual property.

You certainly should be doing this in tandem with the finalization of your business plan. And you should at the very least have this process well under way before making any sales calls.

The mindset here, is that you are the one who is *totally responsible* for both the marketing and the protection of your patented product. And not the big manufacturer that you *could have* teamed up with through a licensing agreement.

Therefore, you are the one responsible for establishing both the *look* of your product and establishing of any secondary levels of protection for your patented invention. I will elaborate in the upcoming section entitled, "Trade Dress and Marks."

Let's be honest, going it alone is a tremendous amount of work. Yet the potential rewards could far exceed your wildest expectations. Depending on your specific product and its market, your profit margins would be many times greater than what you would receive for a royalty derived from a license agreement.

Case in point. These are the types of inventors/entrepreneurs that are far enough along in the process to appear on the show "Shark Tank." These individuals by and large have already been quite successful at both making and marketing a product themselves. As they find themselves pitching to the "Sharks," they're looking for additional capital and hoping to enlist both their experience and business connections in order to help them attain increased sales. That said, notice how control driven and tough-minded the panelists are when it comes down to investing in someone else's dream. If you're presently in this rather enviable position, where you are far enough along to give a presentation to any powerful investor, it's highly advisable that you finish the rest of this book.

Pros and Cons

If I could compare both options, I would say that if you don't want to tackle the immense undertaking of going it alone, you should place your energies toward developing a licensing strategy and capitalize on your patent and your product that way.

Licensing a patent is certainly by no means a defeat, should you decide to choose this option. As a matter of fact, as far as I'm concerned, if you can obtain a fair licensing agreement with an honorable company that will promote your product for both of your mutual benefits, it's nothing short of a home run!

However, don't be misled, obtaining a fair and equitable license deal will require *nearly almost* as much work on your part as going it alone.

As previously mentioned, going it alone will definitely afford you both greater profits and personal control as opposed to striking a licensing deal. But as pointed out earlier, raising the necessary capital is yet a whole other mountain that you must climb in order to go it alone. And just because you have decided to go it alone, doesn't automatically guarantee your success either. Your risks will be enormous, compounded by the weight of the promises that you've made to your investors and stakeholders. As a matter of course, this weighty responsibility will force many inventors to reject this option and push them in the direction of securing a licensing deal. This is exactly why licensing your patent is the normal course of action.

Should you choose either option, our mantra is never going to change. Therefore, don't get sloppy and pay attention to all the details no matter how small they may appear. Keep detailed records and don't share your information too freely with any of the potential manufactures and distributors that you encounter along the way. Document everything and reduce your business plan to a concise written presentation.

Prepare to be robbed and accosted by the greedy interlopers lurking about. This paranoia and way of thinking will only serve to keep you on your guard. By operating under this mindset, you'll be reducing the chances of these bad things actually happening to you, and with a little luck, quite possibly, eliminate it. Simply stated, "prepare for the worst and hope for the best!"

As for the dream... You've already got one and you're going to need it in order to succeed regardless of what option you may choose. You've already committed to becoming an inventor so the master salesman that lies dormant inside of you will come alive no matter which path you decide to follow.

As for the makeup of the market, its trends and cycles; you're already the visionary of your invention. You wouldn't be researching how to make and market your invention if you didn't already believe in its success.

If I were you, I'd carefully consider the pros and cons that both of these options have to offer before making a final decision.

Trade Dress and Marks

Trade dress refers to the total image and appearance of a product, which includes size, graphics, shape, colors, textures and the marketing techniques used to promote an items sale. For the most part trade dress is protected under the statues pertaining to *trademark law*. However, labels and commercial prints that may constitute the key elements of an items trade dress may also be protected under the *copyright laws* as well. The specific trademark laws can be found under United States Code Title 15 Chapter 22.

According to the PTO, it is not absolutely essential to register your mark with them in order to protect your trade dress. But as you might have already guessed, that's not how I feel about it. I know that at some point, hopefully much sooner than later, you should register your mark! The following has been taken directly from the PTO's website entitled:
"Should I Register My Mark?"

- Is registration of my mark required?
- No. You can establish rights in a mark based on legitimate use of the mark. However, owning a federal trademark registration on the Principal Register provides several advantages, e.g.,
- You can establish your rights based upon the legitimate use of the mark. However, owning a federal trademark registration on the Principal Register provides several advantages, e.g.,"
- constructive notice to the public of the registrant's claim of ownership of the mark;
- a legal presumption of the registrant's ownership of the mark and the registrant's exclusive right to use the mark nationwide on or in connection with the goods and/or services listed in the registration; the ability to bring an action concerning the mark in federal court; the use of the U.S. registration as a basis to obtain registration in foreign countries; and the ability to file the U.S. registration with the U.S. Customs Service to prevent importation of infringing foreign goods.
- When can I use the trademark symbols TM, SM and ®?
- Any time you claim rights in a mark, you may use the "TM" (trademark) or "SM" (service mark) designation to alert the public to your claim, regardless of whether you have filed an application with the USPTO. However, you may use the federal registration symbol "®" only after the USPTO actually *registers a mark*, and not while an application is pending. Also, you may use the registration symbol with the mark only on or in connection with the goods and/or services listed in the federal trademark registration. See the PTO's website under "Should I Register My Mark?"

Author's Note. A copyright is an application that comes with yet another set of rules. In most cases a copyright will not necessarily apply to a products appearance. The specific law can be found under Title 17 of the United States Code referred to as 17 USC. For clarity I pulled this explanation from the PTO's website.

- A Copyright is a form of protection provided to the authors of "original works of authorship" including literary, dramatic, musical, artistic, and certain other intellectual works, both published and unpublished. The 1976 Copyright Act generally gives the owner of copyright the exclusive right to reproduce the copyrighted work, to prepare derivative works, to distribute copies or phone records of the copyrighted work, to perform the copyrighted work publicly, or to display the copyrighted work publicly.
- The copyright protects the form of expression rather than the subject matter of the writing. For example, a description of a machine could be copyrighted, but this would only prevent others from copying the description; it would not prevent others from writing a description of their own or from making and using the machine. Copyrights are registered by the Library of Congress' Copyright Office.
- There are times when you may desire a combination of copyright, patent and trademark protection for your work. You should consult an attorney to determine what forms of intellectual property protection are best suited to your needs. See the PTO's website concerning copyrights basics.

As you can see, there is a vast difference between these *marks* and *patent coverage*. So please don't confuse the various protections these marks afford as opposed to the protection that patent protection provides. Similarly, don't further confuse these various marks with one another, or their various applications and protections.

I cannot stress it enough. The very existence of the PTO's website can help to take much of the mystery out of the Intellectual Property Formation Process. For the aspiring inventor, the PTO's website is a vital source of information. So my best advice to you is this, avail yourself to this wonderful tool and explore it thoroughly.

With regard to my actual experience applying for registered marks, as of this writing I have never filed for a registered mark, but I know how they work. As always, consult your practitioner for his or her guidance on this matter. In any case, the person who filed your patent application will do just fine to file for any of the necessary marks that you may be considering.

As for the timing, I wouldn't advise directing too much energy toward this pursuit until your *notice of allowance* for your patent is on its way. In my opinion, it would be very premature for an inventor seeking a patent to expend valuable resources on designing a logo and obtaining trademark protection before ever receiving the patent grant.

Registered marks are important for you to both know about and to secure, but as an inventor, your primary concern is that you stay on task and obtain the patent first.

Two Real World Examples

In my opinion, nothing teaches better than a good real world example. So I would like to direct your attention to two separate real world situations that have been playing out in this arena.

Let's take the rubber shoes that go by the name of Crocs®. You know, the rubber shoes with the all the round holes in them, the ones that come in all sorts of crazy colors. By any stretch, Crocs have been very successful and are a highly profitable product to the tune of hundreds of millions of dollars. But all is not well in Eden. Without going into tremendous detail, the Crocs patent may be declared invalid on a technicality. So far the European Union has already denied giving them patent protection based upon some inherent weaknesses found in their patent.

And what' the fighting all about? The strap that goes over the front of the shoe.

Of course Crocs has a registered logo and trademark protection, but as we've already covered, that's only skin deep.

The second example is Under Armour®, the company that makes the highly popular apparel and undergarments for the sporting community. They have taken the outdoor sporting world by storm and presently dominate that market by capturing seventy percent of the market share. Yet as it appears, before their launch into the fray of the free marketplace, they did not enjoy any patent protection as they entered.

Do you think that companies the likes of Nike®, Reebok®, Adidas®, and Champion®, will be complacent to sit on the sidelines watching as hundreds of millions of dollars are being made in this unsecured market? Yes, Under Armour has a registered logo and trademark protection, but that's only skin deep.

Though I'd personally like to jump at the chance to be in either of their enviable positions, the building maelstrom that could envelope each one of these highly successful companies cannot be discounted. I suggest that you study these two situations on the Internet to see just how important adequate patent protection really is.

This is happening to two fabulous companies all because of what? The answer is before us and it's quite simple. These attacks on their capitalistic gold hails from the fact that Crocs was shielded by a weak patent and that Under Armour discounted the value of entering the game without the advantage that only a strong patent can provide. Really folks, it's that simple.

I'm going to take this opportunity to reinforce that registered marks, and in particular trademarks; protect your product from somebody who may want to duplicate your physical look, logo or the appearance of your product. As noted, both of these companies have their trade dress and marks registered with PTO or they wouldn't be authorized to display the ® symbol. Remember, the ® symbol means that the logo or trademark has been formally registered with the PTO.

I want you to consider this. In a great sense, trade dress is only skin deep, because it protects your invention from the outside. Similar to how your skin protects your body.

Patents on the other hand, work from the very inside of the invention and radiate their strength outward. Patents exclude anybody from duplicating your invention from the inside out. Your patent could be viewed as the muscle of your invention, composed of the inner workings related to the function, novelty, manufacturing processes, or the inventions components list.

In the event that you're granted a patent, it would be highly advantageous for you to consider obtaining a trademark for your invention as well. I would advise this course of action whether your intentions are to license your product to a manufacturer, or whether you have decided to go it alone. The costs of doing this are considerably less expensive than filing a patent application and the rewards are great. Having the proper trade dress protection adds another level of *protection* or *ownership* to your product. This will create yet another obvious fortification that any greedy interloper must think long and hard before attempting any assault against your ownership.

As the USPTO has demonstrated quite clearly, it's to your benefit to establish your claims as to the originality and the look of your product. If you choose to do so, you'll be protecting your rights as the creator of your trade dress material.

If I could make a wish for you, it would be that you would be the inventor of a well-crafted patent with an equally powerful and fully registered trade dress to go along with it.

Just so you know, at the time of my inventing I didn't register my product by employing either the formal or informal use of a mark. During my licensing odyssey I wasn't focused in that direction. I was utterly focused on getting my foot in the door and rather obsessed with obtaining an equitable licensing agreement.

However, that's not to say I didn't consider the possibilities of a trademark. What I am saying, is that I didn't focus on that aspect nearly to the degree that I'm bringing it to your attention now.

Speaking now as an inventor who has already suffered an attack on his ownership, I want your horizons to be much broader than then mine ever were during my journey.

In all due candor, I didn't have any formally established trade dress or *look* established for my new oil filter. And since I was trying to break into a monopolistic market, *I thought rather incorrectly*, that I would just leave this artsy stuff up to the big boys, thinking that a licensing agreement would make us partners. Wrong. In retrospect, that was a naïve approach, which made for a stupid mistake.

In my opinion, you should definitely be focusing on the value and the importance of your patented products overall look as well. If you can come up with something worthy of your invention, by all means pursue it. If you're not artsy, then it's easy enough to get a graphic designer.

As an aside, if you should get an independent artist involved, be certain to document that the artwork being produced, has been commissioned exclusively for you and that upon payment in full, the artist's entire rights to this work are being transferred over, solely to you.

Again getting back to the creation of intellectual property and this most certainly includes all artwork, you have to make sure that you become the sole owner of the work product that the artist is producing for you. Or you could one day find yourself on the receiving end of a copyright infringement lawsuit instituted by the artist. I'm not kidding!

If you still find that you have trouble understanding the concept of trade dress, next time you're out and about on a warm day I want to examine the sea of T-shirt and sweat jackets that nearly everyone sports. People of all ages and cultures have become walking billboards in the name of fashion. Typically, most people are mindless of the fact that others are getting fabulously rich off of their chests and backs. If you consider this phenomenon from an intellectual property aspect, theses t-shirt wearers are either knowingly or unknowingly wearing some creator's trade dress, whether it was officially registered or not. Nonetheless, someone is making some serious money off of this particular trade dress whether they are doing so legally or not.

Additionally, the concept of trade dress along with being bolstered by a registered mark is important for two separate reasons. The first reason being it just may give you the added edge necessary to get your foot in the *front door* of a manufacturer or a retailer. Never lose sight of the fact that getting in the front door is a *huge achievement*, whether you're going it alone, or whether you're attempting to license your widget to large manufacturer.

Remember, you've already done the lion's share of the R&D. How much more advantageous would your position be if you had already addressed the trade tress protection in a tasteful and forward-looking manner?

Secondly from my point of view, the act of establishing a trade dress for your property and by formally registering you mark with the PTO, establishes a secondary layer of ownership. This extra insulation should be enough to thwart any would-be interloper from absconding with your patented widget.

A Home Work Assignment

I don't like homework assignments, but I have two very fascinating cases for you to check out on the internet. These cases have long since been decided and have been boiled down to their basic elements so that any non-legally minded individual can not only grasp, but marvel at what each case has to teach.

As I've already put forth, the laws governing trademark and copyright law are rather straightforward and are a beautiful thing. So, take a breather and look up what happened to the Nestle′ Company® when Taster's Choice® misappropriated a photograph of a male model by *neglecting to secure* his permission to plaster it about their coffee containers for twenty years.

Anyway, after a trial, Nestle′ had to pony up $16 Million Dollars for using the unauthorized likeness of this male model turned schoolteacher.

The second case is X-IT Products vs. Walter Kidde. This one of my favorite cases and it clearly portrays how two Harvard Business School graduates had their IP stolen despite being under a binding NDA. This case involves trade dress or trademark theft, and patent claims theft as well. The patent theft in this particular case, highlights many of the same type of wrongdoings that I personally experienced during my business dealings with Honeywell.

This case illustrates the lengths to which a powerful, well established and very dishonest company will go in order to steal another individual's *already protected IP.* This particular case will teach you this, not me. When you are finished, you will know beyond a shadow of a doubt that what I have been sharing with you all along, is indeed very real.

Though our judicial system is oftentimes flawed; and my personal experience with it was a total nightmare, I still want you to believe that there is hope. As I've told you, hope is the force that is driving your future forward as an inventor, so I want you to take careful notice of something as you review the facts of this case.

The judge, the court, the legal proceedings and X-IT's lawyer[s] are all fine examples of how fairness and justice in American courts should be arrived at, where a small plaintiff takes on a corporate giant in a complex IP battle.

The take away message here is as follows; when it comes time for you to consider trade dress for your product, I hope that you'll think twice before dismissing this additional form of protection. Go back and review what the PTO and 15 USC and *The Lanham Act* has to say regarding these rather coveted protections.

Chapter 9

THE PSYCHOLOGY BEHIND ROYALTY RATES

Beginning the Valuation Process

It seems rather peculiar to me, but there isn't a whole lot of information out there that explains how an inventor should go about establishing a royalty rate.

For instance, if you spend any amount of time examining the PTO's web site, or any of the other sites out there, you'll come away with the notion that being granted a patent is an inventor's golden opportunity. And of course that's true to a point.

After you expand your search, you're apt to uncover a ton of material that promises to help you bring your idea to market, but yet there seems to be a void regarding royalty rate analysis and licensing.

The general impression that I'm left with is almost as much to say to the inventor, "Establishing a royalty rate for your invention is not that important, so don't worry about it, because it will all work out when the time comes."

As an inventor, you need to be aware, that the art of obtaining a fair royalty rate for your patented invention is no small thing! In reality it's a whole other mountain that must be climbed.

As you may have expected, I'd like to fill in some of those blanks for you. What I'd really like to teach you is that establishing a royalty rate is *not* solely based upon on the facts, the figures and some mathematical principals. It would be lovely if it were. But the reality is, the establishment of a royalty rate is a bit more involved than you might expect. Once again this process will be driven by any number of intangible elements that I can only refer to as the *human factor*.

Before getting started, a quick review is in order.

As previously discussed, there was the *outright sale*. Which by the way, I still counsel against. My reasoning is simple. You will not earn a fraction of the financial reward that is due you, based purely on the fact that this is your first invention and you have no established track record. The achievement of discovering a valuable emerging market, along with all that went into the process will be greatly discounted should you choose this option.

There was the option of *going it alone*. This option affords the inventor the ability to manufacture and market his invention under his or her own control. While that may sound alluring at first, a closer look will reveal that pulling this one off is a Herculean task. Even though this option will afford the highest potential for both profit and personal control, the level of responsibility will be at its greatest level. This option will increase both the inventor's responsibility and workload dramatically, because the inventor must build an entire business from the ground up in order to dispose of his invention. Truly a monumental task.

Then of course there is *licensing*. Though this is by no means a cakewalk, licensing is still the most practical of all the options. Most importantly, the financial rewards of securing a good license can certainly justify the inventor's odyssey of getting there.

The upcoming pages of this chapter will be touch upon the key elements behind the establishment of a realistic royalty rate.

Licensing is the Norm

The first two paths *are not* the norm, licensing is. As such, I have already touched upon the factors why licensing would be the only way to go with regard to striking a deal with a monopoly or an oligopoly. And of course that still holds true. So licensing even with all of its various pitfalls, and there can be many at times, would still be the option of choice for most inventors.

That's why when you first begin to research the inventing and the patenting process; the goal of entering into a licensing agreement should become one of your primary objectives. The only exception would be if you already own the means of production and can get the invention to market through the channels that you've already established. In that case you *should* go it alone.

In the final analysis, the inventor's *most realistic option* will be to license his or her patent to someone who can do all of these things for you. In most cases we are talking about teaming up with an established manufacturer.

From a practical standpoint, licensing will work in just about nearly every type of market and in practically every type of scenario. That is however, with the strict understanding that the tighter the market, the more difficult it will be for the inventor to successfully attain a license agreement. As previously illustrated, the fewer the number of players in any given market will tend to restrict entry dramatically, thereby *decreasing* an inventor's chance of *ever* attaining a licensing agreement.

So again, when the idea first arrives, if it should fall into a monopolistic type of market, the inventor must think long and hard as to whether he or she should even proceed with the patenting process at all. Simply stated, the odds of your success in achieving a licensing agreement might be so tightly stacked against you from the get-go, that it may not be worth the risk to begin with.

I suggest that if you need any further clarification, go back and review my personal scenario and the pressures exerted by the constraints of an OEM driven oligopoly/monopoly.

It must be noted, if you are fortunate enough to enter into a licensing agreement in this particular environment, it will only be due to the fact that your invention has been found to be quite valuable by the *licensee*.

Again, the inventor must be brutally honest with himself from day one concerning his invention and the probability of ever attaining a license agreement in the first place.

Lastly, you don't have to be an economist to embark on this next step, just a realist. I'm not an economist, nor do I pretend to be one; but you must have a clear understanding of the market conditions that your invention has positioned you in.

That's right! Your invention is going to position you in the market, not vice versa. For example, I developed an oil filter and subsequently I was locked into that particular market whether I liked it or not. That was my fate and there was nothing that I could do to change it. Even if I wanted to place this invention into let's say the more relaxed tool market, it would have never fit. So keep in mind the adage, "square pegs fit into square holes and round pegs fit into round holes." Don't fight it.

Just so you know, do you have any notion how many times that I pondered to the point of exasperation, why it was my fate to become an inventor of oil filters? Think with me for a moment. As a backyard inventor, you really can't stray much further off the beaten path or have picked a more tightly regulated market than I did. Yet despite the incredible odds, I chose to follow my dream.

The question still remains for you to wrestle with, will you follow yours?

However, there is a bright spot to all of this. If I could figure out the oil filter market as an industry outsider, then there's a very good chance that you can figure out your market as well.

What Licensing Is

As previously stated, before you can ever begin to calculate what your royalty rate might be, you're going to be required to conduct nearly the same amount of research to manufacture and market your product as the inventor who is attempting to go it alone.

That's right. I don't want you to miss this point. For you to effectively market and obtain a fair license agreement, it will virtually take you the same amount of research as it would for the inventor who plans on manufacturing and marketing his product.

However, there is one major difference. In the pursuit of a licensing deal, you are *not* going to be personally engaged in raising the necessary capital to enter the marketplace like the inventor who chooses to go it alone.

That is why in the truest sense; most inventors will choose to license their patents. Simply stated, most inventors don't own a suitable means of production. Nor do they have a guaranteed pipeline into a specific market. Nor do they possess the necessary funding.

As discussed, these responsibilities will fall squarely on the shoulders of the manufacturer and it's your job as the inventor to clearly understand this.

Be ever mindful that the manufacturer is taking a calculated risk by teaming up with both you and your patent. To be fair about it, your patent is unproven to everyone and the manufacturer is no exception.

Think of it this way. Instead of you going out and raising the capital to produce your product, the manufacture must dip into his pocket to finance this venture.

In summary, there are a myriad of hoops that even a manufacturer must jump through with regard to the manufacture and the marketing of your newly presented invention. Therefore, the inventor who is seeking to license out his product is going to be required to jump through those same hoops in order to sell the manufacturer on his/her vision.

So if it's your desire to enter into a license agreement don't play it down, because that in of itself is a very tall order. In essence, you will be required to force-feed everything necessary to close the licensing deal with your licensing partner.

Some Good Psychology Never Hurts

Before we delve into the specifics of royalty rate calculations, I think it's best to touch upon some of the intangibles that you're going to be up against. In all probability, the manufacturer that you wish to team up with hasn't studied the emerging market like you have. More than likely, they haven't studied this opportunity ever before!

Here are the facts. You've already been granted the patent[s] pertaining to the emerging market and the manufacturers that you're about to call on, don't own any such patent[s]. In addition to that, you've already obtained some trade dress protection as well, and again, the manufacturer doesn't own any of this either.

Now here's what sets you apart from the pack. You've seen the emerging market and you've taken the initiative to lay claim to it by obtaining a patent. This of course, is what qualifies you as the visionary of this particular emerging market and *not* the manufacturer that you're about to deal with.

Yes…, this took lots of time, lots of study and lots of your hard earned capital, but nonetheless, you did it! As a result of your great investment, you understand this emerging market better than *any* manufacturer ever might.

So here's the point to all of this. It's now time to figure out how you're going to profit from all of your hard work and farsighted vision. Now that you've finally arrived at this point in the odyssey, it becomes necessary for you to switch gears once again. It's imperative that you begin to start thinking more like a salesman, because from this point forward, it's going to be your job to *sell* the potential *licensee* something they may not know anything about. Hence it's crucial that you know your product and the universe that it fits into, both inside and out.

Here's how it works. When a company is introduced to your new patent for the first time, they might be intrigued *just enough* to entertain how they may gain some additional market share and increase their bottom line. Initially that's what will grab their attention.

What you may not be aware of, is that often times the manufacturer that you may be calling on could be skittish, standoffish or even downright negative towards your patent.

This is where you must begin to put yourself in their shoes. As a visionary turned *master salesman*, you must be able to *anticipate* what it's going to take in order to sell your patent and its corresponding emerging market. Here are some of the questions that a potential manufacturer that you might be talking with *will* be asking themselves:

- Does the market opportunity that the inventor is talking about really exist?
- If it does exist, how much money can we make from this product?
- Is this idea too good to be true?
- How did we miss this opportunity? It's impossible, because we're already major players in this field.
- Is this inventor just a crackpot? Is he or she for real?
- How can he/she possibly have a patent on this idea and we don't? We make tens of millions dollars in this market each and every year. How'd we miss it?
- We've never partnered with an outside inventor before. How do we approach this situation with this so-called inventor?
- Where's his/her proof to back all of this up?
- How much money does he/she want?
- How can we get any leverage over this guy?
- Are there any weaknesses? How can we wrestle this technology way from him?

When an industry outsider such as a backyard inventor, catches a major player flatfooted by obtaining a patent in their field of expertise, well you can only imagine some of the reactions and situations that this can create. There is however one reaction you will not get. Nobody is going to toss out the welcome mat, put their arm around your shoulder and say to you, welcome home… we've been expecting you!

- Every manufacturer who expects to stay ahead of their competition is in a perpetual state of prospecting to discover what you now already own!

Then suddenly out of the blue, you show up with the patent. Unsolicited. But not only that, you show up with a solid business plan for an *emerging market* opportunity that has been right under their noses, in the very business category that they dominate. Think of the embarrassment that they must feel! And now if they want to participate in *your new find*, they have to deal with you.

Even though you're in the catbirds seat, and you might be capable of delivering this new profit center to the manufacturer, don't get cocky! Because in most cases, it's going to take some doing before they can come to grips with what you've actually accomplished. Not only that, the big question they'll soon be asking themselves is how they plan on dealing with you.

If they are the interested in what you have to offer, their first order of business is to get a copy of your patent and have it examined with a fine tooth comb. They need to be convinced of a couple of things:

- How strong is your patent?
- How appropriate, relevant and *value added* is your trade dress?

Actually all of this, or any part thereof is quite rare. So for the most part, many companies may find themselves dealing with an outside inventor like yourself for the very first time.

Sure they're going to make money with your idea if they choose to go with it, and so will you. That of course is the whole point. But sometimes it's not so obvious to them at first, because their judgment may be clouded by all the negative emotions that you've just stirred up *in them, because so badly beat them at their own game*. Therefore, they're going to need some time to digest everything before they can allow themselves to move forward with you.

- Although licensing may be the norm, it's certainly not an everyday occurrence for a manufacturer to be approached by a backyard inventor with a patent[s].
- It's certainly not an everyday occurrence for a manufacturer to be approached by a backyard inventor with a valuable idea that can be supported by verifiable market data.
- Rarely is a manufacturer approached by a backyard inventor who has all of the above, and in addition to that, has a registered trade dress that hits the marketing bullseye.

This is where it becomes your job to finesse your way inside that company by making the proper contacts. As an inventor, you need to cultivate allies within a company to gain support for your idea. The whole object is to have them embrace what you're presenting so that they will want to team up with you!

The reason for all this dancing on their part is quite simple:

- Your patent was not birthed from inside their company. It was given birth outside of their company by you. Your invention will immediately be branded with the *not invented here* label. With that label can come much resistance.

Just so you know, I excelled at breaking through the NIH barrier. When I approached the various filter manufacturers I caught every one of them flatfooted, because not one of them had dreamt of my particular improvement[s].

Fram was no different than the rest of the players. When I initially met with their filter engineers, not one of them held a single patent for an oil filter. Not one. As a matter of fact, I couldn't find one oil filter patent that the Fram Filter Division could lay claim to.

On the other hand, I came calling with two benchmark oil filter patents. The NIH factor at Fram was very strong indeed, and nearly impenetrable. The VP of Engineering was dead set against my idea and made it nearly impossible for me to even make a marketing presentation. However, I was very lucky. I had cultivated a staunch ally in the marketing department and it was this individual who initially was able to open the door, enabling me to make my way into the company. And before the project was over, Fram's entire senior engineering staff from both the US and Canada were collaborating with me toward the development and the production of the Double Guard oil filter.

A significant truth from that experience leads me to teach you this:

- It's critical that the inventor is capable of leading the engineering team forward, especially if you have invented a mechanical or technical product.
- It is just as critical that the inventor be as capable of leading the marketing forward as well.
- It's critical that the inventor sets the proper tone and assumes the role of product visionary.

Just so you know, I was responsible for leading the engineering department forward where the products manufacture was concerned. And I was also responsible for leading the marketing department forward as well.

Here's a key. Although manufacturing and marketing are two mutually exclusive tasks, these tasks must be accomplished simultaneously if the project is to succeed. Therefore, it's imperative that the inventor must be capable of leading the development of his or her product on both fronts.

Here's my point. If I had proven incapable of doing this, the project would have flopped and my patents and the emerging market would have wound up in the toilet. If left to their own devices, Fram would have blown this opportunity altogether. Not plugging my book here, but all the intricate details have been chronicled for you in "The Geed of a Dime."

Humility, Diplomacy and Vigilance is Key

Although I've been advising you all along to become the lead sled dog, there are some important things you should be aware of while pulling the sled.

Sometimes when an outside inventor introduces an entirely new concept to the manufacturer, the status quo can be thrown off kilter and the *fear of failure* can get extremely heightened. The introduction of a new idea; especially one that's being introduced by an outside inventor can oftentimes breed envy, jealousy and maliciousness on the part of company employees.

It can become easy for the people on the inside of the company to begin saying to each other, "Who the heck does this outsider think he is? Waltzing in here and telling us what to do with our market, just because he has a lousy patent or two." And that's really easy for them to do, because they don't have the slightest clue of what it actually took for you to have gotten past the front door.

This particular sentiment can manifest itself in any number of ways.

Just so you know, in my particular case, Fram's upper management reacted to my presence this way. The head of the engineering department and the senior management eventually got the bright idea that they could violate our confidentiality agreements and simply take my trade secrets for their own to profit at my expense. During our relationship, that's how their feelings of insecurity manifested behind the scenes. However, in my wildest nightmares, I never dreamt that they would stoop to such a low level as to violate our trade secret agreements and basic contract and patent law.

You can only imagine what a total heart break and disappointment it was, when I found out some five years later, that's what they had been spending the bulk of their energies on.

How You Conduct Yourself Matters

I think it's also appropriate that I warn you of yet another pitfall. This one however can be self-inflicted and goes something like this; don't get caught up in your own celebrity in the event that the company should begin to fawn over you and your patent. Nobody takes too kindly to a self-indulgent individual given to gloating.

And another thing, just because you are the inventor and the visionary, you must always use tact and humility when teaching these individuals how your invention fits into the emerging market opportunity. If you attempt to bull your way into a license agreement, you will be sadly mistaken. For the most part, you're going to be playing to delicate egos here, so courtesy and strength through humility will put you up and over the bar.

Don't ever lose sight of the fact that you are an uninvited guest. Remember, that things were just fine before you came calling, so don't tick anyone off. Because if you do, the people with whom you've been dealing with, won't hesitate to flush your licensing opportunity down the toilet and there won't be a trace of interest left.

So why did I bother to tell you all of this? The answer is quite simple. In nine out of ten cases you will have to romance each other for quite some time before the topic of your compensation will ever come up. The company will need both time and convincing that your product can be manufactured and then successfully marketed. In addition to that, the company will have to be sold on the fact that they'll be able to work with you.

In the event you were to kick in the front door with guns-a-blazing, and tell the company that you want so much money up front, and that you want so much money per piece, you'd wind up shooting yourself in the foot instead of securing a license. By the way, if you're able to kick in the front door and get everything that you're asking for; I just want you to know way ahead of time that you're a far better salesman than I'll ever be, and that you should be the one writing this book and not me.

In the final analysis, just because you have a patent or two, or you happen to own a pretty trade dress, it doesn't mean that everyone you're going to be dealing with is going to roll over and give you the candy store. In my experience, it simply won't happen.

You must be able to justify your royalty rate, because in the end, no manufacture really wants to pay *any inventor* a royalty. Period.

Here's the moral.

- Be ever mindful that the licensing process is as much a game of psychology and sales, as it is anything else.

Just so you know, during my interaction with AlliedSignal / Fram I conducted myself with humility, decorum and total respect toward the people and the process that I found myself an integral part of. Obviously that was the case, or I wouldn't be capable of advising you to do the same.

But despite that, two things must have happened on the way to the dance...

As a group, they collectively must have taken my kindness for weakness. Therefore, they felt obliged to take whatever liberties they wanted with my IP, despite what the law called for, and despite the Trade Secret Agreements that we had already signed.

Unbeknownst to me, they also had a corporate culture that was inherently dishonest that paid little care about destroying a weaker business partner's future. And believe me when I tell you, this mentality went as high as the men and women who ran this company. This would include, but is certainly not limited to; the VP of the Automotive Division, the Senior attorney for the automotive division, VP of Human Resources, the Chief General Counsel and the CEO. So please learn a lesson here, because you just never know. It's all been documented in T*he Greed of a Dime.*

Trust me, I wasn't sloppy at all. I know for a fact that I had never given them the opportunity to rob the candy store, however they just couldn't resist.

So… if you have invented something valuable, and you have secured all the proper protection for your invention, yet you haven't bothered to study X-IT Products vs. Walter Kidde before striking out on your marketing campaign…well, then shame on you.

Chapter 10

A ROYALTY RATE PRIMER

Establishing a Value

I had advised you early in the process to try and visualize how your invention would be manufactured. In that vein, I had also encouraged you to build a working prototype if it was at all practical. Back then, the rationale behind envisioning your invention and the building of a prototype, was twofold:

- First. It would go a long way towards demonstrating whether your invention was practical or not.
- Second. It would go a long way toward the development of strong patent claims.

Now where the *valuation process* for your royalty is concerned, I'm going to be advising that you should once again consider building a working prototype. Except this time, the purpose of having a working prototype is going to be crucial in helping you figure out what a fair royalty rate might be.

Before you can come up with a fair royalty rate, you have to figure out with as much certainty as possible, what the *manufacturer's pretax profit* is going to be from the sale of your product. In order to figure out the manufacturer's pretax profits, we must first begin by considering how much it will cost the manufacturer to put this item on the retailer's shelf. I'm now going to explain how to do all of this.

The valuation process consists primarily of two parts: *ramp-up costs* and *opportunity costs*.

- Ramp-up costs refer to the costs incurred by a manufacturer when changes to his assembly line are required to accommodate the production of any new product.
- Opportunity costs refer to the *total costs* incurred by a manufacturer to deliver an *improved product model* to market. These costs will include such things as new materials, graphics, packaging, marketing activities *as well* as the ramp-up costs.

Let's take a moment to discuss the importance of ramp-up costs. For our purposes we are going to break out the ramp-up costs and look at them separately. Depending on the complexity of the product being manufactured, ramp-up costs can eat up a significant amount of the capital needed to build any new product. The stopping and the starting of assembly lines, along with making any significant changes to them can be quite a significant expense.

In nearly every case, the manufacture will have to institute some sort of change to their production facility so that they will be able to manufacture a new product. Remember, even the smallest change to an existing product will require the manufacturer to make some sort of change to their assembly line.

So again, for the manufacturer to be able to make your product, his assembly line is going to require an investment on the company's part in order to make the necessary line changes. The costs of those changes will vary depending on how much or how little they have to adapt their assembly line to accommodate the production of your product.

Depending on the complexity of the proposed product, this could be a sizable capital investment that could potentially take a large chunk out of the manufacturers pretax profits. If these costs should prove to be too high, the project could get axed before it ever gets off the ground. Therefore, it's imperative that you begin to calculate what the potential ramp-up costs will be for the manufacturer to produce your new product.

I have to stop you here for a moment and tell you something. In order for you to accurately ascertain what the true ramp up costs will be, you'll have to wait until the manufacture that you're going to partner with actually shares them with you. That however doesn't get you completely off the hook. Because in the interim, it's still your duty to try and calculate to the best of your ability what these costs might be.

The very same goes for the other half of the equation; *opportunity costs*. Opportunity costs refer to the costs incurred by a manufacturer to deliver a finished product to market. Those costs will include such things as the new materials needed to make the product. It will also include such things as graphics, packaging, marketing activities and the like.

Again each separate area is responsible for taking a chunk out of the manufacturers potential profits. If any one of these costs should get out of line, the project could get axed before it ever gets off the ground as well. All in all, the inventor must have an intimate knowledge of how these costs will affect the overall profit margin of his or her new product.

Your first order of business is to figure out what your *improvement costs* are going to be to produce your new and improved product. In order to begin figuring out your improvement costs, you must first identify a *pre-existing product* that's as closely related to your invention as possible. The basic product that you want to add your improvement to is referred to as the *products platform.*

Once you have identified that product, the first order of business is to *reverse engineer* it. Reverse engineering, in simplistic terms means that you are going to break down a pre-existing product into its most basic parts.

Once you've accomplished that, you're going to put it back together again by using those same parts. The object of building it back together again is so that you can begin to understand the manufacturing process with more clarity. This process will not only open your mind as to how many steps there might be involved to manufacture the products basic platform, but it will begin to teach you how to go about adding your improvement to it. Once you understand the products basic *platform*, it will enable you to envision how to go about adapting your improvement to it.

As an inventor, you must be capable of understanding *to the best of your ability* how to manufacture your product. This exercise will not only help you figure out how to build your product, but it will help you break down the various costs. Most importantly, this exercise will enable you to figure out what you're your products *improvement costs* are. Improvement costs refer to those additional costs needed to improve the pre-existing product into your new and improved product.

The reverse engineering process will enable you to get a handle on the following:

- What it costs the manufacturer to produce the pre-existing product that you intend to add your improvement to.
- What your *improvement costs* will be to change the pre-existing product's platform into your new and improved product.
- What the *overall manufacturing costs* are to manufacture your new and improved product.

As an aside, the Japanese became masters at the art of reverse engineering after the conclusion of World War II. They have successfully held that position for a generation, and now the Chinese have stepped in and have become the new masters, as evidenced by nearly everything that we buy is stamped made in China.

You see as an inventor, it's going to be your responsibility to target the specific manufacturers in your field of invention and study them, just like the Chinese have been studying our manufacturing practices. In fact, it's going to be your mission to not only figure out how to make your product, but how much it's going to cost.

Here are two very important things you need to be mindful of when going through the reverse engineering process:

- First. Study how a particular manufacturer makes their product.
- Second. Investigate how much it costs a particular manufacturer to produce their product.

This knowledge is very important, because these costs will eventually be factored into what you will end up receiving as a royalty. As a master salesman, you should be as knowledgeable as possible regarding both ramp-up costs and opportunity costs.

In truth, you must become a master at playing down these costs. One fine day when you're sitting across the negotiating table hammering out your royalty, the manufacturer will be doing just the opposite, because he will be playing up these costs!

When the situation finally presents itself, you can rest assured that the manufacturer will begin to bemoan the fact that he is going to be required to make a significant investment for both the production and the marketing of your new product. Most assuredly, these costs will come up when he begins to justify what he thinks your royalty should be.

Here is the key. You must do all this research well in advance of ever sitting down at the licensing table with a potential *licensee*. To be more accurate, you really must have all this information down cold, before you ever make your first sales call, because you *never know* when the topic of your compensation is going to come up. So when it does, you had better be prepared!

If by chance you find yourself reading this book, and you happen to be on the cusp of entering into a license agreement, and you've yet to cost out your product, you shouldn't go a step further until you have gathered as much information in this area as possible.

My admonition is this. Do not enter into licensing negotiations *without* having a clear-cut idea of what your contribution to process is worth beforehand. You will deeply regret going into this exercise blind.

The Manufacturer's Pre-tax Profits

After the ramp up and opportunity costs have all been accounted for, what's left behind is something that's referred to as the *manufacturer's pre-tax profit*. I am going to detail how you can realistically go about calculating what *any* manufacturer's pre-tax profit might be to produce *your* invention. The manufacturer's pre-tax profit is very important to the inventor, because this is the money that your royalty will come out of.

No, I didn't say that this money is yours. Nor did I say that all of this money belongs to the manufacturer either. What I will say is that any inventor who is a *party* to licensing agreement, is entitled to a *percentage* of the manufacture's pretax profit.

- As a rule, every inventor should perform this sort of analysis well in advance of ever filing for a patent.

The main objective of this exercise is to arrive at handful of key numbers. Only after you have arrived at these numbers, will you be able to calculate what a fair royalty rate might be for you to receive.

My advice is simple. If the royalty that you've come up with seems reasonable enough for you to pursue the inventor's path, then by all means you should pursue it. If it's not, this would be a good time for you to bail out.

So to be clear, *you must know* what the manufacturer's pre-tax profit is, before you can *ever* begin to figure out what your royalty will be. In a very real sense, you are about to conduct a detailed appraisal as to what the value of your patented invention is going to be worth to the manufacturer. And as you're about to find out, in the real world of licensing, that's what really counts.

The very first bit of information that you'll be seeking can be broken down into three separate categories:

- The information that will be representative of the target industry as a whole.
- The information that will be specific to each specific manufacturer that you have placed on your list of potential partners.
- How much your raw improvement costs will be to produce your *much-improved product.*

The manufacturer's pre-tax profit can be calculated by utilizing the information that these three sources can provide. The final royalty that any inventor will receive is going to be based upon a percentage of the manufacturer's pre-tax profit. The final royalty an inventor may receive is specific to each manufacturer and should only be considered on a case-by-case basis.

Warning. This exercise is critical, and no one is going to do this for you, especially not the manufacturer!

The following illustration is a purely hypothetical example. To keep things consistent, I am going to return to the hammer illustration. In order to more realistically illustrate what you need to learn, I'm going to use a real company; Stanley® of New Briton, Connecticut.

Let's begin.

During your research on the production of your much-improved hammer, you have concluded that your *improvement costs* will add an *additional* $1.00 in raw materials. That means it will take one dollar in additional capital to transform the pre-existing product into your much-improved product. In the case of our example you are proposing to transform an ordinary claw hammer into your revolutionary new hammer.

That's a good start. But in addition to that, you're going to need to find out how much it *presently* cost's Stanley® to make a standard claw type nailing hammer that is most similar to yours. As you might expect, that's going to take some digging to find that out.

Another bit of information that should be high on your list, is to find out how big the US hammer market is. It is imperative that you not only be able to find out how many individual hammers are sold on an annual basis, but how much revenue is generated.

In the case of our example, let's say that the hand held claw hammer market that's most similar to yours, sells approximately 5 million units annually. You've also found out that the national average retail price for this particular type of hammer sells for around $12.00 dollars apiece. Therefore, you're confident in assuming that the *entire* hand held claw hammer market generates approximately $60 million dollars in annual *gross revenues*.

During your investigation, you further discovered that there is approximately $7 million dollars' worth of specialty hand held hammers that are sold annually. Upon careful inspection, you have also discovered that there is at least another dozen other types of hammers, such as masonry hammers, drywall hammers, hatchets, ball peens and the like.

Although these specialty hammers generate additional revenue, they do not have any particular bearing on your particular market. Therefore, this additional revenue will not figure into your calculations. However, knowing this information does a couple of things:

- It builds your knowledge base as to the universe that your new product fits into.
- It demonstrates to any potential licensing partner that you have thoroughly done your homework.

Once again as the inventor, it's critical that you're keenly aware of the specific *market segment* or *niche* that your invention directly falls into. Yet at the same time, it's also important that you're aware of the other *niche markets* that don't directly affect the one that attempting to sell into.

I bothered to point this out, because as a master salesman it's your responsibility to be aware of these and any other relevant facts that may pertain to your market as a whole. By being aware of this type of information, it will also serve to reinforce to any potential licensee that you have an in-depth understanding of your market.

It's also important for you to understand that your much-improved hammer *is not* going to *replace* the existing claw hammer market. In all practicality, it's going to capture a certain *share* of the claw hammer market by converting potential sales of that existing style of hammer into the sales of your new hammer.

The logic here is rather straightforward. The hand held claw hammer has been around for a very long time and has been universally adopted as an indispensable tool. The individuals who need a claw hammer will most certainly continue to buy them. The people who feel comfortable using a claw hammer will continue to use them. And likewise, the people who already own a claw hammer will continue to own one.

In addition to that, people tend to go out and purchase a hammer when needed, and once purchased, they tend to keep them around forever. As you know, hammers are very durable and have a very long service life. Therefore, hammers seldom ever need replacing. Many times, hammers just seem to get passed on from one generation to the next.

So be realistic. You didn't reinvent the hammer and do away with the existing market like the CD nearly did to the phonograph record.

Nonetheless, the introduction of your much-improved hammer is going to do some notable things:

- First. It's going to create its own market segment or niche.
- Second. Even though it won't *replace* the existing claw hammer market, it will capture a certain *share* of the claw hammer market and convert those potential sales into the sales for your much-improved hammer.
- Third. The manufacturer who decides to team up with you, has the potential of capturing a percentage of their competitor's market share.
- Fourth. Depending on the magnitude of your innovation, your much-improved hammer may increase the overall demand for handheld hammers in the future.

Getting back.

During your investigation, you have identified that there at least twelve hammer manufacturers of any note in the US. The biggest player is the Stanley® Tool Company of Connecticut. You have also figured out that this market has plenty of freedom for entry, because there are many players. Therefore, the US hammer market is *not* an oligopoly nor is it a monopoly. That means if you were to pursue the licensing of your hammer, there wouldn't be any firm barriers that would keep you from participating in this market.

The next step would be to study the biggest and most successful player in your market, and that of course would be Stanley. Study them inside and out, because they are going to be the yardstick by which you'll be measuring all the other competitors against.

Besides that, in most cases it will generally be to your benefit to approach the biggest and most successful manufacturer in their respective market category. Teaming up with the biggest and best players may have several advantages for the inventor with regard to the future sales of his invention. There is an awful lot to be said for rank within a specific industry.

Here are some notable advantages of teaming up with a market leader:

- Strong Trade Name recognition.
- Large sales volume.
- Efficient means of marketing and distribution.

On the other hand, sometimes a less notable player may be more eager to enter into a licensing agreement than the number one or number two guy. Sometimes a less notable player might be hungrier and want to run harder with your new product than the market leaders, so that's always something that the inventor should consider as well.

Unfortunately, it is impossible for me to tell you who will be best suited for you to team up with when it comes time to market your actual invention, and which direction is best for you to initially follow. That is going to be your decision and that's precisely why you have to become the visionary where your invention is concerned and why others are not.

For the sake of our example, you found out from an industry source that that Stanley sells approximately 2 million hammers annually and enjoys 40% of the US claw hammer market.

As a matter of practice, you've already studied every possible hammer category and every hammer type that Stanley makes. So after all of your research, you are convinced that if they were to introduce your patented hammer, their claw hammer sales *could potentially* increase by an additional 20%. The majority of this 20% gain will be the result of taking market share away from the other manufacturers. Some of this gain will also be the result of drawing new hammer buyers into the market and some as a result of upgrading their standard claw hammer to your much-improved hammer.

That means that after Stanley introduces your much-improved hammer, they might end up with a possible 60% of the overall claw hammer market.

That would mean that sales for their claw hammer category *could potentially* increase by an additional 1,000,000 units for the first year. Of course this additional jump in sales will equate to substantially higher revenues that would be generated from the sale of this improved hammer.

Needless to say, this tremendous growth potential could be huge! Furthermore, it would be directly attributed to your relatively inexpensive and simplistic innovation! And that's the key to being able to strike a good licensing deal.

For our calculations, we are going to assume that the introduction of our much-improved claw hammer will generate the *additional sales* of 1,000,000 units sold the first year.

So before going any further, let's review what you've uncovered.

- You have identified the various players in the US market. There are at least twelve major players.
- There are no barriers to entry, so this is a free market.
- You have identified the annual gross dollar volume for the US claw hammer market to be $60 million dollars.
- You have identified that there are 5 million claw hammers sold every year in the US.
- You have identified the various players' percentage of the US market share.
- Stanley already has a 40% market share.
- Stanley sells 2 million claw hammers per year.
- The Stanley claw hammer retails at the industry average retail price of $12.00.
- You have projected that your improvement will increase Stanley's overall US hammer sales by 20%.
- You have projected that if Stanley partners with you, it will increase their market share of the hand held claw hammer market by 20% or 1,000,000 units for the first year.
- You have identified that the *raw cost* of your improvement to upgrade the standard claw type hammer will be $1.00. This is the raw cost for your improvement and does not take into consideration what the final ramp-up and opportunity costs are going to be.

As you can see, you have gathered a lot of crucial information. Some of this information will be *industry specific*, some of it will be *manufacturer specific* and some of it will be *specific to your patented improvement*.

In the final analysis, you must be able to reduce your patented improvement into a simple spreadsheet. You must not only be able to do this in order to sell your idea, but you must be able to do this in order to earn a fair royalty from it. So please, don't run from this exercise.

Just so you know, I'm not a math person by any stretch. Yet I reveled in this process, because I knew that locked up in my analysis was the true value of what my patents were worth. By the way, it was the numbers as much as anything else that got my foot in the door at Fram. And in the end, that's what's going to get your foot in the door of your company as well.

There is no rhyme or reason as to how you go about collecting this information. Some of this information will fall into your lap. Some of this information will require months of digging before you will be able to uncover it. Yet some of this information you may never learn about, until you're actually sitting down with the manufacturer and hashing out the numbers.

The point is, this is a paint-by-the-numbers type of operation and your goal is to have the picture as fully developed as possible before making your first sales call. So before we are able to figure out what Stanley's pre-tax profit is, we still have some important pieces of the puzzle to color in.

Here's what you still have to figure out before you can begin to calculate what Stanley's pretax profit on your new product is going to be.

- First. You're going to have to find out what it costs Stanley to manufacture their standard claw hammer since this is the platform that you're going to add your improvement to.
- Second. You have to get an approximate handle on what the total opportunity costs are going to be to manufacture and market your new product.
- Third. You're going to have to establish what the *true manufacturing costs* are going to be for Stanley to produce your much-improved hammer.
- Fourth. You must determine at what price Stanley is going to *wholesale* this much-improved hammer to the retailer.
- Fifth. You must determine what a *realistic retail price* the consumer would be willing to pay for your much-improved hammer.

Here's the key.

- The difference between the true manufacturing costs and the wholesale costs, will give you the manufacturer's pretax profits on your new product.

So if you can figure out what it will cost Stanley to produce this new hammer, and if you can figure out what they can wholesale it to the retailers for, you will be closer to figuring out what Stanley's pretax profit margin is going to be for this much-improved hammer. Once we have compiled these figures we will have the last major piece to the puzzle!

When analyzing this data, try to be as accurate as possible. Do this despite the fact that you are not privy to the same financial information that the manufacturers have access to. As a matter of practice, all manufacturers go to great lengths to shield these figures from the outside world, because these numbers are closely held. That aside, you still have to be able to approximate what these figures might be as accurately as possible.

So keep these two things in mind:

- Your calculations and projections are only as good as the information that you uncover.
- Your calculations are only as valid as the supporting data.

Getting back to that hammer.

Through some incredible research and some luck on your part, you have discovered the coveted key to your royalty puzzle! You have uncovered that it costs Stanley Tools $4.00 to manufacture their standard claw hammer. This is truly a Eureka moment for you, since you already know that their standard claw hammer retails for the industry average of $12.00.

The simple math clearly shows that there has is an $8.00 *gross profit to be split* amongst Stanley and the big retailers.

Again as a result of all your rooting around, you've also uncovered that Stanley usually splits the $8.00 *gross profit* 50/50 when they sell into the big retail environment. That means that Stanley would wholesale their standard claw hammer to the big retailers such as Lowes® or The Home Depot® for around $8.00.

In addition to that, you have also concluded that Stanley probably makes an even greater profit margin when the sell their claw hammers to the smaller retailers. That assumption is based upon the fact that the smaller retailers don't have nearly the same buying power as these two giant retailers do.

Therefore, you *estimate* that Stanley's *profit margin* for this particular claw hammer can range somewhere between $4.00 and $5.00. To play it safe, you figure on the conservative side and base your calculations on the $4.00-dollar profit figure, because you've yet to get a true handle on what the opportunity costs might be to produce your much-improved hammer.

Based upon the information you've gathered; you *guesstimate* that the *total opportunity costs* to manufacture your new hammer will be in the neighborhood of $2.00. The first one-dollar represents the additional material costs and the second dollar represents all of the other associated costs to put this product on the shelf.

Even though it will be *nearly impossible* for you to get an exact handle on both the ramp-up and opportunity costs, you must do your best to try and figure this out. Be conservative when figuring your products potential profits, lest when negotiation time comes, you'll come across as an uninformed and greedy inventor. And that's exactly what you don't want.

Allow me to bring something else to your attention. Although a fifty/fifty split is actually quite possible, I don't want you to come away thinking that this would always be the case either, because it certainly won't. Therefore, it will take additional detective work on your part to actually figure out what the real profit split may be for your actual product.

To uncover this sort of information it might come down to you paying an actual visit to the tool department and asking the person in charge this kind of question. You might ask how much Lowe's pays for one of Stanley's standard claw hammers closest to the model that you envision improving. Or better yet, you might be able to ask the vendor who comes around periodically and takes care of the display and does the inventory for the store. You could even ask the manager of the tool department. Or it could even be as simple as asking your friend at the local hardware store to find out what he pays wholesale for a Stanley claw hammer.

As an aside, a company's Annual Report or 10-K filing could be a source for some of the general kind of information that you might be seeking. Investigating trade groups and specialty organizations that report this type of information could be another source of information.

Now with the advent of the Internet, it's possible to uncover this type of information by paying a fee to a company that collects and sells this type of data. Even studying the various competitors' information can help project the financial data that you're looking to secure. Sometimes a company's *stock prospectus* could tell you what their market share in a particular industry might be.

I not only encourage you to study your market and all of the various competitors, but I want you to focus on becoming an authority on the entire market and as well as its inner workings.

To repeat, I'm well aware that you may not have a handle on what these specific costs might be. In addition to that, I want you to be aware that many of these figures aren't so readily attainable. That's exactly why when you begin to figure out what a manufacturer's profit might be, you must do so conservatively!

As your licensing negotiations progress, the manufacturer will begin to share with you what some of his *true costs* will be to produce your much-improved product. So please don't expect to be able to calculate your royalty with *true accuracy* until after you've sat down with the manufacturer and discussed these numbers. Nonetheless, you must go through this process ahead of time for the following reasons:

- First. So that you don't just accept the manufacturers royalty offer on face value.
- Second. That you understand the process of how to arrive at a fair royalty rate, so when you finally get the real numbers, you will be able to plug them into the formula.
- Third. So that *you* can determine for yourself what a fair royalty might be for you to accept.

At the conclusion of this chapter, we will revisit how some of these costs as well as some of the psychological factors will play a major role in determining what your actual royalty might be.

Getting back.

After analyzing the hand held hammer market in addition to understanding the basic profit structure between Stanley and their major *vendors*, you have concluded that the retail customer like yourself would be willing to pay $18.00 for your much-improved hammer. This is your call and it's going to be your best guesstimate. This figure will be based upon your research and your intimate knowledge of the market data.

As a result of being able to answer the last remaining questions, you can begin to engage in figuring out Stanley's pretax profit margin for your much improved hammer.

Here's what you found out:

- It will cost Stanley approximately $6.00 to produce your much-improved claw hammer. This figure takes into account that it already costs Stanley $4.00 to build their standard claw hammer, plus the additional $2.00 for the total opportunity costs of your new improvement.
- Stanley splits its profits 50/50 with the big box stores such as Lowes and The Home Depot.
- Stanley presently wholesales its standard claw type hammer to the big box stores for $8.00.
- You have calculated that Stanley could retail your much-improved hammer for $18.00.
- You have calculated that Stanley could wholesale your much-improved hammer to the big box stores for $12.00.

Here's how the math will break down.

Your best guesstimate tells you that your new and improved hammer could reasonably retail for $18.00. This is a total gain of $6.00 or a 33.3% increase over the retail price of Stanley's standard claw hammer, which presently retails for $12.00.

Again, you have figured out that your new hammer could be manufactured for $6.00 and sold in the retail stores for $18.00. That would leave a gross profit of $12.00 to be split between Stanley and the giant retailers. That means the gross profit would increase from $8.00 for their standard claw hammer to $12.00 for your much-improved hammer. There would be a total profit gain of $4.00 for both Stanley and the retailer, which would reflect a profit increase of 33.3% for your new hammer.

That means the individual pretax profit to be realized by both Stanley and the retailer for this much-improved hammer would increase from $4.00 to $6.00, for a gain of $2.00 or 33.3% apiece.

To summarize let's compare the figures of Stanley's standard claw hammer vs. your much improved model.

<u>Stanley's standard claw hammer bullet points.</u>

- You found out that it costs Stanley $4.00 to produce their *standard* claw hammer.
- You found out that Stanley's standard claw type hammer retails for $12.00 in the large retail environment.
- You found out that there was an $8.00 gross profit that was to be split between Stanley and the large retailers on the sale of their standard claw hammer.
- You found out that Stanley earns a pretax profit on this hammer of $4.00 dollars.
- You found out that Stanley sells 5,000,000 million of these hammers annually for a pretax profit of $20,000,000 dollars.

<u>Your much–improved hammer's bullet points</u>

- You calculated that Stanley's opportunity costs to manufacture and market your much-improved hammer was an additional $2.00 more than their standard claw hammer, which presently costs them $4.00 to manufacture.
- You have concluded that Stanley could manufacture your much-improved hammer for $6.00.
- You have concluded that your much-improved hammer could retail for $18.00 in the large retail environment.
- You have concluded that you much-improved hammer could earn an overall profit of $12.00. As opposed to the overall profit of $8.00 generated by their standard claw type hammer.
- You have concluded that your much-improved hammer will generate approximately 33.3% or $2.00 in additional profits apiece for both Stanley and the large retailers.
- You have concluded that your much-improved hammer will generate a pretax profit of $6.00 for Stanley.
- You have projected that the first year's annual sales for your new hammer be 1,000,000 units.
- You have projected that addition sale of 1,000,000 units would equal an additional $6,000,000 dollars in additional pretax profit for the company.
- You have projected that if they teamed up with you, Stanley would add 33.3% to their pretax bottom line the first year in business with you.

Folk's these are not just numbers. This is business, and this is serious business. This is why you license and this is exactly why a major company will want to take a license from you.

Goldscheider's Rule

Once you've finally figured out what the manufactures pretax profit might be on your value added product, the burning question still remains. What's the magic formula that gets applied to the company's pretax profit so that an inventor can determine what his fair royalty rate should be?

Look no further, because here's the best answer that anybody can give you.

Robert Goldscheider has been defending his 25% royalty rate rule since 1959. In a landmark case, Mr. Goldscheider represented the Philco Corporation in a European licensing dispute involving 18 licenses for its radio and phonograph patents.

In that case Mr. Goldscheider in the capacity of a damages expert, calculated that the *Licensee or the manufacturer*; assumed 75 percent of the risk. On the other hand, the *Licensor; the one who granted the license* assumed 25 percent of the risk. As a result of that analysis, the "25% Rule" was born.

The major impact of that case laid the groundwork for his ***25% Rule*** which has more or less been the gold standard defense for royalty rate analysis. Goldscheider's rule basically states that 25% of the responsibility falls to the *licensor or the inventor*; and the remaining 75% of the responsibility falls to the *licensee or the manufacturer*. His groundbreaking analysis provided that the relationship between inventor between and manufacture should reflect a 25/75 percent split of the pretax profits.

For our purposes the terms *gross profit margins* and *pretax profits* means the same thing. It's the profit that a company makes on a product before paying taxes.

Therefore,

- The inventor is entitled to 25% of the manufacturers pretax profits.
- The inventor who owns the patent is always referred to as the one who *grants* the license, known as the *licensor*.
- The manufacturer who *receives* the license is known as the *licensee*.

To keep the nomenclature straight, just think of the inventor as the *giver or licensor* and the manufacturer as the *receiver or licensee*.

During his career, Mr. Goldscheider has testified in over a 100 intellectual property cases. As a result of being an intellectual property expert it has been said that he had amassed a small fortune doing this sort of work. "Goldscheider is oftentimes referred to as the Father of the 25% Rule, a method used for calculating royalties when measuring damages in infringement litigations which has been used for over 50 years by countless attorneys."

I said all of this, because whether you agree with Mr. Goldscheider or not, his rule is brought to bear in nearly every lawsuit where the value of an inventor's patent or an inventor's contribution are in dispute.

Since the adoption of this rule, no one has put forth another ratio that even comes close to competing against Mr. Goldscheider's inventor-manufacturer's split. Mr. Goldscheider passed away in July 2014.

Just so you know, I have personally dealt with Mr. Mr. Goldscheider's 25% rule during my court case. To set the stage, let me just start out by stating that as defendants; Honeywell by any account had been most uncooperative when it came to the *discovery process*. Since you may not understand what the term *discovery* means, allow me to explain what it is.

Each party in a lawsuit has a duty to produce the evidence that the other side requests. As such, discovery is the collection of documents, tangible items and the testimony produced by each side. This is to be performed to the best of each of the warring party's abilities and it must be done in an honest manner. Therein lies the rub. Really now, if you think about it, how can we expect the party who already broke the law to suddenly become law abiding, just because they got caught stealing and now they're in court? I still haven't figured that one out yet. But that's how our system is set up.

Anyway, the court in conjunction with the Federal Rules of Civil Procedure mandate strict adherence to these rules where the exchange of *documents and things* are concerned. As such, the discovery process has a starting date and an ending date and both sides are supposed to be equally bound by these parameters. In most instances, once discovery is closed or has ended, neither party is allowed to introduce any new evidence into the lawsuit whatsoever.

Now was that so hard to understand?

Just so you know, Honeywell had a strong aversion towards providing me their financial documents during our formal discovery period. I have documents proving that I had made at least *four formal requests* for their *readily accessible* financial data. Yet Honeywell never provided all of the information that I had reasonably requested during the discovery period.

So after formal discovery had been closed some two and a half years, Honeywell conveniently stumbled upon over 600 pages of documents relating to their past licensing history. Though this information wasn't something that I had ever requested, they brought it forth so that they could make a run at debunking Mr. Goldscheider's 25% rule.

Of course this was a joke, and the judge should have never of admitted this into evidence, but he did. On the other hand, if Honeywell had been on the ball, they could have easily of introduced this material in a timely fashion. Instead, they pleaded with the court to have it introduced some 2 ½ years after discovery *supposedly* had been closed.

Honeywell should have been barred on the grounds that they employ an entire department that monitors their 12,000 patents and their worldwide licensing activities and could have easily introduced this discovery in a timely fashion.

The point is, this was all done on the eve of trial in an all-out attempt to vilify Mr. Goldscheider's 25% rule. Honeywell had no other option, but to defame Goldscheider's rule, since they were already on the wrong side of it to begin with.

They were on the wrong side of Goldscheider's rule in my case since they were only paying me a mere 10 ten cents a filter when they were making a pretax profit of $2.50 for every filter that they wholesaled.

According to Mr. Goldscheider's rule it doesn't take a rocket scientist to figure out that the royalty rate they should have been paying me all along was something more like 50 cents for every filter that they wholesaled, and not the dime I had agreed to accept.

As a result, Honeywell spent at least a half million dollars to derail Mr. Goldscheider's 25% rule and they tried with all their might during the battle of our financial experts to further reduce my royalty rate to zero cents! This little stunt was not only expensive for me to respond to, but it was a down right crime for them to be allowed by the court to pull this kind of charade on the eve of my jury trial.

Nonetheless, the Federal District the judge who presided over my case allowed them to introduce this new material in an attempt to debunk the Mr. Goldscheider's 25% rule.

So here's what I'm saying to you.

- As an inventor, you want to be on right side of Mr. Goldscheider's 25% rule before you *ever* sign anything.
- As an inventor, you are entitled to 25% of the manufactures pretax profits.
- As an inventor, you must fight like hell during licensing negotiations to etch into the contract your fair share of the pretax profits.

By the same token most manufactures, their defense attorneys and their financial experts will try and make Mr. Goldscheider out to be some sort of a greedy crackpot. Well crackpot or not, it's far better that you learn about him now, as opposed to later.

I highly suggest you look him up Mr. Goldscheider on the Internet. Have this information in hand and be ready to justify to any prospective licensee where you're coming from as the visionary and the market maker.

Oh, one last thought. If Mr. Goldscheider's 25% rule was a figment of the inventing community's imagination, then how come Honeywell spent well over a half million dollars shadowboxing a ghost?

Now What's Your Share?

Plain and simple, the formula that you would apply to figure out your royalty rate is as follows:

- $\frac{\text{(Number of units sold annually) X (the company's pretax profits)}}{25\%}$

Disclaimer. Before this formula can be applied in earnest, the company must substantiate to your satisfaction how they arrived at their pretax profits. That means that the company must share with you what their *real* costs are to put this product on the shelf.

Remember up until this point, you are doing your best to guesstimate what the company's ramp-up and opportunity cost would be to put this product on the shelf. By going through this exercise well in advance of ever receiving their figures, you will be in a far better position to judge whether they are being truthful about their accounting or not.

For the sake of keeping things simple, let's take the figures that you've already gathered and plug them into the royalty rate formula.

You already projected that Stanley could secure an additional 20% in new market share from the existing claw hammer market if they decided to produce your much-improved hammer. That number would equate to approximately 1,000,000 additional new hammers sold annually. You projected that the pretax profit would be approximately $6.00 for every new hammer sold. Mr. Goldscheider has already informed you that you are entitled to 25% of the manufacturer's pretax profits.

Therefore, the equation should look like this:

- <u>1,000,000 units X $6.00 = $6,000,000 million dollars in pretax profits</u>

  25%

However, before you run out and begin to count your first year's royalty of $1,500,000 dollars, I'd like to make you aware of a couple of things.

There are two possible mindsets that can be applied toward Stanley's new profits.

- The first scenario will be the *company's mindset*, which will *favor* the company.
- The second scenario will be the *inventor's mindset*, which will be *fair* to the inventor.

Let's consider the first scenario. Under this scenario the *company* would take the pretax profit figure of only a $2.00 for every new and improved hammer sold. Their argument would be as follows, "We are already producing the standard claw hammer for which you intend on adding your improvement to, and we have been receiving a $4.00-dollar profit from the sale of that item long before you ever came along. Therefore, we feel that you should only be entitled to a *percentage* of the profit that can directly be attributed to your improvement, and not what we've been earning on our preexisting product's platform."

Pure and simple, the company will do the math by multiplying the additional new sales of 1,000,000 hammers by $2.00. The company would insist that the $2.00 figure be used, because they will claim that's the pretax figure that is directly attributable to your improvement. Under the company's analysis, they would claim that their additional revenues would total approximately $2 million dollars. By their way of thinking this figure would be the direct result of your patented improvement.

Under this *first scenario*, Stanley's would take their pretax profits of $2 million dollars and divide that by 25% and they would come out with a royalty figure based upon first year sales of $500,000 dollars.

Keep in mind, this will only happen if they are fair-minded enough to apply Mr. Goldscheider's 25% rule to their pretax profits, and of course there's no guarantee that they will.

Under the *second scenario*, you would take overall pretax profit figure of $6.00 and multiply that by the sales of 1,000,000 hammers. This profit figure would be derived by taking Stanley's former profit of $4.00 in addition to the $2.00 profit brought about by the institution of your invention.

As the inventor, you would insist upon the $6.00 figure be used. You would argue that $6.00 is the company's pretax profit figure that is directly attributable to your *total improvement*. Under that analysis, you would come up with the additional revenue figure of approximately $6 million dollars. By your way of thinking this figure would be the direct result of your patented improvement.

Under this *second scenario*, you would want Stanley to take their pretax profits of $6 million dollars and divide that by 25%. In that case you would come out with a royalty figure of $1,500,000 dollars, based upon the first year sales.

Again, that would only happen if they were fair enough to apply Mr. Goldscheider's 25% rule to their pretax profits for the entire product, and there's no guarantee that they will.

Both from my vantage point of being an inventor and in light of all that you'll have to go through to get this far, *I most certainly favor the second scenario.* In my mind this is a very fair and reasonable assumption. One only needs to ask the following questions to see if my point of view has merit.

"If it were not for you and your patented improvement, then what was the mechanism responsible for generating the additional sales of 1,000,000 new hammers that Stanley benefited from?"

By what miracle did Stanley add $6 million dollars' worth of pretax profits to their balance sheet?

By what miracle was Stanley able to add an instant 20% market share in less than one years' time?

Did Stanley discover and evaluate the emerging market?

Did Stanley secure the patent(s) and trade dress?

The answer of course, is that you're the logical reason for their newly found prosperity. The other half of my supporting argument goes something like this:

The much-improved hammer that you've invented is *an entirely new device*. To my way of thinking, it doesn't matter whether the underlying platform for this new hammer had already existed or not. In truth, the inventor is entitled to 25% of the pretax profit on the *entire* new device regardless of whether there was a preexisting platform or not.

Remember what I taught you earlier. Chances are real good that you're not going to be a Thomas Edison. Therefore, you were never expected to come up with a stand-alone invention, nor were you going to receive a pioneer patent. Of course the product's platform already exists in some form out in the marketplace! However, that shouldn't discount the fact that you were able to take a previously existing platform and create an entirely new and improved product.

Therefore, no matter what line of reasoning the company may put forth, the fact remains that you did create an entirely new profit center for them to capitalize on.

Just so you know, I'm not claiming in any way shape or form that I created the spin-on oil filter, far from it. What I will tell you is that I was able to take a *pre-existing products platform* and come up with a couple of very good patents and some extremely valuable trade secrets in order to improve it. Information was good enough to enable Honeywell to file an additional 17 patents and earn them $100,000,000 dollars generated from the IP that I know about.

I certainly can't speak for Mr. Goldscheider, but I would tend to think that he would favor the *second scenario* as well. I believe that this is how he would view your contributions, when he says that you are entitled to 25% of the pretax profits for the invention. I know that's how I view it.

Nonetheless I must warn you well in advance, neither situation that I just described may play out so neatly. So before you begin to rely strictly on this formula, I'd better share some real world pressures that could very well eat away at your royalty rate.

Pricing it Right and Splitting Up the Profits

There are a couple of things you should be aware of:

- First. What's going to be the profit split between the manufacture and the retailer?
- Second. Are they capable of pricing it right?

In our example the large retailers such as Lowes and The Home Depot would earn a $6.00 profit by selling your much-improved hammer made by Stanley. In a great sense how these two giants propose to price your article *will* have a direct effect on what you will earn as the inventor. I purposely included this information so that you can better understand how the total profit structure is set up, and to make it clear that the retailer is in business with Stanley so that they both can make as much of a profit as possible from every item they sell.

Just be mindful that the more money that the retailer makes, the less money there is for the manufacturer to profit from. As a result, the smaller the profit for the manufacturer, the smaller the royalty is going to be for the inventor.

- No matter how much your invention may increase the overall profit of an item, as the inventor, your royalty comes out of the manufacturer's side, and not the retailer's. However, the retailer's profit will directly affect what you might receive.
- The retailer's gross profit is the difference between what he paid to obtain the product and what he can eventually retail it to the public for.

In the event that both the manufacturer and the retailer happen to get crazy, they can push the retail price of your product up so high, that nobody will buy it. If that happens, the entire project is in jeopardy of going bust. If the project should go bust, due to either the manufacturer's or the retailer's greed, the inventor is sure to get the short end of the stick. This can all happen, because the inventor has placed his trust in a licensing agreement that specifies that he will be making his fortune one piece at time.

This bears repeating.

- If either the retailer or the manufacturer pushes the price too high in order obtain a larger profit, the product may not sell and the inventor will lose.

Just so you know, I have intimate and personal experience as an inventor concerning just such an issue. Initially, the Double Guard's retail price was set way too high. From the onset, both Honeywell and Walmart set out to exact profit margins from the Double Guard that were unheard of in this *product category*. Prior to the advent of the Double Guard, there had *never been a value added oil filter offered for sale with such an incredible profit margin for both the manufacturer and the retailer.* Never.

As a result of overpricing this filter, it drove a considerable number of consumers to *steal* the product by switching out the more expensive Double Guard into the boxes of Fram's lower priced oil filter. From the products initial offering, the number of thefts quickly skyrocketed into the several hundreds of thousands of units. As a result of the product being pilfered, the entire product line had to be withdrawn from Walmart and subsequently repackaged into theft proof packaging.

As a result of this pricing fiasco, and being caught flatfooted as to consumer demand, the Double Guard lost six months of *critical rollout time*. This cost the company millions of dollars and over the first few years of my license I personally lost hundreds of thousands of dollars in royalties myself, because I was automatically a partner to their screw up.

Anyway, this simple illustration goes to the very heart of what licensing is all about. Therefore, you better view it as something other than dry bones!

I hope *you* can begin to fathom just how valuable a novel patent can be to both the manufacturer as well as their retailing partners. You better believe that they do! This is all documented in *The Greed of a Dime*.

Royalties vs. Reality

I have already established that it would truly be ideal if the inventor would be entitled to a clean 25% pretax cut of the profits.

Yet in most cases, that's not necessarily what you might end up receiving as the end result of your licensing negotiations. There are various reasons for this, so you better be aware of what some of the factors might be well in advance of you sitting down at the negotiating table.

It could just be your fate that you wind up negotiating with a monopoly, or a very hardheaded company. Or the company that you might be dealing with could be very stingy. Or you may even be dealing with a greedy company. Just remember, companies come in all sizes and flavors. The reality of it is this, you won't know what flavor you're going to get until you actually get deep inside one of them. And you really won't know, until the ink is dry on your license agreement and your product is out in the marketplace.

They may be terrified by the prospect of failure, or they may not have done anything innovative in recent memory. You name it.

Here's what I've learned about money. In my experience, most people are neither very fair, nor do they tend to be overly generous when it comes time to part with their money. So how can an inventor rely upon a nameless and faceless corporation to be any more benevolent when they have the facade of business to hide behind?

My answer is simple. Don't expect the company that you end up partnering with to be generous when it comes time for them to part with their money either.

My point is this. It might not be so obvious at first, but companies do have their own individual personalities. So try and be aware of this ahead of time. In my personal case, I never considered Honeywell's initial greed to figure so prominently into my relationship with them, but it did. As a result of my naiveté, I nearly got crushed.

That's why it's so critical that you begin to prepare to calculate your royalty rate by employing as many factors as possible. In the final analysis, many factors will influence what a fair royalty will be, and chief among them is:

- How valuable is your idea?
- How strong is your patent?
- How well documented and protected are your trade secrets?
- Do you have an established and powerful trade dress?
- Is your trade dress officially registered with the PTO?
- Is the company that you are negotiating with greedy or stingy?
- Is their corporate culture riddled with the fear of failure?
- Do they cringe at the prospect of investing in the development of any new product?
- Is the manufacturer willing to recognize that without your contribution to the overall process they would have nothing where this new emerging market is concerned?
- What are the ramp up costs to introduce this product?

- What are the overall opportunity costs to roll out this product?
- What is its lifecycle of the product going to be?
- How big is the emerging market?
- Are the projected pretax profits sizable enough to justify the company's involvement?
- How good and how strong is the total package that you've put on the table for their consideration?

As you can see, these are some very important factors when considering your negotiating strength. And by no means, is this meant to be a definitive list.

These are just a few of the factors that you will have to deal with. And of course, the results that you will achieve can only be measured on a case-by-case basis.

I want to remind you once again, not to get caught up in the fantasy that being a successful inventor is the same thing as being a successful sports figure, a movie star or rock star. You are not going to be one of the chosen few who gets to negotiate one of those unimaginable contracts.

Being an inventor and spurring industry onward and upward is not a high profile line of work. So before you get immersed in the inventor's odyssey, you better not expect to be treated the same way that superstars get treated when they go into one of their deals.

Now you know why I've been stressing all along that doing your homework was the key to becoming a successful inventor. In realistic terms, you have a much better idea how to determine what your contribution to enterprise will be. In the final analysis, it will be up to both you and the manufacturer to divvy up the pretax profits fairly, so that you can wind up with a fair royalty rate.

Chapter 11

MOUNT MARKETING

Who's Going to Make the Phone Ring?

Let's just assume that you've already received your patent grant and it's been a while. Perhaps you've let a few weeks slip by, maybe it's even been a few months. Whatever the case, your phone hasn't been ringing off the hook with companies looking to license your patent.

Why not?

You do realize that shortly after your patent is granted, the USPTO is kind enough to publish a condensed blurb for every patent that they grant in a publication called the *Official Gazette*. Today that publication can be found online through the PTO's website for all to see. In fact, prior to the Internet, all of the newly issued patents were announced to the public in that humble little bi-monthly newspaper that you once needed a subscription for.

But in today's world that's all changed. This type of information is way more accessible to the public than it ever was. To see what I'm talking about, I encourage you to log on to the PTO's website and check out the Official Gazette for yourselves.

Anyway, the Official Gazette is the Patent Offices' way of announcing to the entire world that all of these newly granted patents are ready to assume their exciting new roles in business and industry. Likewise, you would think that the Official Gazette would be the perfect place for enterprising companies to troll the waters of innovation and discover the new inventions of tomorrow that might give rise to the next great emerging market.

Also remember that your patent application becomes public knowledge after 18 months. So there is every opportunity for business and industry to monitor whether you got the big grant or not.

So let me ask you something. After your patent has been publicly announced on the most prestigious website in the world for patents, why hasn't business or industry called on you?

Haven't they read about your patent?

The only rational answer I have to offer is that they are not paying much attention to the Gazette, because I never got a call either and my ideas earned around a hundred million dollars for Honeywell.

Just so you know, no one had ever called me after either of my two patents were issued and asked me if I would like to grant them a license. And just so you know, I did ask all of the engineer's and the marketing people if they had read this publication. Most were baffled, and without exception, none of them were familiar with this publication.

So if by chance, getting this phone call was the ticket that you had been counting on to secure a licensing deal, I'm afraid that you're going to be disappointed with the outcome.

Becoming a successful inventor entails much more than just coming up with a good idea and receiving a patent for it, which leads me to reinforce what I've been teaching you about all along. As back yard inventors we have the power to control much of our own destiny and as such we are also responsible for creating our own opportunities as well. That's precisely why I'd like to tell you about the next challenge that you'll be facing. Marketing.

In my estimation, in order for a patent to reach its full potential, it must enjoy a life of its own in the marketplace where it can not only compete, but earn its keep by generating a monetary return for the owner. In short, a successful patent is something that is going to flourish and reward the inventor with real dividends both monetary and otherwise.

If my past inventing odyssey is any indication of what you may experience in the future, I can virtually promise you that nobody will be beating a path to your doorstep, just because you "invented a better mousetrap." By and large, that cute expression just like so many other things about inventing is nothing more than a well-worn myth. In reality, nobody is going to beat a path to your door, just because you invented something. What really happens, is that you as the *visionary*, must beat a path to the various potential manufacturers *who might*, if properly marketed, license your invention.

With that said, the primary purpose of this chapter is to help you understand some of the basic mechanics behind the successful marketing of your patent. Specifically, I would like to show you how to organize that information so that you might present your invention to a potential manufacturing partner, and how to do so in a more powerful and convincing manner.

As you might expect, the marketing aspect of this journey is yet a whole other mountain for you to climb, and it shouldn't be taken lightly. Simply put, the proper marketing of your patent is going to play the most essential role in the pursuit of attaining a licensing agreement.

You have the Ability to Market

If I could venture a guess, most of you reading this book are neither professional salespeople nor are you individuals who are actively engaged in the marketing of a product or a service on a daily basis. And that's quite all right, because to accomplish this objective you don't have to be a sales person nor a marketing professional to get the job done. The very fact that you have successfully arrived at this point in the odyssey is a good enough indication that perhaps you are more of a salesman than you might have given yourself credit for.

Need I remind you, that you have already sold your idea to the US Patent Office? That's right! In effect, being granted a patent was your first big sale! If the Patent Office didn't "buy" your idea, then they wouldn't have granted you a patent for it in the first place. All that you need to do at this point, is to build upon that first sales experience and hone your presentation for this next level.

The next level of course, is marketing your invention to the manufacturers. In that regard, my advice to you is twofold:

First. You need not question your abilities, because as a visionary, you are already supremely qualified to perform this task.

Second. Do not to let the aspect of marketing your invention to any company intimidate you, because you already have proof enough that you are capable of scaling this mountain.

A Marketing Tutorial

The first step is that you have to establish who your favorite company would be to enter into a license with and there are various criteria for establishing this. The following are two important considerations that immediately come to mind:

- Consumer exposure and brand recognition.
- What is ultimately best for you and your invention?

What I simply mean is this; the greater the consumer exposure, the stronger the company's brand recognition will be. The stronger the company's brand recognition, the more apt the consumer will be to place his purchasing trust in that company's product. Strong brand recognition combined with consumer confidence gives any new product that such a company may roll out, a fighting chance to succeed in the marketplace.

So usually, the more prominent the player, the greater the market share that they'll enjoy. In most cases, the greater the market share that a company has, the more likely they will be positioned to sell the highest volume of your value-added product. Since most licensing arrangements are fashioned where the inventor makes his profit one widget at a time, this is a chief consideration when deciding which company to team up with.

To sum it up, the company that can sell the most widgets for you will ultimately be doing what is best for both you and your invention. These factors in conjunction with you being paid a fair royalty will bode well toward your chances of earning a respectable financial return.

Let's explore in greater detail what I just laid out for you.

This is how I want you to look at it; the marketing plan primarily consists of two parts. The first part of the marketing plan is the systematic gathering of information. Indeed, that is simple enough and we have already covered that in quite some detail. By this stage in the odyssey, you have already done most of the legwork. You should have acquired about as much information as possible, absent from calling on the separate manufacturers themselves. So we can begin by checking that exercise off our list.

The second part of the marketing plan is rather straightforward as well. It is the process where you are going to take all of that information which you have gathered and present it to your selected group of manufacturers.

My job is to present you with a straightforward road map that will better help you organize the marketing of your patent and maximize your chances of success.

Here are three key things for you to keep in mind:

- First. You must put together a list of who you might consider going into business with.
- Second. You must obtain as much information as possible regarding any of the potential business partners that you might be considering to team up with.
- Third. The specific order in which you call each company is going to be extremely important.

Of all the possible companies that you could team up with, you need to decide who is going to be your first choice to go into business with and who would be your last choice. Most importantly, you need to be able to justify why. This process is like building any ball team where the manager is responsible for cutting and positioning players; separating the starters from the benchwarmers. You get the point.

The placement of a company on your list is going to dictate the order that you call upon each company.

Here's how it's going to work.

You're going to begin your marketing calls by contacting these companies by telephone. That's right, I said telephone calls, not letters and not emails. Use the power of your voice over the airwaves before ever resorting to the pen or the keyboard. Letters and emails are anonymous and are easily thrown in the trash. Telephone calls if they get through can be so much more personable, and most importantly, can catch the receiver off guard. If you can stay relaxed and present your idea in an articulate, yet passionate manner you can take full advantage of the sudden turbulence that your call has created.

Here is my experience with the telephone. I have found that if you have done your research and you are able to project with confidence that you know exactly what you want and with whom you want to speak with, you can make your way into the most guarded office. The principal is very simple; you must believe with conviction in what you are doing.

This is key folks! Why do think I've been referring to you as inventor, visionary, entrepreneur and market maker? Because that is what you must believe about yourself deep down where you live to be able to succeed at this next level. I don't want to dash your hopes, but if you don't have the fire down below at this point in the game, then I can't make you any promises going forward.

Back to marketing.

At first blush what I'm about to say here might not make much sense, but it will after you hear me out. I want you to call your least favorite company first. Then work your way down your list until you wind up making the last call, to your most prized company.

You see, up until this point you have been barred from contacting any of these companies directly during your intelligence gathering, because you didn't want tip anyone off. Now that you're your able to contact the manufacturers, keep in mind that this isn't a race and that there isn't a time limit as to how long this process may to take you. So please don't rush this, because you're only going to get one shot at each company.

The point is, after finally breaking this long period of secrecy and being able to communicate directly with these companies, this process should yield you a whole host of information. In most cases these contacts will produce the only form of *closely held* information that you may ever get. You'll learn things that you wouldn't have otherwise been exposed to, such as how the manufacturing community in general may view your emerging market. You may come away with information pertaining to *real* profit numbers, production costs, means of production, ramp-up costs, opportunity costs, true market shares, competitive edge and the list goes on.

Think of it this way. The more calls you make, the more you will grow into your role as the expert of your emerging market. View each phone call and each ensuing discourse with the various manufacturers as a correspondence course on marketing your invention. In the end you will come away being way more of an expert than you ever were before you started this process. Plain and simple; knowledge is power.

You see, talking intelligently to people in a pleasant and engaging manner gets them to talk about themselves and their job. In most cases, they will want to talk about your patent and how you came up with your idea. This dialog will eventually lead to how the both of you view the emerging market.

The main advantage here, is that your particular type of call is going to be rare; exceedingly rare. These gatekeepers of industry seldom if ever, field these types of calls from inventors, so be enthusiastic and make the best of this opportunity.

If you sell your idea with genuine enthusiasm, the person on the other end of the line will be more inclined to drop their guard. Then as an outsider you can begin to work your way towards becoming an insider.

This exercise has a dual function:

- First. It is done in preparation for that great moment that you have been living for, giving the presentation of a lifetime to your most coveted company.
- Second. Which is just as important, it will enable you to prepare yourself to realistically engage in royalty rate negotiations for a license once you get to that stage.

As covered in the previous chapter, to be really effective during licensing negotiations, you need to have as much accurate information as possible to do this effectively. This is your golden opportunity to grab it!

How May I Direct Your Call?

This marketing exercise is a one shot deal when it comes to contacting a potential company. Likewise, their response to your phone call can be more or less summed up on a pass-fail basis. First impressions are key. If they happen to like both you and your idea, the talks will progress. If they don't, your talks will die on the vine.

Chances are real good, that the company that you'll be calling on won't be accepting a second and third call from you, once they've expressed that they're not interested. So besides having your facts well-rehearsed, it's crucial that you know how to have your call properly directed.

Allow me to explain.

If the company that you're calling on is large enough to support both a marketing department and an engineering department, your phone call will be directed to either one of those departments. Typically, most companies will have an individual or two in either department that might field these specific types of calls. Their job title usually includes the phrase, "… director of new product development or chief technology officer…"

The point is, I don't want your call being directed in a wilily-nilly fashion. From the onset, I want your call to be both purposeful and well directed. Therefore, I want your call to be directed toward the proper individual in the marketing department. That's right, the marketing department.

Now if you don't have the name of a specific individual, this is how you would go about making this call. When you first place your call and get the central operator, tell her or him how you would like to have your call directed. This is your job and it's critical. Politely direct the operator to forward your call to the marketing department. Specifically, tell the operator that you'd like your call to be directed to the individual in the marketing department who happens to be in charge of new product development. Tell the operator that you are an inventor and that you have been just issued a patent and that you would like to discuss your patented invention with the individual who would be most responsible for handling such a call.

You are not doing this to brag, and this is certainly not the appropriate time to be blowing your own horn. But this is the appropriate occasion to let the switchboard operator know that you have been granted a patent and that you certainly would appreciate being directed to the proper person in the marketing department in order to discuss it.

My best advice is that you should give the operator enough information in a slow, pleasant and deliberate manner. This will enable her to make the proper decision. If you do this right, the operator on the other end of the phone will actually want to try and help you reach the right person.

"Why would they want to help you?" The answer is simple. They answer tens of thousands of calls in any given period. Most of the calls that they field are mundane, and many, if not most of the callers know the party's name and extension. Now all of a sudden, here comes your call out of left field. Trust me, this kind of call is a bit intriguing, to even the most seasoned switchboard operator. Furthermore, your idea will sound like it could actually provide a benefit to the company. You have to trust me on this, but virtually everyone will respect the fact that you have a patent as a calling card. In addition to that, everyone that works for a company wants try and bolster their job security, and the main switchboard operator is no exception.

I'm not being melodramatic here, but these central operators are generally great people and they're smart! It's their job to help you and thereby help their company, so don't underestimate their ability to get your call going in the right direction.

However, before making such a *blind call*, it is highly advisable that you first check out the company's website. If the company is large enough, you can read through the company's various press releases to aid in your search of finding the right contact. The company's legal filings are another source for you to consider; such as the annual report or 10K. Professional listings and organizations are other good sources. LinkedIn.com, is an excellent internet source for this kind of information as well. If you can specifically tell the operator with whom you'd like to be connected, your chances of getting past the front door will increase dramatically.

As your call begins to hurtle it way towards your party, don't be the least-bit let down should it get intercepted by that individual's assistant. Rather rejoice, since fate has presented you an opportunity to explain why you would like to speak with her/his boss. Speaking to an assistant can be highly beneficial, since it gives you the chance to cultivate an ally. So sell the assistant, just like you would be selling her boss. Generally speaking, these relationships are very solid between the boss and assistant and your polite and respectful handling of the assistant will go a million miles towards creating an opportunity to speak with her boss. Before you finish, make sure that you get the assistants full name, including both her and her boss's phone numbers and email addresses! And do send her an email that recaps your conversation and thanks her for her courtesy.

Now in the event that you can't reach either the assistant or her boss, don't hesitate to leave a short, but pleasant message with your cell phone number. If you don't hear back in a couple of days, then it's ok to call back. Many of the people that you might be trying to speak with have intense travel schedules, so don't get discouraged. Don't leave more than a couple of messages, and don't appear too anxious or desperate. And whatever you do, don't come across like a pest. If you have a desire to see how I did this in the flesh, then I direct you to my first book.

By all means, you *do not want* your first call going to the engineering department. If it does, you might be fighting an uphill battle from the start! In my experience, it's best to have your call directed to the marketing department first. Now I'll tell you why.

Marketing people tend to be the creative thinkers of the company and if they are doing their job, they're hard at work trying to figure out how to develop the next emerging market. In that respect, they are just like you! So in most cases, they'll not only take your call, but they'll speak with you for a couple of simple reasons:

- First. This type of call is very rare and it's *somewhat* welcomed.
- Second. If for no other reason their *curiosity* will get the better of them, because if they're doing their job, it's always about monitoring their industry.
- Third. They just can't resist hearing how you may have beaten them to the punch.

So in your first few breaths, you're going to make it perfectly clear that you have an exclusive on your idea, because you've come calling with a US patent. This is the clincher, because inventors calling with patents are indeed rare. Since this exercise is all about credibility, owning a US patent makes you credible.

Yea sure they occasionally get calls from inventors, but often times these people are like the side show freaks that try out for American Idol in the beginning of each season. What I mean is that their ideas are written down on matchbook covers and on the backs of dinner napkins. Few if any of them, have been granted a patent, and essentially, most of these callers have done little to no homework whatsoever. They just call companies, because they have the guts to do so, and their presentation isn't capable of carrying them any further than that.

On the flip side, we have gone to great lengths throughout this book to differentiate who you are as an inventor. Therefore, it's imperative that you announce in a humble, yet genuine manner that you have just been issued a US patent and that you would be happy to discuss this incredible emerging market opportunity with them and would love to hear what they think.

At this point, about all I can offer you is this; if they are doing their job, they should be glad to hear what you have to say. Again if they are doing their job, they should be on the constant prowl looking for the next-best-new-and-improved widget to market. And again, if they are doing their job, they are looking for that once in a career, emerging market opportunity.

Discovering an emerging market is indeed a rare occurrence even for a well-positioned company. Therefore, they would be extremely foolish not to at least spend a few moments and entertain what you have to say, since you have already discovered one.

Generally speaking, marketing people have a tendency to be more abstract in their thinking than their engineering counterparts. Marketing people tend to think more with their emotions and have a penchant for entertaining any reasonable concept that might increase their company's profits. Generally speaking, they tend *not* to be preoccupied with the manufacturing details, which they unabashedly hand off to their engineering counterparts when confronted with those sort of issues.

As a whole marketing people tend to be more excitable and think with a bent toward the emotional side. They simply know that excitement sells. That's why they are in the marketing business and that's why you want to speak with them first. At this point you are selling an emerging market opportunity and that fact alone should be excitement enough.

This is what I want you to realize. You are not so much selling your patent. What you are selling, is an emerging market! As a matter of fact, all your patent does at this point is establish your credibility and offer the *smart* marketing guy or gal a chance to figure out that they may be looking at the next big *exclusive* here! For the time being, and until you can get your foot in the door, I want to think of your patent as nothing more than your calling card! You are selling the sizzle with plenty of meat on the bone.

On the other hand, if your sales call gets fielded by someone in the engineering department, your invention may get picked apart before anyone ever gets a chance to evaluate its potential worth as a *value-added product*. Chances are most engineers will begin to dissect your invention from a manufacturing and production standpoint before ever considering its true market potential. Nothing against engineers, but that's their job. They're more inclined to be skeptical as to whether your product can feasibly be produced in their facility without causing them a major assembly line disruption.

Engineers tend to be more cerebral in their thinking and take a very pragmatic view about every product that rolls off their assembly line. Engineers tend to be more practical and dollar conscious as to how products are produced and they can sometimes guard their production lines to a fault, since they're the ones in charge of that operation.

That's why when you finally get to the pre-licensing stage, you'll thank the Lord above that you bothered to go through the prototype and cost analysis exercises as carefully as you did. Because someday, this is what you'll have to discuss in great detail with the engineering department. As a matter of fact, before your journey is over, there's a good chance that you'll be responsible for telling the engineers how to manufacture your product, or it might never get off the ground!

Just so you know, the marketing guys and the engineering guys who are working for the same company can often times be at odds with one another as to how any given new product should be approached.

The object of your call placement is most important in helping you avoid this potential scenario right out of the box. The truth is, no matter the circumstances; this call is going to be difficult enough. There will be plenty of opportunities along the way for you to be facing some real opposition to your invention, the least of which may be an encounter with *Not Invented Here*. So why bring this all upon yourself during your first contact, just because your call simply ended up in the wrong hands?

My advice is simple. Give yourself at least a fighting chance to penetrate each company as far as you can. Strive to come away with something new and valuable from each new exchange. Build upon each call and prepare for the next one. In order to be able to do this effectively, you must first understand some of the how's and why's of directing your call.

One Call at a Time

Here's what I want you to comprehend.

This marketing journey is all about calling on your first choice one day and being able to close the deal. Based upon my experience, I don't believe that there are too many salesmen walking around who are skilled enough to close a licensing deal with their first choice on a cold call.

Hence, knowing that I was an industry outsider, I chose to call on my first choice last. I did this for the following reasons:

- First. So that I could gain experience by presenting my marketing presentation several times.
- Second. So that I would be more capable of isolating their various objections and readjust my sales tactics accordingly.

- Third. So that when the opportunity finally presented itself, I would have given myself the necessary experience to mature into the master salesman necessary to close my first choice.

All I can tell you is that you might not go into this process as a master salesman, but if all goes well, you'll emerge from the process as being one.

I warned you well in advance, securing a licensing agreement is by no means a guarantee and it's most definitely not a get rich quick scheme. Yet what we are embarking on is a noble enterprise and there are many individuals that are no smarter than you or I who are succeeding at this endeavor every day of the week. Inventors are signing licenses every day in this great America of ours. It's your job to figure out where you fit into the new markets that are emerging every day and how you plan on signing your own licensing deal.

Just so you know, here's how I did it.

My game plan was simple. I called on one manufacturer at a time and followed a specific calling order. I knew who I was going to call first, and who I was going to call last. I purposely contacted one manufacturer at a time so that when the objections to my invention would come up, I would be able to consider their implications before I contacted my next prospect.

Look at it this way. If you adopt a splatter gun approach by calling on every company in a bang... bang... bang manner, you won't be able to apply what you've learned from each successive call. You'll be incapable of applying what you have learned from your first prospect and you won't be able to apply it to the next. And so on.

If each company should happen to reject your idea all at once, you could theoretically poison the entire well. Should you adopt the splatter gun approach, you could wind up with no prospects left to call.

Again, be mindful of what I just said. Once you contact a company, making a second and third call may not be an option. So don't forget, making a first good impression is everything when it comes to sales.

Therefore, you must pace yourself and take it one company at time. This will allow you to figure out the lay of the land by isolating the various manufacturer's objections as you go along. This approach will also afford you the advantage of exploring your target industry in a much deeper manner since you have never been afforded this opportunity until now.

So as you might expect, finally being afforded the opportunity to directly contact a specific company will begin to help you develop the much-needed real world insights that you are going to need for success. You will need to probe as deep as possible in order to collect the information that you will eventually need to close your licensing deal. As you can see, there is a lot of preparation that must be done before this phone call is ever placed.

Obviously, this is going to take considerably more time for you to be able to accomplish this, but as I told you previously, this entire odyssey is about investing large amounts of time. The art of prospecting takes time. It *might t*ake you anywhere from six months to a year or two after you have received your patent, before you conclude your journey with a license agreement.

Just so you know, it took me two years of prospecting and marketing calls before I entered into my license agreement with Honeywell.

The time that it might take you to secure a licensing deal has many, many variables such as the trend wave of your invention and how it will energize the emerging market. It will depend on whether you are going to be selling your idea into a free market where there is plenty of freedom for entry or if you are selling your idea to a closed market, such as an oligopoly or a monopoly.

It might also depend on whether your product has to meet certain industry wide certifications such as OEM requirements or Underwriters Laboratories certifications. And most importantly, it will greatly depend on the companies that you are calling on.

I cannot begin to stress how important the people factor is. In fact, the inventor who is seeking to license his or her invention is entrusting his entire future into the hands of these individuals and anything can happen. Your project will either fly like an eagle or it will crash and burn to the ground. In the final analysis, your success is highly dependent upon the people at the company who'll be in charge of your project.

So I want you to look at this realistically. It may not take you two years like it took me, but companies simply do not routinely license other people's patents and adopt them as their own. And furthermore, they aren't in the habit of immediately rolling out a brand new product, just because you called on them with your patent.

If someone has led you to believe otherwise, I wholeheartedly disagree and you are only setting yourself up for a major let down if you allow yourself to believe in that line of reasoning.

There are no overnight sensations in the inventing game. Just study the various products that you use every day and ask yourself why the simplest of innovations have taken so long to come into existence?

As an inventor and a consumer, it's most helpful if you keep your eyes wide open and constantly study the myriad of products that surround us. As you begin to think like an inventor, pay careful attention to the evolution of the products around us. Then for an exercise, take a specific product's development and study their corresponding trend waves.

Practice this as a mental exercise and two things may happen:

- First. You may come up with an original improvement or invention of your own.
- Second. If you are presently working on an invention, it will reinforce how you might better develop your idea and help fine-tune your marketing plan.

Here's a perfect example of what I am talking about. We have all eaten at diners and restaurants and have faced that dreaded new *glass* catsup bottle. You know, the one that's staring you in the face, that when your burger and fries finally arrives, it defies you to get the catsup out. I know that you have stuck a clean knife in there as well to pull it out. Glass catsup bottles have been around for eons and this scenario has played out for eons as well.

For argument's sake, let's say that plastic bottles have been around and have commonly been in use since the 1980's. So why would it take a multi-billion-dollar company eight times over with a fleet of marketing people and all sorts of engineers, twenty years to finally figure out that catsup dispenses much easier from the bottom of the bottle than from the top? And that catsup dispenses much easier by squeezing a plastic bottle compared to shaking a glass one?

Why would it take so long for a multi-billion-dollar company like Heinz®, to redesign a catsup bottle and make it out of plastic and put the cap on the bottom, instead of the top?

I'll answer this one for you. For one thing, glass bottles are perceived to be classier than plastic bottles. If you want to argue that point, think back and see if a Coke® doesn't taste better out of that old green bottle than it does out of a clear plastic one.

But even more confounding, is the concept of putting a cap on the bottom of a bottle. This idea goes against all conventional thinking. Especially when everybody at the company's focus group is screaming that it simply can't be done due to things such as leakage, the central gravity of the bottles design and potential product damage. Not to mention, whether the consumer will accept this rather *unconventional* design.

Just so you know, I had this exact fight with Fram's *senior engineering staff.* You see for eons, when oil filters are produced, they come off the production line with the tapping plate down and then get boxed. The tapping plate is the part of the filter that attaches to the car's engine block. It's made out of a heavy piece of metal and it's very stable when placed on end. Filters traditionally come off the line tapping plate down in order to provide stability for the product to move on down the line *before* it's placed in the box. In contrast, the other end of the oil filter is always somewhat rounded and not nearly as stable. During production, should the filter be placed on its rounded end, it would fall over before reaching the packaging area.

Anyway, in order to manufacture this filter, we needed to spray or deposit a mixture of Teflon and carrier oil into the filter, tapping plate up. We also needed to package the filter tapping plate up in order to keep this liquid contained in the filter until the filter media could absorb it. Seems rather simple, doesn't it?

Initially, the Fram engineering department took the position that to manufacture such a filter was impossible, "Because all filters come off the production line tapping plate down!"

Here's the key for you to understand. I possessed the knowledge of how oil filters were made and how their production lines functioned long before I ever dealt with the Fram engineers.

Though it was an exasperating process, not unlike building the bridge over the River Kwai, I was finally able to teach the engineers how to cost effectively invert the filter so that the tapping plate would face the sky and thus solve this engineering dilemma. True story.

In my opinion, that's why as a backyard inventor you have such an advantage. As a group we don't necessarily think conventionally and our thinking is not constrained to the fate of focus groups and long standing traditions. That's exactly why as a person who has a penchant for inventing, you must always be studying the product development of the things around you and how they are made.

The moral of this story is that there are numerous caps, spray tips and bottle designs and lots and lots of other very ordinary things that we take for granted on a daily basis. All of which are patented. My question to you is simple, wouldn't you like to own one? I know that I would.

The point is, as backyard inventors we can often times make unconventional wisdom become a reality for the betterment of us all, if only we pay attention to product evolution and jump on the right trend wave.

Resistance to Change is Normal

The previous illustration in many ways typifies how manufactures can resist the opportunity to innovate. One day you could be challenged with that type of resistance where your invention is concerned too. The fact is, one day you could be hearing more *no's* than *yes's* where your invention is concerned. So, I not only want you to expect rejections, but I want you to learn how to anticipate them.

Experiencing rejections doesn't mean that your idea isn't any good or that you're some sort of crackpot with a patent. We have already covered much of that psychology and the mindset of industry; so don't be subscribing to any of those negative thoughts. Most of all, please don't take any of these rejections personally, just chock it up to everything that I have been teaching you thus far and forge ahead.

During this stage of the game you have to pump yourself up by continually feeding your soul with positive thoughts. One way that was especially helpful to me was that every time that I got scared, and there were many; I would just remind myself that *I was the innovator and the patent holder and not them*. Certainly neither the stranger other end of the phone nor his company was in possession of the patents, and neither one of them was the visionary responsible for discovering the emerging market.

What I'm saying is absolutely true regarding any inventor who might find him or herself at this stage. So you best believe it. Take strength in the fact that you have enough guts to make a cold call to an entrenched industry that very well may be subscribing to the not invented here mentality. Frankly folks, you're about to make a highly technical sales call. And in the world of sales, it doesn't get any tougher than what you are about to do.

Don't discount the fact that when you begin this leg of the odyssey that you'll truly be alone. Remember, you are doing the same job as a salesman who's employed by a large company, except you'll be doing your selling minus the backing and support that only a large company can provide.

So my best advice to you is this. You better start filling yourself with faith and not with fear concerning this monumental task. Alas be proud of yourself. This is the highest art form in all of sales! Period.

The Basis for Your Invention is Critical

The best way to teach you about marketing your invention is to share with you how I went about it. I want to clearly put forth what had inspired me to file for a patent. The following will illustrate how I defined the emerging market, the trend wave for my product and the basis for my invention.

- Taken together, the emerging market, the trend wave for your product, along with the basis for your invention, will end up providing you with the necessary foundation from which to build your marketing plan.

Let's take a closer look.

My rational was simple. I based my invention on the Teflon treated oil additive market. The size of the overall market was huge, valued in the hundreds of millions of dollars in annual sales at one point. My attempt to capitalize on this emerging market was based upon the facts and was not based upon *other people's uninformed opinions*.

What I just said is vitally important. As inventors we must always pursue our goals based on what we have verified as being true and *not* based upon what the naysayers might be saying at any given time. As always, we must pursue our inventions based on solid information that we have uncovered and not some undocumented negativity offered by the peanut gallery.

Fact. The Teflon Additive market was birthed sometime in the late 1970's, and Slick-50® had cultivated this market and had established itself as the industry leader. Before I had become acquainted with this market, Slick-50 had already been around for better than a decade and had sold hundreds of millions of dollars' worth of their magic elixirs.

As far as I was concerned, Slick-50 had stood the test of time and had been highly profitable. That overview motivated me to do some investigation and this is what convinced me to push onward.

First. None of the junkyards that I knew anything about were filled with hulking wrecks and blown motors due to their owner's use of Slick-50.

Second. The automobile manufactures weren't circulating any service bulletins that prohibited the use of Teflon oil additives in their motors. Nor were they threatening to void the engine warranties of anyone using this material either.

Armed with that bit of information I allowed myself to move ahead with the development of an oil filter that would be treated with basically the same material found in Slick-50. That was the basis for my invention, and that's what gave birth to my vision of wanting to compete head on against this giant with my '842 patent.

That in a nutshell, was the basis for my invention.

My plan however *wasn't* to go up against Slick-50 in a bottle, because there were already a dozen companies out there already doing that, and frankly, I wasn't out to reinvent the wheel. Instead, I decided to compete against them in a totally different venue. So after some careful soul searching and thinking of how I could improve my first oil filter patent, I came up with a delivery system that *nobody would ever expect.*

I chose a delivery system that I was convinced *no other competitor* would be able to successfully defend themselves against. This time instead of incorporating an additive package in an oil filter as cited in my '901 patent, I would employ a material that would be universally appealing to the majority of consumers. So I chose a material with tremendous brand recognition to be the star of my show; Teflon®.

I have to admit, the premise for my invention was rather simple, but as we've already gone over, often time's simplicity is the genius behind a good invention. Nonetheless my invention had never been put forth in any fashion prior to my doing so.

So there you have it. Depending on your motivation level, rejection and obstacles can drive an inventor to reevaluate and reengineer his/her product which may result in refiling for a new patent. This time around, I chose to compete in an established Teflon treated oil additive market by using a device that nobody in the history of Teflon additives or in the field of oil filtration had ever dreamt about..., an oil filter. That's when the light bulb came on full force! And that's essentially how I invented the Teflon treated oil filter in my mind!

My business plan was straight forward. I planned to compete against all of the Teflon elixirs in the marketplace and my premise couldn't have been simpler. My game plan was to beat all the competitors on two major fronts; price and convenience.

Since I had already done my homework, I already knew that I could treat an oil filter with the same amount of Teflon found in the Slick–50 product for around *¢ 35* and I used *$1 dollar as my total improvement cost.* At the time I came up with my invention, Slick–50 was selling their product for close to *$24 dollars* a bottle. During that same time frame, a premium oil filter was selling in the retail environment for well under *$5 dollars*.

From previous research gathered in the attempt to license my first patent, I already knew that it cost the major filter manufactures somewhere around *$1.50* to produce their *standard size* spin–on oil filters.

Let's stop her a moment and reflect upon how I began to put the gross profit margin picture together, since this is a perfect real world example.

- Improvement costs for the raw material that I wanted to employ. Around ¢35 cents to treat one oil filter.
- The retail cost of a standard spin-on oil filter most similar to my invention. Around $5.00 and under.
- The product that I was going to compete against. Around $24 dollars.
- Manufacturing costs to produce a standard size spin on oil filter. Around a $1.50.

It was my original intent to introduce to the consumer a premium oil filter that would in fact perform two jobs and do it more economically. For the first time ever, I was the one who dreamt up taking a premium oil filter that would perform two jobs.

First, it would perform its standard function of keeping an engine's motor oil clean by functioning as an oil filter.

Second, the filter would introduce a recognizable and beneficial additive in a microscopic form that would be liberated into the engines oil system to enhance performance.

The additive that I chose to employ was something that everybody at least in America was already persuaded had a positive benefit. It was on our frying pans and on the bottom of our irons, it was in our paint, it was in our plastics and it had even found its way into the space program. It was a marvelous material and it was everywhere doing tremendous things! That material of course was Teflon® made famous by the DuPont Corporation®.

I simply took the decades of marketing genius behind the DuPont Corporation and their desire to make Teflon a household product and piggybacked that with the Petrolon Corporation's® promotion of their Slick-50® product. All I did was capitalize on both of their achievements by inventing a Teflon treated oil filter!

The premise for this product was just as simple. Oil all by itself is slippery to begin with, but if the right amount of Teflon were added to it, it would become even slipperier. Therefore, this Teflon fortified oil would be better yet at reducing the harmful friction inside of a car's engine. Friction of course is the main culprit for both pre-mature engine wear, heat generation, loss of power and poor fuel economy.

Armed with that information, I was more convinced than ever, that it would be realistic to go ahead and file for a patent.

That in a nutshell was the target market for my invention.

On the surface, inventing can be as simple as developing a better peanut butter cup. I took an emerging phenomenon, in this case the Teflon oil additive market and bet that the introduction of a brand new one of a kind product such as my Teflon treated oil filter would reinvigorate and redirect the market demand toward my product. I also believed that the introduction of this wildly new product would not only *extend the trend wave* for the Teflon additive market, but also extend the trend wave for my product as well.

My Teflon treated oil filter concept was conceptualized to take advantage of three dynamic factors that were already in place:

The first factor, was that many millions of bottles of Teflon treated oil additives were already being sold each year in the US. The manufacturers such as Slick-50 had already done the marketing for me by shaping the consumer's mindset that the Teflon material contained in their product provided a real benefit to the consumers by reducing the amount of wear in their engines.

Secondly, over 500 million oil filters were being sold annually in the United States alone. The oil filter category at the time of my invention was beyond dull and there hadn't been a value added or a "new and improved" oil filter that had met with any level of success in nearly forty years! This provided a very real opportunity to *reinvigorate* a whole product category and drive demand toward my product.

Thirdly, my marketing plan was twofold. First, I envisioned teaming up with a world leader in oil filtration; Fram. Second, I envisioned *co-branding* this product with the world-renowned DuPont Corporation by utilizing their material in my filter and placing their Teflon *trademark* on my finished product.

Fourthly, the US had morphed into a service economy and more and more car owners were having their oil changed by someone else. It was now time to give these consumers not only a choice, but an upgrade when they visited their local oil change shop.

Here is the marketing angle that propelled me up and over the bar.

First, I had envisioned how to introduce the first viable dual function value-added oil filter in history.

Second, I had developed a marketing plan that included co-branding my invention with another world-class trademark.

Third, I had envisioned teaming up with a world leader in the oil filter business. This company had to possess both tremendous brand recognition and the best channels of distribution in the industry. Fram was that company, as a result, Fram was my first choice.

My position was simple. The company that teamed up with me had a real opportunity to gain some significant market share in the oil filter market by introducing this value added and co-branded product. With the proper execution, this product could expand their business in three separate market venues: *retail, installed sales and heavy-duty.*

That in a nutshell was my inventions trend wave.

I shared all of this with you for a reason. I want to convince you that even as a backyard inventor and as a total industry outsider, it's very possible for you to envision the emerging market long before the big boys ever do. And most importantly, you can be right! This is what I had brought to the Fram Oil Filter Company and that is why they had bothered to team up with me!

Just so you know, prior to my vision of co-branding this product, this type of marketing angle was rarely if ever utilized by the mainstream companies that were selling products. I can tell you that my brainchild of co-branding this filter with the DuPont Corporation was indeed a first for the Honeywell Automotive Division, because they were required to enter into a separate license agreement with DuPont for the use of their Teflon trademark.

This process went much smoother than it may have gone otherwise, due to the fact that I had already established a formal relationship with DuPont and their licensing department. Nearly two years prior to my calling on Fram, I had already signed a licensing agreement with DuPont that covered the full scope of their trademark requirements.

Consequently, I was able to instruct Fram on how to properly follow DuPont's guidelines.

Now that you have a basic understanding of how to develop that simple little peanut butter cup, let's go forward and explore some of the gymnastics required to market that little gem.

Making it Come Alive: An Overview

To better make this process come alive for you, I'm going to share how I approached my particular market, including the particular factors that had influenced my marketing strategy. So here's how it went for me.

First of all, there were only six oil filter manufactures of any note in the United States of America at the time in which I assaulted Mount Marketing. I'll list them in the order of their consumer brand recognition; starting from the top they were; Fram, Purolator, AC Delco, Wix, Hastings and Champion Labs. I don't care how you cut it; those were the players who made up the US oil filter market at the time I came calling with my patents and my trade secrets. The market dynamics were such that I was trying to break into an oligopoly that was about as tightly packed as any monopoly without morphing into one.

My only advice to you during this stage in the odyssey is to take heart in your endeavor and persevere. At this stage in the game, failure only comes to the inventor after he has decided to quit before reaching the summit.

In all likelihood, you probably won't be setting your sights on introducing an invention that will either compete against or put forth a new OEM designated product like I did. And chances are good that you aren't trying to break into such a restricted market either. But if you are, study well what I have been teaching you, because there will be many obstacles to face. Yet despite the particular circumstances, your dream can certainly come true if you have a valuable idea and there is enough J.P. Barnum in you to promote it.

At the time, both Fram and Purolator were the two most publicly identifiable producers of oil filters in America. Wix was a much weaker third. As such these three companies were my top picks in this order; Fram, Purolator, Wix.

Just so you know, I never called on AC. I didn't call them despite the fact that every GM vehicle that rolls off their assembly line is originally equipped with an AC brand of filter. AC oil filters are a product of AC Delco, and they are a division of General Motors. These filters are primarily manufactured to be sold as original equipment, or as replacement filters for both General Motor's cars and light trucks. Though AC filters will cross over and fit nearly any other manufacturers motor, selling oil filters into the *aftermarket* was not an aggressive part of AC's business model. From what I had discovered, I simply didn't believe that AC was actively seeking to cultivate new horizons in the oil filter *aftermarket*.

Though AC sold many hundreds of thousands of filters annually, I passed on them for a few reasons:

First, their oil filter brand was not that visible to the front line consumer.

Second, I simply didn't believe that AC had any desire to produce a value added oil filter that would compete in the aftermarket.

Third, and perhaps most importantly; it's my belief that the automakers in general are too heavily entrenched in their own engineering morass and NIH mentality to have been open minded enough to embrace an outsider's oil filter idea.

Anyway, I felt that selling a new oil filter concept to General Motors would have been tantamount to my selling a new missile defense system to the Pentagon. So right off the bat, I had whittled down my list to five players before I ever began.

Despite never calling AC, I had studied them sufficiently enough and had gathered as much intelligence about their company as possible. In the event that I had struck out completely with the rest of my list, I would have called on them and would have been prepared to do so. This is a rare case where a company can be so big and so powerful that it might be best not to bother with them at all. That's unless you get desperate and they become your very last resort.

The first company that I called upon was Hastings; a small Michigan based metal stamping company that also was more or less a regional player in the oil filter business. Hastings definitely made a decent oil filter, but they would not have been a very good choice based upon the criteria that I've already presented to you thus far.

Again if at all possible, you want a publicly recognizable company that is a major player in the field of your invention. Nonetheless, I called on Hastings anyway to gauge the market and as such I came away with some valuable insights, but as far as I was concerned, the fit certainly wasn't there.

I then reached out to Champion Labs, a fairly big player, except their specialty was in the manufacturing of oil filters for other people to put their names on. We refer to those companies as *private label manufacturers*.

Because of their business model, Champion Labs does not enjoy a lot of public product recognition, even though their filters can be found in some retail venues marketed under the Champ® brand name. Their Champ filter did not command anything near the brand strength of a Purolator or a Fram.

On the other hand, many garages and quick lube establishments that routinely do oil changes use their filters. Shop owners and mechanics alike, love the Champ brand filter, because it still gets the job done at a much cheaper price compared to using a high profile premium brand filter.

Again, Champion Labs wasn't a good first choice either, for my value added filter concept. Although garage mechanics were familiar with the Champion brand, the general consumer was not. And since I envisioned my filter being marketed as a value added product that was going to be marketed directly to the consumer as a premium oil filter, the only way to have successfully approached this market was to go through a company that had already enjoyed strong *brand recognition.* I realized before I had ever launched out, that it would be critical for me to align myself with a company that the buying public could readily identify with in the retail setting.

My new concept would need to be propelled by a company that had garnered as much consumer awareness in the market as possible. Analyze it this way; a company such as Champion Labs simply could not develop consumer awareness overnight. It often times takes decades for a company to develop strong brand recognition. Because I had already determined that they lacked the critical component required for a successful rollout of a value-added product, Champion Labs was yet another company that had to be scratched off my list.

In addition to that deficit, there was no selling them based upon the mindset of the engineering department. Their VP of engineering told me on my first call, that he considered Teflon additives to be *snake oil.* Champion Labs had made my decision not to go with them rather easy. As you can see, my list of potential manufacturing partners had shrunk by nearly half before I even got out of the gate.

Although the lead engineer's objection was nothing new to me, I was more determined than ever to overcome the snake oil obstacle on my next couple of calls.

Notice something here; I just got done referring to rejection as an obstacle, because in this game, that's exactly what it is. Therefore, it's your job as the visionary of an emerging market to engineer around these various rejections as they begin to come your way.

I personally believe that as long as your invention is not some fantasy, you will be able to isolate these objections and successfully be able to get around them. Yet it's only fair that I warn you, these rejections do hurt, and as a consequence I was crushed on many occasions. As in all of life's endeavors worth pursuing, this is something that all inventors must find a way to overcome.

As you can imagine, I had the rather daunting task of convincing any major oil filter manufacturer with OEM status to roll out a brand new product line consisting of Teflon treated oil filters. It was an extremely difficult sale. And it was extremely difficult to prove to them that if we *both teamed up*, we could capitalize on the emerging market that I had discovered.

I was then on to Wix. This company was another large player. Wix enjoyed a good deal of recognition amongst mechanics and people who know their way around cars and trucks. They produced a private label filter line for a NAPA®, who at the time happened to be the largest automotive retailer in the United States with over two thousand retail locations.

NAPA retail stores not only cater to the local garage mechanics, but they also focus heavily on the *do it your selfer* segment of the automotive retail aftermarket. These *DIY's* as they're referred to in the trade, are the weekend warriors who replace their own brakes, alternators, starter motors and routinely change their cars oil on any given weekend, of which I'm still one.

However, for the most part, Wix definitely lacked the public brand recognition and the consumer impact that either a Fram or a Purolator already had going for them. Unfortunately, Wix was not the best first choice for my value added oil filter either. Yet to this day, I still believe in my gut that if Wix and NAPA had teamed up with me, and if they had done a proper rollout for my product, I would have made millions of dollars in royalties from that relationship. My rational for this was simple, they were a fixture on the rising NASCAR circuit.

Here's an important insight as to why I knew that specific combination could have produced a potential winner. Both Wix and NAPA were NASCAR sponsors, which made them *readily identifiable* to over *sixty million loyal NASCAR fans at that time*. That's not a too shabby of a consumer base from which to launch any new product.

Just so you know, after my initial contact with Wix, the company had allowed nearly a year to pass before they finally wanted to meet with me. By the time that they wanted to meet with me, it was too late. I was already committed to Fram and we had already signed the first of two NDA's.

Incidentally, while we're still discussing Wix and their affiliation with NAPA, I did have a brief conversation with a top marketing manager from NAPA regarding my Teflon treated oil filter. This fellow happened share the same mindset as the head of engineering for Champion Labs; he too believed that Teflon oil additives was nothing more than snake oil.

I have to tell you, I found that to be rather an oxymoron, since every NAPA store that I've ever been in, carries some sort of Teflon based oil treatment for sale, and usually it happens to be Slick-50. So go figure.

I shared the NAPA story with you so that I could expand your thinking a bit. The normal route for an inventor to take when marketing his invention is to go directly to the source by calling upon the manufacturer. In this particular case, NAPA is a giant automotive parts retailer and not a parts manufacturer.

However, as the inventor and market maker, you are not limited to just call upon the manufacturers. For instance, if you find that the manufacturers tend to be close-minded about your invention, then it's worth trying to contact either a prominent marketing source or a powerful retailer that may already carry your particular type of product. The point is, keep both your mind and your options open.

For example, if you come up with a great idea, you can call Walmart's corporate headquarters in Bentonville, AK. And if your idea has merit, they will invite you to make a sales presentation directly to one of their in-house buyers. There's also QVC and the Home Shopping Networks as well. My point is this, if your invention is valuable enough, and if you have a will to succeed as an inventor, then you'll find a way.

As an aside, if you happen to strike gold with a major retailer like a Walmart or a QVC, then by all means you should reconsider whether you want to pursue the licensing process if at all. And if you should happen to be so lucky, I would urge you to seriously investigate what it would take to manufacture and distribute the product yourself.

So to conclude…

After Wix's slow as molasses response… And after NAPA's outright no… I was down to just two players on my list of hopefuls…, Purolator and Fram.

The Second Trend Wave

From the onset of this teaching I have been emphasizing how important your invention's trend wave is, and how it will affect your future success as an inventor. But do you realize that there is a second trend wave that will come into play during the marketing phase?

In fact, you must consider this second trend wave and all of its implications before you begin to make your final decision as to which company you're going to partner with.

Allow me to break it down for you. Aside from the products trend wave, the second trend wave that must be considered is the company's trend wave. At first blush, this trend wave may not be nearly as obvious as the products trend wave, but each company will follow their own separate and distinct trend wave as well.

A company's trend wave is made up of two separate components; business and psychological.

From a business standpoint, a company will conduct business operations in a market where they know their profit center lies. Each company will adhere to a particular business model and profit structure and will tend *not* to deviate from it. This is a very important consideration, because in great measure this will determine if a company will even entertain the possibilities of your invention or not.

For example, I brought out the fact that AC primarily made original equipment replacement oil filters for General Motors cars and trucks and for all intended purposes the bulk of their sales are generated from their dealer networks.

I then went on and pointed out that Champion Labs was primarily a *private label manufacturer*, and their approach to the market was to generally produce oil filters for other companies to put their names on.

Case in point. Each company on my list had a separate and distinct business model that they adhered to. Through my research I had discovered that each company had its own set of self-imposed limitations as to how they approached the marketing of oil filters in general. This is a very important consideration when it comes time to find a home for your invention.

To this day, the only thing that these companies share in common is that their general business model regarding both the development and marketing of oil filters hasn't changed much since I first began studying them over twenty years ago.

Just so you know, I dare say that most of their marketing plans at that particular time didn't coincide with my value added approach. The reason for this discrepancy was rather obvious, at least to me. Until I had arrived on the scene with my two patents, the oil filter category wasn't necessarily known for its innovation. As a group, the oil filter industry wasn't seeking a value added concept, because none of them had independently developed one up until that point. It took my persistent marketing campaign to finally open up the floodgates for that change to begin. Yet despite my best efforts to make inroads into this industry, in the end there would only be one taker.

Now from a psychological aspect, each company that you might entertain calling on will operate in a particular *market niche* and they do so for some simple reasons as well. Primarily, a company will conduct business operations in a market where they feel most comfortable operating in. In a word, many companies are not nearly as aggressive as you might think when it comes to pursuing new products and new markets.

In my experience with oil filters, I have been exposed to large companies that were apprehensive to venture out of their comfort zones where they had been accustomed to conducting business as usual for long periods of time. The main culprit for this behavior needs little explanation. As individuals we all must deal with it on a personal level and companies must deal with on a corporate level as well. Simply stated, it's the *Fear of Failure*, and some companies are riddled with it.

This leads me to conclude that in many ways companies can react like people. Meaning, companies don't always embrace change. Often times these companies possess corporate cultures that seem to be based more on feelings and personalities than anything else. These general attributes will in great measure determine whether a company will entertain the possibilities of your invention or not. These are in effect some of the more psychological components that make up every company's trend wave and you need to be aware of them.

To sum it up, every company that you might be considering will be guided by their own unique corporate driven trend waves. Simply put, they're going to follow their own marketing philosophy, whether you bring them a revolutionary product or not.

The reality is, when you first present your invention it will be nothing more than a diamond in the rough and not every company is going to be able to conceptualize your invention and its corresponding emerging markets full potential. The rational for this is very simple; you are the prospector who dug it up out of the same ground they have been trodding on for decades, yet they never saw it.

In turn, some companies will tell you flat out on the very first phone call that they think your idea is crazy and not for them. It could be that simple and there's very little that you can do to change this. All you can do during that exchange is to keep that individual on the phone for as long as possible in an attempt to try and find out why there's no interest in your invention. After it's over, about all you can do is to add that bit of information to your database and prime yourself for the next phone call.

On the other hand, some companies may be interested, but their viewpoint as to how your invention should be marketed, might dramatically differ from that of your own. Just be prepared for this, because you might just end up with a partner whose marketing strategy could be totally crosswise to yours.

So without getting into some incredible hair splitting, let's just say that once there is an initial meeting of the minds as to your inventions potential, there is a better than average chance that the company you might be talking with will have different viewpoints about how the invention should be marketed. As you might expect, these opinions are as varied as the colors of the rainbow and only personal contact with the company will provide how they truly feel.

Therefore, it's of paramount importance that once you find a company that seems to be as excited about your idea as you are, it's best for you to try and compare that company's general trend wave to that of your inventions as soon as possible. What I mean by that is the following: just because a company may like your idea and might even be excited about it, doesn't necessarily mean that they are going to market it the way that you would.

Like I said, just be aware of this situation, because it could wind up being a bone of contention for you and something that you might have to live with for a very long time.

Now if all of this is beginning to sound incredibly like trying to find a suitable marriage partner, you would be right.

- For an inventor to find the right licensing partner, it's about as close to getting married as one can get.

Best-case scenario, you are seeking a company whose general business operations and marketing philosophies are as closely matched to your inventions trend wave as possible.

When you finally arrive at this point, and begin to speak directly to these manufacturers it will become quite apparent, that what I've been priming you for is for sure real. During your marketing campaign you will have an opportunity to not only find out their mindsets, but their strengths and weaknesses as well.

So the bottom line is this; you don't want to go into business with just anybody. Because if your licensing agreement is to run for the life of your patent, you are looking at a relationship that may last a good twenty years, or so.

A Bit of History

Before venturing any further, I would like to put into perspective some important things about my marketing calls. As you well know, I am the sole inventor of two separate oil filter patents. The first patent that I had been granted was in June of 1988. The second patent that I had been granted was in May of 1993. As you can clearly see, these patents were granted five years apart.

To eliminate any confusion, I had attempted to initiate a possible interest in a licensing agreement with both Purolator and Fram on two separate occasions.

The first marketing campaign I embarked on began in 1988. That was an effort to license my first patent, which was the '901 patent for an additive treated oil filter. So after a year or so of trying, my efforts turned out to be unsuccessful at obtaining a licensing agreement with either Purolator or Fram and our relationships ended.

But before we parted ways this is what got out of my efforts. After speaking rather extensively to both companies, they both told me that though my idea was a good one, the general public would not be able to identify with the benefits of my invention and therefore they would not be able to market it. *However, they both said that if I ever came up with a new idea that the consumers could identify with..., then call us back.*

Now really... That was either a veiled dare or a polite kiss off, because really..., what were the chances of the same backyard inventor coming up with another patented oil filter improvement, when they were incapable of coming up with something new on their own?

Just so you know, after being told to pack it in, I totally removed myself from the situation and I didn't contact either company after they had made it known to me that they weren't interested in my invention. It was done. It was over, and I walked way without ticking anyone off. Therefore, I left the door open just in case I was able to come up with another idea.

This is key. You can't let your emotions get in the way if you should meet with failure. If you do, when you get your next great idea, there won't be anybody to sell it to, should your new idea fall under the same category.

By the same token, I just knew that I was on to something and I couldn't allow myself to quit. I had no other choice, but to immediately begin the inventing process all over again. So I began to formulate the idea for my second patent, which I hoped would be more universally appealing to the oil filter manufactures than my first idea. As a result, I threw myself once again into the entire inventing, patenting and investigation process for the second time.

Then approximately five years later in 1993, I was granted my second patent, this time for the '841, my Teflon treated oil filter. During 1993 and 1994 I attempted once again to generate interest in my newly granted second patent, placing the greatest emphasis on enticing either Purolator or Fram. I did so, because I had already identified both of these companies as being the world leaders in oil filtration.

To make it perfectly clear, I failed to gain Purolator's interest over the course of two separate marketing campaigns and both of my inventions were summarily dismissed by the company.

However, in 1995 I was successful in obtaining a licensing agreement with Fram and I was able to license my second patent for the Teflon treated oil filter to them.

The point that I'm trying to make here, is that I called on both of these companies on two separate occasions regarding two separate and distinct inventions/patents. So out of a total of four separate tries, I was only successful one out of four times, which means that I was batting only 25%.

So as you might expect, prior to contacting either Purolator or Fram for the second time, I had already established a bit of history. Just so you know without getting into tremendous detail, you can imagine that not all of this was pleasant for me to swallow.

Unfortunately, due to circumstances that were specific to this particular industry, I was once again in the predicament of having to market my idea to this very small group of companies. So after I was granted my second oil filter patent I had no other choice, but to revisit these same two companies with my new patent.

Now here's the sticking point, and this is what I want to leave you with. If you are going to be successful in a particularly tight industry the simple truth is this; you'd better hope that you can strike a licensing deal with either of the key two players. The reality is if you don't, then you might have to go packing, at which point your dream of attaining a licensing agreement could be finished forever.

If this should befall you, I'm afraid that you will be left with only two choices; go and file for another patent like I did, or go out and manufacture and market the product on your own.

In my particular case, though I was extremely persistent, I was also very lucky. I was fortunate enough to get a second bite at the apple. And as I've already pointed out, that's certainly not always going to be the case.

So here's the key. Never shut a door that you won't be able to open at a later date. And don't burn any bridges no matter how tempted you might be to do so. Rejection hurts! Yet you must always leave with dignity and on a pleasant note, because after all, you just never know when you'll need to be crossing that same river again.

The moral of this exercise is simple. If you're a jerk, the people that you'll be dealing with will tend to have very long memories.

My Last Two Companies: A Case Study

As you can see, I had methodically whittled my list down to just two companies. I had done so by following the exact same methodology that I've been instructing you to employ. At long last, it was time once again for me to contact Purolator and then Fram.

In an effort to shed further light on the process, let's take the last two remaining companies on my list and use them as a case study. I invite you to follow along as I provide you with a thumbnails sketch of what I had to contend with on my journey towards the marketing of my invention.

I had collected about as much information on both of these companies as I could find. My intelligence report was rather good, but as you might expect, it was still rather limited. Remember, I wouldn't allow myself to contact either one of these two companies until I had followed my calling sequence. That meant calling all of the other companies on my list first, in the sequential order I had previously disclosed. Now I made those calls, despite the fact that I would have been elated to skip this process and jump right into business with either Purolator or Fram. But as I told you, this process shouldn't be compromised to accommodate your convenience.

So let's see what some digging and personal contact revealed during the final stages of marketing of my invention.

It may seem coincidental, but both Fram and Purolator claim to have invented the oil filter. Yet despite who may have actually gotten there first, both companies' roots can be traced back to the very beginning of this business in America.

From the late 1940's through the early 1980's the majority of red-blooded American men changed their own oil. The simple fact was that most people couldn't afford to do otherwise. So this practice had become an automotive staple and this ritual was performed in vast numbers on any given weekend.

As such, the oil filter business remained a rather predictable business and this crucial bit of engine maintenance continued unchanged for nearly a generation. Hence, the guy who regularly changed his own oil was referred to in the oil filter trade as a *do it your selfer*, or *DIY*. Both Purolator and Fram blossomed in this environment and these market conditions enabled both companies to become leaders in the US oil filter business for both passenger cars and light trucks.

But in the early 80's, this all began to change. The trend began to shift away from the do-it-yourselfer as the trend moved toward the *fast lube* garages that were springing up all over the place. This growing segment of the business was referred to in the trade as the *installed sales market*. People had become more affluent and were quickly adopting a *service mentality*.

Just so you know, as I began developing my inventions and studying my products trend wave, I had become acutely aware of this major shift in the consumer's behavior. As a result, I was under the firm conviction that in order for my filter to enjoy *maximum success*, it would need to play a major role in the in the *installed sales environment and not just be limited DIY retail environment*.

Let's drift back in time for a moment, shall we. When I first began to drive a car in the mid 70's, it was a natural fact that I would become a do it your selfer. I can vividly remember going to my neighborhood auto parts store on a Saturday morning and having to wait in a line that would be five or six guys deep. I also seem to recall that the majority of the men waiting in those lines were there to purchase oil and filters. These lines were thing of beauty for a young man to take part of, almost like a scene from a Norman Rockwell painting. Yet like so many others scenes from a simpler past, those Saturday morning lines that used to be an auto parts staple, no longer exist today.

Now fast-forward with me to late 1980's as I began my inventing career. I drew much of the inspiration for my invention from those early days waiting in the auto parts store. I can remember listening intently as the men waiting in line would hotly debate which brand of filter was better; Purolator, Fram, or some other guys.

I had envisioned that perhaps one-day, my invention would be able to create the same stir, except this time, I didn't want my value added product limited to just the retail environment.

Although retail was definitely a great venue, it was a *rapidly shrinking market* and I knew it. To put the shifting market into perspective at the time in which I invented my oil filter, the *installed sales market accounted for nearly forty-five percent of all oil filters sold in the US and this figure was increasing with the passing of every year.*

So quite logically, I envisioned giving the installed sales customer the same opportunity to be given a choice of which filter to purchase, just like he was buying an oil filter in an auto parts store on a Saturday morning.

The fact is, when you frequent an installed sales location, there is only one type of filter that is being offered for sale. The consumer is not given a choice. Usually the filter offered is a very inexpensive *house brand* and it's more of a *throw-on* than anything else. This is so, because the profit is derived from the sale of the motor oil and the labor. Not the oil filter.

There's simply no choice of filters at these establishments and as an inventor of a value added oil filter, I was convinced that there should be. It seemed only natural that the consumer should be given a choice in this matter, given that a major diver of our economy has become the concept of *upgrading* or *up-selling* after we make the initial purchase.

This pervasive mentality has its tentacles in every market, from cars, to televisions and computers, where extended service contracts and warranties have become the norm for any big ticket item we purchase. The epitome of this is upgrading mentality has been honed to perfection at the fast food drive-through.

Needless to say, when it came time for me to market my invention, the oil filter sales model was rapidly moving away from the *do it your selfer* and giving way to the specialty quick lube shops that began to dot the landscape to perform this service.

So when I called on these two filter giants in the mid 1990's, each company enjoyed approximately the same market share of around 28 percent apiece, making for a combined total of 56 percent of the US oil filter market. And in all due candor, that's about where their similarities ended.

So, let's take a closer look and examine each one of these companies' separately. Pay especially close attention to their different market dynamics and how each one would react to the rapidly developing service economy, which began in earnest to sweep across America in the early 80's. During this era, America as was rapidly moving away from a manufacturing based economy and was becoming more of a serviced based economy. Today it is estimated that over 90% of our economy's gross domestic output is directly tied to the service sector!

Just so you know, at age fifty-seven I'm still a diehard DIY. I have to admit, I still enjoy climbing under my car and tinkering in oil. But I have to tell you; I'm in the ever-shrinking minority.

Just for the record, during my entire foray, I never ran into either a filter engineer or a marketing person who changed his or her own oil. I might add, that goes doubly for all the lawyers as well, because I asked just about everyone that I ever came in contact with the same question, "Do you change your own oil?

Invariably, the answer always came back as a *no*.

So let me ask you something, where do you think these individuals go when it comes time to have their oil changed? Would an installed service center, or their car dealer seem too far-fetched?

I told you upfront, this invention stuff wasn't all rocket science, just applied common sense.

Purolator's Dynamics

Just so you know, I had deliberately decided to call on Purolator before I called on Fram. My rational was simple, based upon my intelligence gathering; they were probably *not* going to enter into a licensing deal with me. Nonetheless, I still persisted and maintained a dialog with them for nearly a year, before ever reaching out to Fram. As a result, I gained some very valuable information as to the oil filter market in general. But most importantly as an outsider, I gained some valuable insight as to how an industry leader viewed the oil filter market's dynamics.

Here's what I knew about their business model…

They did less advertising than Fram. Yet despite that particular shortcoming they still enjoyed very strong *brand recognition*, which they had built upon over the course of two generations. The company marketed their flagship oil filter on the retail level under their Purolator® brand name and sold approximately one hundred million oil filters each year.

Purolator possessed strong *brand recognition*, strong sales and was in tune with the installed sales trend. Over time they began shifting their business model and began focusing on how they could deliver a better quality filter to the installed sales market. As a result, Purolator had cultivated a very big private label business and began supplying this segment of the fast lube industry with an oil filter that they dubbed the Group Seven® oil filter. This filter had captured at least sixty percent of the installed sales market and was sold to both big and small installed service sites that performed oil changes. As a result, Purolator supplied the lion's share of filters to this growing market segment and had acquired the Jiffy Lube® account, which at the time was the largest fast lube franchise in the US.

As I began to conduct my research, Purolator's business model by all accounts seemed to be the perfect match for my inventions trend wave. They enjoyed a strong retail presence, which I felt was a priority, but at the same time they were in synch with our growing service based economy. I was certain that if I could just team up with Purolator and market my value-added product through their installed sales outlets such as Jiffy Lube, it would have been nothing short of a match made in heaven. But that wasn't meant to be…

Just prior to contacting them, I had discovered that Purolator had recently been bought and sold a couple of times by larger conglomerates. Unbeknownst to me, this would have far reaching affects and consequently would have a negative impact on both the marketing and engineering departments. As a result of being recently spun-off, this terrific company was in terrible state of internal flux. What I didn't realize as an idealistic inventor, was that these variables were going to make it impossible for me to license my patent to them.

Here's a thumbnails sketch of my quest to close Purolator. As a result of getting knocked around a bit by other filter companies on my previous sales calls, I was aggressively seeking a positive response from Purolator. So out of sheer determination, I placed a call to the highest company employee I could find.

So who do think I called?

I called the CEO's office and Roman Boruta the CEO of Purolator came to the phone. We had a very promising dialog and he assured me that my patent would get the full attention that it deserved. He then personally directed me to call his VP of Marketing. I was ecstatic!

Unfortunately, the VP of marketing didn't share the CEO's enthusiasm and as a result, he passed me on to the VP of Engineering. At which point, the senior engineer and I dialoged for nearly one year. Yet little of what we discussed had anything to do with the value of my invention or the emerging market that I had discovered. The simple fact, was that I couldn't sizzle either the top marketing man or the head of engineering. In hindsight, I was foolish to spend nearly a year trying to cultivate them.

So let me give you some precious advice. In the future, if you should encounter an environment such as this, I want you to realize that it's a waste of time to market your invention to a company that's either in a state of internal flux or too negative.

I dare say, even if you had invented the first light bulb, you'd be incapable of marketing your idea in such an environment. So learn whatever you can, but don't camp out for a year like I did. Spending a year chasing any company is a waste of your precious time and resources.

Here's why. Unstable or negative companies create unstable work environments and in this type of atmosphere, most employees are way more concerned about the basics, like job security and paying their bills at the end of the week. Understandably, creativity will take a back seat and so will your invention.

Launching an innovative product line and taking on that additional responsibility will be the last thing on anyone's mind. The last thing that any employee needs at this particular point in time is the additional risk that comes with creating and launching a new product line that could possibly flop. Understand, as great as your invention might be, if a company is incapable of making a fairly quick and positive assessment of your idea, you're best to move on.

In the end Purolator would serve only as a good test subject. The experience combined with the gathered intelligence would prepare me for my ultimate quarry, Fram.

Fram's Dynamics

Now with everyone else eliminated, I found myself down to just one company. Believe me this type of situation can create an insane amount of pressure for the inventor to deal with, but I had something even greater breathing down my neck.

My initial attempt at marketing my first oil filter patent, the '901 to Fram was almost unimaginable. After calling on the company, I was referred straightway to Director of New Product Development. From the onset things were going swimmingly between us and there was strong interest in my invention. Needless to say, Mr. Kennedy was a real gentleman.

As a result, I immediately mailed him off a copy of my newly granted patent. As for his part he boxed up a couple of the company's thick master filter catalogs and sent along a non-disclosure agreement for me to sign and return.

The meeting that I'd been dreaming about was about to happen!

It wasn't too long before the meeting was set, and I was invited to come up to Fram's Rhode Island headquarters to meet with the company's representatives which included the VP of Engineering, the VP of Manufacturing and Director of New Product Development.

To make a rather insane story short, my first marketing meeting with Fram went something like this. After spending some four hours with these three gentlemen on a beautiful warm spring day back in '89, I was abruptly told to go packing after what seemed to be a rather pleasant and promising exchange.

I could feel my heart sinking to my feet as I glanced over toward the Director of New Products, only to see a total look of surprise on that the young fellows face. The VP of Engineering didn't skip a beat as he abruptly ended our luncheon meeting at the Rustler Steak House.

I couldn't figure it, we were in the middle of a very pleasant cup of coffee, when he said, "Young man, your idea is too good to be true and besides that, I don't believe that you even have a patent on this thing." As I began to fumble for the latches on my brief case to pull out an extra copy of my patent for him to reconsider, he stopped me. Then in a stern, but polite voice he said, "Don't bother…"

At the time, I was a very green thirty-one-year-old inventor armed with not much more than my first patent. It just so happened that I was staring down the barrel of a manufacturing mentality that I wouldn't have believed, unless I had experienced it for myself.

Now that I can reflect back, I picked up on those very same vibes when I was calling on Purolator, except it wasn't nearly as rabid. Anyway over time I would come to learn that it was that little something that I already taught you about. That little something I've already identified as NIH or Not Invented Here.

Boy, talk about being green. I was so green at the time I couldn't even recognize it for what it was. The point is, if this should happen to you on your first marketing call, then all I can tell you is that you are pretty much done for. Hopefully you have another company to call on.

I told you all this, just so I could properly set the stage for my attempt at marketing my second patent to Fram Oil Filters.

Now let's see why I was determined to team up with Fram despite my prior treatment at the hands of the senior engineer. Allow me to explain why they were still my first choice and why I still wanted to team up with a company like that.

For starters, the Fram filter company was the acclaimed world leader in oil filtration with over 28 percent of the market share. Besides that, they were an important cog in *AlliedSignal / Honeywell's* multi-billion-dollar automotive aftermarket conglomerate. By all indications, AlliedSignal and their Fram filter division appeared to be more stable than Purolator, and hence, the most logical first choice for me to go with.

Of all my possible licensing options, Fram was still my first choice and that's exactly why they were the last company I called upon.

Before I ever called on Fram, I knew that they did more marketing than Purolator. I also knew that they were not just an oil filter company like Purolator, but were a wholly owned subsidiary of a much larger industrial conglomerate.

Before I called on Fram, I was armed with some pretty impressive information concerning the oil filter business in general. My hard won information regarding Purolator combined with the intelligence that I had gathered by strategically going down my list of filter companies had enabled me to present my marketing plan to Fram as if I were a true insider.

As I launched into what might have been my final marketing campaign, I was under the impression that Fram was the more stable of the two companies and better able to make a sound business decision concerning my invention.

Ideally, this is precisely where you want to end up by the time you are ready to place your last marketing call, but I have to remind you of something.

- Only personal contact can reveal the true inner workings of any company that you are calling on.

Now I would like to share with you what I didn't have a clue about until I had made personal contact.

I didn't have any idea how much influence AlliedSignal's powerful CEO exerted on this multi-billion-dollar business unit. And I certainly wasn't aware of the fact that although this was considered to be one of the top filter companies in the world, it was more or less looked upon as a bastard stepchild by the parent company.

I was totally shocked to find out from Fram's marketing managers, that Allied's Automotive Aftermarket business unit was perpetually in play and could be sold off at any time if the right buyer emerged. To put it bluntly, Allied's filter business was also in play, and I had no idea about that little detail until I had gone deep inside and discovered it for myself.

To put this in perspective, this information didn't become known to me until many months after the pre-license agreements had already been signed. Actually the first time that I was hearing anything of this sort didn't come up, until I was on the cusp of entering into a license for my patent. And that only came about, because one of my main contacts was abruptly leaving the company.

I also wasn't aware that Fram's market niche was so highly focused on the DIY, despite the sea change in the market trend toward installed sales. Fram adamantly resisted the installed sales venue and treated venue as if it didn't exist. To say that I was baffled by their indifference toward this exploding market would have been an understatement. Their mentality was simple; they made more profit by selling their premium filters under the Fram brand name in the retail environment than producing house brand filters for themselves or for other customers to put their names on. So when the notion of selling a value-added premium line of filter to the installed sales market presented itself, they just couldn't fathom how to go about it. Despite the fact that the filter was going to have the Fram name emblazoned on it.

Pure and simple, the retail market was their niche and my invention wasn't about to change their business model. As a whole, the company's profit center and comfort zone was selling their premium brand filter line in the various retail outlets like the Walmart's, the Pep Boys and the Auto Zones across America and that was their mentality. Even *"The most innovative oil filter in history,"* which they had appropriately dubbed my invention; wasn't powerful enough to sway how they viewed the oil filter business.

So once deep inside, I learned firsthand that Fram lacked the necessary gusto to go after the installed sales market that Purolator pretty much had a lock on. I was truly convinced that my value added product would have given them the necessary edge to do so, but again, that wasn't to be. Prior to my entrée deep inside, I simply wouldn't have been able to believe all that I had experienced, unless I had witnessed it for myself.

As a whole, Fram pretty much chose not to become a player in the lucrative heavy-duty market for big trucks and diesel applications either, even though they had an established presence in that market as well. Again their thinking baffled me, because this product segment by and large generates at least twice the profit margins per unit sold as compared to selling automotive oil filters. And the operators of these big, heavy and expensive engines were always on the lookout to find a simplistic avenue to reduce their operation costs and downtime.

Coming from my perspective as someone who understood both the cost mechanisms and the general mindset of that business, I was truly mystified by their non-entry into that market with my value added product. I knew the trucking business from the ground up and it wasn't just something that I had read about in a book. In addition to being an over the road truck driver, I had owned and operated my own rigs and knew that a cost saving oil filter would be most welcomed by both owner-operators and fleet owners as well.

Perhaps most disappointing, was their arrogant dismissal of getting involved in a little upstart sport called NASCAR. Coincidence or not, in the mid 90's about the same time that I came calling on Fram, NASCAR was really beginning to hit its stride.

NASCAR wasn't just for rednecks anymore and it was going mainstream; Fifth Avenue style. Instead, Fram stubbornly chose maintain their marginal involvement in the much smaller and somewhat stagnate NHRA racing circuit.

If only they had invested the necessary funds and made their presence known in this sport. If only they had capitalized on their already established brand name with my value-added product, they would have reaped incalculable dividends.

My question to you might be, 'who doesn't advertise in NASCAR?'

Again once inside the Fram filter division I camped upon these issues to the point that if I persisted with any more vigor, they would have surely shown me the door. Since Fram was in all probability my only hope of striking a licensing deal, I had to control myself and therefore tone down the vision for my invention.

Unfortunately, that was just the way it was and that was eventually the mindset of the partner I had ended up going into business with. On the surface they appeared to be the biggest and the best, but as whole they were loaded with incredible deficiencies.

Just so you know, as an inventor you have no other option than to live the best you can with a company's weaknesses. And it is up to you to do your best to prosper from that relationship. I am telling you all of this, because even though you might have the best-laid plans, there are still yet a million variables that can affect your success.

So as I told you early on, if you don't like your options, then perhaps it's best that go out manufacture and market the invention yourself. Under those circumstances, you won't have anyone to limit your dreams except yourself.

Chapter 12

PRE-LICENSE AGREEMENTS

What You Sign Will Matter

You've finally arrived, well almost.

At this point in the odyssey there are many things to be thankful for, such as all of the many details that you've executed correctly to get this far. As a result of all your hard work and careful follow through, you've been able to secure your idea, evaluate its worth and protect it by the best means available. As a result, you've forged ahead and been fortunate enough to have gotten your foot through the front door of the company that up until now, you've only been dreaming about.

So what's next?

The next big thing on your agenda is that you're going to meet with the company. But before we get started, let me ask you something. Have you ever experienced dancing with a king cobra before?

Well hopefully, this round won't resemble that, but then again it just may. So before you go meeting with anybody, allow me to make you aware of some things that you *definitely must know*. This information is so important that I am going to devote this entire chapter to *pre-license agreements* and the world in which they operate. What I'm about to share with you is going to prove that what you might be signing one day, will indeed matter.

Setting the Stage for the Pre-Licensing Phase

By now it should be rather apparent, that an inventor's odyssey in many ways is similar to that of a salmon swimming up steam to spawn. If you think about it, so far the journey has been no different, chock full of challenges and littered along the way with many unknown hazards.

So after a long and arduous swim, the fledgling inventor is finally rewarded by his arrival at the pre-licensing stage. Your dream by this point is so real that you can taste it.

This is the point in the odyssey where the company that you've been pursuing has finally seen the merits of your invention. As for your reward, you've been invited to give them the marketing presentation of a lifetime.

This is certainly a time to rejoice! And if you are anything like me, this moment will not have come a moment too soon! As a result of swimming upstream for the past few years or so, your patience will have worn thin and you may be inclined to have your emotions take over. That's exactly why it's necessary for you to slow down and rekindle your vigilance, because for the first time ever, you'll be discussing your invention in great detail with a *prospective* business partner.

Therein lies a significant danger.

Based upon my own personal experience and bolstered by my study of the case law, this next phase of the odyssey will expose you to a situation like none other. Nothing that you have experienced in the journey thus far can adequately prepare you for this next stage. Therefore, it's imperative for you to know well in advance that with this most auspicious of occasions, comes an entirely set of new dangers to be wary of.

The pre-licensing phase will include many things. Chief of which, will be the signing of one or more, *pre-licensing agreements*. These agreements are intended to protect both you and the company from each other. By design, they are intended to define both of your roles in this partnership and to protect any of the information that either of you may divulge.

The pre-licensing phase means that at some point, you *might* be meeting with the representatives of the company on their turf. But before you meet with anyone, you will be signing an NDA or a non-disclosure agreement.

Meeting with the company on their turf means that at some point, you'll be delivering a sales presentation that's powerful enough to make them *want* to go into business with you.

Once that's accomplished, and the company has decided to go into business with you, a timetable with various project milestones will be drawn up. Should any of these objectives fail to be met in a timely fashion, the entire project could get scrapped.

Keep in mind that up until now, you've only had to deal with self-imposed deadlines and possibly a few response deadlines imposed by the PTO during the prosecution of your patent.

So I want to warn of something ahead of time. The added pressure of dealing with real-time project timetables while collaborating with the company can weigh heavily upon the inventor who's doing his best to see his deal materialize.

As such, your dealings during the-licensing phase will undoubtedly include close contact with both the marketing and engineering departments of the company. Just be aware that your *future* interactions with these departments will be critical for both the development and the marketing of your patented product. These interactions will telegraph to the inventor if the manufacturer is fully capable of running with his idea or if they are just going to stumble along. Hence the inventor may feel compelled to help a stumbling manufacturer along in an attempt to prop up the success of this project.

That's all well and good, but if the inventor should decide to help the manufacture with the task at hand, he must do so by exercising the greatest of care!

Allow me to explain.

The dangers that this new relationship can present are quite simple. The inventor is about to have intimate dealings with a company that can squash him like a bug, both from a legal and a financial standpoint. Once the pre-licensing agreements are in place, there is nothing much standing between you and this speeding locomotive except for what you've signed.

As if this isn't enough for you to consider, these meetings will be taking place behind closed doors and under circumstances that nobody from the outside world will be privy to. Nobody will be around to witness what will take place behind these closed doors except you and the company.

- Therefore, it's critical that whatever you share with the company must be meticulously documented!

An Overview of the First Document

Though the term *pre-license agreement* may sound rather similar to *license agreement* as you might imagine, they are worlds apart with regard to both their purpose and function. As a consequence, both types of contracts have completely different functions and will mean different things for the inventor during the different stages of interaction with the company.

During this section we will concentrate the rest of our efforts on pre-licensing agreements and pick up on licensing agreements in the next chapter.

First of all, the pre-license as its title implies, comes first. As previously mentioned, both parties will eventually sign one or more of these documents before consummating their business relationship with a final license agreement.

Pre-licensing agreements are any type of document that the parties may sign prior to the signing of the license agreement. Again, some of the various labels put on these agreements are:

- Non-Disclosure Agreement, also known as a *NDA*.
- Confidentiality Agreement, also known as CA.
- Proprietary Information Agreement, also known as a *PIA*.
- Trade Secret Agreement, also known as a *TSA*.
- Test Marketing Agreement, also known as a *TMA*.

As you might expect, these agreements do vary as to what they might cover, but they do share a common thread. The main thrust of these contracts is to keep each side honest and accountable to one another under the law. That means; contract law, misappropriation of trade secrets and patent law will govern as to how each party handles these contracts.

In the greatest sense, the spirit of these contracts is *a promise to promise*. What that means, is that neither side shall either disclose to a third party or divulge in any manner, any of the information, which has been shared between the two parties. Each party is strictly forbidden to unfairly exploit any of the shared information furnished by the disclosing party. In addition to that, it's also forbidden to use this information in any way to gain an unfair advantage over the disclosing party.

Usually, the first document offered to the inventor would be either a *Non-Disclosure Agreement*, a *Proprietary Information Agreement* or a *Confidentiality Agreement*. As the various tiles imply, secrecy is at the heart of these agreements.

These documents basically establish that whatever the inventor divulges to the company will be held in the strictest of confidence and will not be disclosed to any third party.

This document has three purposes.

- First. This contract promises to keep secret, *any* information that is disclosed by the inventor to the company. Likewise, this contract promises to keep secret *any* information that the company might disclose to the inventor.
- Second. This contract is offered to the inventor so that the company is protected under the law to interact with the inventor concerning his idea. The existence of this agreement also establishes the fact that the relationship between the company and the inventor is above board or what the lawyers like to refer to as *an arm's length agreement*.
- Third. Neither party can use the information divulged by the offering party for their own economic advantage, without first obtaining the express permission in order to do so.

Here's something very important to note.

The very notion that this document is offered by the company to an outside inventor is a clear indication that the company has acknowledged the *possibility* that the information about to be presented *may be new and possibly valuable*. It also recognizes the fact that the information being presented has originated from an individual outside of their company.

Essentially, *both sides* are admonished to play fair with each other and to keep a secret. On the surface, what could be more straightforward?

Now here's what I really want to draw your attention to. These documents are drawn by the company and they are only enforceable for a *specified period of time*. The time period can vary anywhere from several months to several years. What is especially important where your protection is concerned, is that this is the only document that protects your *trade secrets!*

The reality of it is this. You are the one who's going to be providing the trade secrets, so the flow of information is going to flow in one direction..., from you to them. Trust me, they won't be sharing any of their trade secrets with you.

That said, the company that you are about to deal with is the one who's going to draw the NDA or any other agreement that *proposes to protect your trade secrets.* That means that they *are also going to specify the time period* that will govern these documents as well.

An example is in order. The agreement that they offer you states that your trade secrets will be held in strict confidence for seven years. Yet, *you both know* that your patent still has eighteen years left remaining on the clock. So you might ask yourself, "What happens after the seven-year period ends and I still have eleven years remaining on my patent?"

Well, we already covered the fact that your trade secrets don't have a lifespan like your patent does, and we also covered that in most cases your trade secrets are the secret nucleus that makes your patent work.

So let me ask, do you think it's wise to leave your trade secrets hanging out there unprotected in the hands of some company for the eleven remaining years? I think not.

That's why you have every agreement that you sign cover your trade secrets *for the remaining life of your patent and nothing less.* That's why you have an attorney on your team, so he can make the necessary changes to these agreements in order to protect you.

- Before you visit the company or discuss your product in any detail, your attorney must approve this contract. [NDA]
- Any document that proposes to cover your trade secrets must run for the life of your patent.
- Only after your attorney's approval and the signing off by both parties can you proceed to meet with them.
- A *properly executed and properly documented NDA* can be your very best friend should your trade secrets ever get high jacked by the company that you shared them with.

An Overview of the Second Document

The second document though similar to the Non-Disclosure Agreement or Proprietary Information Agreement is much weightier and a little more complex. This second document is normally offered to the inventor *only* after the company has shown significant interest in the inventor's idea. This document could be labeled as *Trade Secret Agreement* or a *Test Marketing Agreement*. No matter what the label, this document is going to frame out the relationship between the inventor and the company. As such, this document will specify in much greater detail, the parameters that will govern their relationship with you.

Additionally, this contract will contain certain milestones and timetables that if successfully reached, a license will then be offered to the inventor.

In the event that both parties are unsuccessful in obtaining the stated objectives for the project, or if they fail to come to terms concerning any of the important elements such as royalty payments, both sides can be released from the contract.

There is one major caveat that provides for the severing of this relationship and it bears repeating:

- Both parties will be held responsible to keep all of the information that's been shared in the strictest confidence. As such, none of that information or your trade secrets can be disclosed to any third party, nor can either party exploit it for their own use for a *specified period of time*. So make sure any and all documents that you sign regarding your trade secrets run concurrently with the life of your patent[s].

Just so you know, Honeywell violated these pre-license agreements we had entered into and went ahead and filed seventeen patents with the confidential information and the trade secrets that I shared with them. This behavior is a perfect example of what sharing confidential information with a third party could look like. It's easy enough to understand, in my case the PTO would be viewed as a third party since it's not directly affiliated with either me or Honeywell. And most importantly, they used this information for their own enrichment and not mine.

For the purposes of this teaching, it's not practical to delve into the specifics of this agreement, because each one is as unique as the two parties and the circumstances surrounding their relationship. These agreements can be as varied as the colors of the rainbow and accordingly, each company and each situation will create a different spin on both the language and the coverage.

The key thing to grasp, is that these documents are critical, extremely legal, and you will be signing one or more of them at some point in your relationship with the manufacturer. So therefore, it's of paramount importance that *your attorney* provides you with an exact break down of what your specific document means with regard to your situation.

Though these documents are commonplace in the licensing business, I feel that both the inventors who sign them, and the lawyers who review them for their clients, oftentimes overlook their great significance. I know that in my particular circumstance this was the case!

This is not the inventor's fault! If anything, this responsibility lies squarely on the lawyers whom the inventors are depending upon for legal counsel. An inventor wouldn't know the difference between this contract and what his life insurance contract says. In fact, it's the lawyer's job to not only explain the significance of what these contracts mean, but to anticipate what the future implications might be as a result of signing them.

For starters, these documents are so foundational that they will actually establish the framework for any lawsuit that the inventor might be compelled to bring against the company where his patent[s] and his related trade secrets are concerned.

In the event that the company should breach this contract, these documents will come to bear upon what *causes may be actionable*, as well as set the limitations of any possible damages that may be levied against the offending party.

Just so you know, when it came time for my lawyer to go into detail about the significance concerning these documents, he rather glossed over them. Instead, he should have been teaching me all that I'm sharing with you. And in case you might be wondering, I had a patent lawyer with plenty of experience on my team! Enough said.

I made it quite clear from the onset of this teaching that the inventor's odyssey was about cultivating an idea, identifying an advantage in the marketplace and then securing a position by obtaining a patent. I also reminded you several times that this journey was about the money. Perhaps in the beginning, you may have thought that my emphasis on the money may have been a bit crass, but as you'll soon see, these documents and what they contain will either make you a prince, a pauper, or a federal litigant.

Pre-License Agreements are Like Stop Signs

Let me begin by posing a simple question. Do these contracts actually protect the inventor?

From a legal standpoint that's what they're supposed to do. But from a practical standpoint, the sad reality is that they really don't. These contracts like nearly every other contract contain a major flaw, an unenforceable flaw. What it boils down to is that sometimes, "Contracts are just written to be broken."

Pre-licensing agreements and all the like, are just like patents… they are nothing more than stop signs. If the company that you're teaming up with wants to violate the contract, they're simply going to break it. Sadly, enough, this situation is reminiscent to the patent and stop sign analogy, which I had presented to you earlier.

Even though the consequences can be grave for the party who chooses to violate these contracts, the truth is, the companies that issue these contracts violate them rather routinely, and I might add, rather blatantly.

You may recall, I have already made you aware that the big players in this game routinely infringe upon patents. And in case I didn't make myself clear, the little guys very seldom violate either patents or pre-licensing agreements. The reason doesn't have to do with anything as noble as the inventor yielding to a higher ethical standard, though I would tend to believe that we do.

No. What it really comes down to here is pure economics and raw power. If you're going to violate either someone's patent or pre-licensing agreement you'd better have both the money and the power in large quantities in order to do so. Of course I am speaking from both my personal experience and what I've learned by researching the case law.

All of this leads me to conclude the following; the overwhelming majority of thefts that occur to inventors takes place during the pre-licensing stage. And this theft is premeditated and perpetrated by the very same companies that the inventor is seeking to team up with. Therefore, I would like to put forth my observations as to why this is likely to occur to the unsuspecting inventor:

- The unspeakable joy of finally arriving at this stage tricks the inventor into getting way too comfortable with the company. Therefore, it's quite easy for the inventor to lose the vigilance that he once had.
- The inventor places way too much trust in the documents that he's signed.
- The inventor begins to believe that the company and the people that he is interacting with have his best interests at heart. They don't.

- The inventor begins to spill his guts and share his most treasured secrets and fails to adequately *protect himself during the entire process.*
- The inventor's documentation habits get thrown to the wayside.

Just so you know, as an inventor I was guilty of all of this and it was my downfall.

Therefore, armed with this knowledge that I gained after the fact, I'll be teaching you once again how to navigate around yet another hazard. As I've done all along, I will attempt to arm you with the proper information so that you won't become just another victim. My objective is to get you through this part of the odyssey, minus the need for ever having to contemplate a lawsuit, because you got screwed during the pre-licensing period.

Once again, your greatest protection against this type of activity lies squarely on your shoulders. You can play this game, and you can play it to win. But what you really need to do is to remain vigilant throughout the *entire* journey. I want you to never lose sight of the fact that you're sitting cross-legged while playing your flute to the cobra.

Why All the Caution?

In a word, trade secrets.

During your experimentation and prototype development it's quite probable that you've improved upon your invention and have developed some new claims that aren't specifically covered by your patent. These new discoveries could include anything from a new material, an application for that new material, to a new twist on your manufacturing process.

- The definition of a trade secret is something that is not readily available in the public domain.

The key thing, is that trade secret information will provide its owner an advantage over all of their competitors. A trade secret could be anything from information, to the physical material, to the application of a special formula. A trade secret certainly would cover the specific application of a specific material or a process as well.

The facts are, if you persist in the never-ending struggle to perfect your invention, it's inevitable that you're going to generate new discoveries that will fall outside the scope of one or more of your patents and their attendant claims. As we've already covered, trade secrets are *much different* than patent claims. So in order for trade secrets to remain truly protected, an inventor has only a few options available:

- Trade secrets *must* remain a secret and known only to the inventor.
- In order for trade secrets to gain protection in the public domain, they *must* be incorporated in a set of formal patent claims that in turn must be granted in the form of a patent in order to gain protection.
- Trade secrets if divulged, *must* be protected by a formal contract such as a non-disclosure agreement, a proprietary information agreement or some type of confidentiality agreement.

Unless these new discoveries are incorporated in the form of new patent claims and formally recognized by the USPTO, they will be classified as trade secrets.

Keep in mind that the patent that you've already been granted *will not* cover these trade secrets if they *were not included* in the claims at the time that the application was submitted. Therefore, as the inventing process progresses, it's highly possible that *even the original inventor* if he so chooses, could without too much effort, *engineer around* his original patent claims!

Just so you know, after I was under the protection of 2 separate NDA's, I began sharing in excruciating detail with Honeywell how my initial patent application for a Teflon treated oil filter got rejected by the PTO. I also shared in the strictest of confidence how the application battle played out between me and my patent examiner.

And since Honeywell and I were partners, I didn't hesitate to school them on how to get this new set of claims for my improved Teflon treated oil filter accepted by the PTO. In so doing, I shared with them my numerous trade secrets, chief of which was the key element for both a new patent and the filter that they were about to produce. Now keep in mind the exact material that I divulged, and its proposed use hadn't ever been put forth in a patent application for an oil filter before. Furthermore, my idea was not something that had already existed in the public domain. It was my personal trade secret and it was my IP.

I divulged my trade secrets to Honeywell for a few specific reasons:

- I was protected by two separate NDA's.
- We were partners and a license had been offered to me.
- I was definitely going to be the co-inventor.
- They needed all of the help and confidence that I could give them to get this project off the drawing board.
- I trusted them, because I believed that they wouldn't violate any of the laws.
- And most importantly, if any patent applications were filed I would automatically be named as the co-inventor.

So… To make a long story short, they went and filed for the exact same patent that I had taught them about. To add insult to injury, they also filed and received several other patents regarding the various claims that I had taught them about as well.

Now here's the rub. They began doing all of this while I was under 2 separate NDA's; and later, when I was under a fully executed licensing agreement. Their actions violated US patent law 35 USC § 115 & 116 regarding inventorship, contract law, and the misappropriation of trade secrets.

So here's the lesson. If an inventor *improperly discloses* his trade secret information to a company during the product development stage a couple of things can happen:

- First. The company could choose to *engineer around* the original patent's claims and they could produce the product without adhering to the original patent.
- Second. The company could take your trade secret information and file for their own patents and cut you out altogether. And they will do this despite what the law states, because they totally understand that the only way that you can enforce your IP rights is to sue them.

Pay attention! This holds true even if you have signed disclosures in place!

- Once an inventor divulges his trade secrets to the company, there is nothing to protect him, but the agreements he has signed.

This can all be so innocent on the part of the inventor, but if it happens it can be totally devastating, because a very serious legal action is on your horizon.

Just so you know, I did this very thing and it cost me nearly everything! Yes, I shared my trade secrets with Honeywell, and yes, they violated the both of our trade secret agreements and went on to file 17 patents, cutting me out of tens upon tens of millions of dollars in royalties. And yes, the only option that they left me was to sue them.

By now you must be screaming, how heck did you let all of this happen to you?

My answer to you is simple so pay attention.

- I didn't document nearly to the degree that I've been admonishing you to do.
- I trusted that the non-disclosure documents that we had both signed would maintain an honest and arm's length relationship between us.
- I trusted them and bought into the myth that a highly respected company also has integrity.
- I did not document nearly like I should have.

So, before you begin to teach the company anything, at the very minimum you must put your presentation in writing. Make sure that you give them a copy. Document everything until your fingers bleed. And I do mean that you should document e-mails, phone calls and personal visits and contacts. Send certified letters that memorialize everything that you've talked about to the point that you should own stock in the US Post Office's certified mail department.

The key here is this. You must develop a paper trail that will prove beyond any reasonable doubt that you are the first and true inventor of anything that you might share with the company. The paper trail must be so convincing that even the most arrogant company will think twice before facing it, and that the most wayward judge would be afraid to ignore it!

Never lose sight of the fact that it's you who will be giving birth to this project; not the company! That's why you have to be very careful, because the information that you disclose to them could be very valuable! Know this, when you throw something as valuable as your trade secrets into the mix, people and the companies that they work for can tend to do some crazy stuff when they begin to see dollar signs.

At this point in the game, the company has everything to gain, while you on the other hand, have everything to lose. Here's what this dilemma is all about in a nutshell.

- You can *never ever* be too certain that the company will abide by the agreement that's going to be signed by the two of you!

Let me state this for the record. If anyone is going to breach the contract it's going to be the company and not the inventor! One only needs to look at the case law to see that the inventor rarely if *ever*, acts in bad faith in one of these deals.

Why is that you might ask? Simply because, if an inventor was to breach this contract it would be as stupid as walking in front of a speeding locomotive! That's why.

Controlling Law

Before moving on, I think that it's only appropriate that I give you a crash course in c*ontrolling law*. And since we are going to be dealing with contracts and the laws that will govern them, now would be the proper time to bring your highly qualified attorney into the game. Once again it's crucial that you choose someone who is very well suited for this particular job. Your attorney is going to represent you in the capacity of *licensing negotiator* and as such, it's going to be his or her task to review and approve *anything* that you might be asked to sign.

Some of the various documents presented to you may include the following:

- Confidentiality Agreements.
- Non-Disclosure Agreements.
- Trade Secret Agreements.
- Proprietary Information Agreements.
- Test Marketing agreements.
- License Agreements.

By way of definition, all of these documents are considered to be contracts, because two or more separate parties are making an agreement concerning specific terms.

Here is a key. After your attorney has reviewed *any* of these documents, one of the very first things to note is what particular state's law will govern the agreement. In the world of contracts this is known as *controlling law*.

Allow me to explain, because unless you're fresh out of law school, you may not have a clue as to what I'm about to share with you.

As you know, each state in the Union has their own governing body or legislature. The legislature is responsible for enacting the laws; these laws are also referred to as *statutes*. Each of our fifty states has their own set of laws on the books and they don't necessarily line up with one another. Even when the states happen to share the same laws, they can differ on any number of key elements! The laws that are shared by each state *can vary* on any of these key elements:

- The *standards* for the same law can vary from state to state.
- The *application* of the law can vary from state to state.
- The *enforcement* of the law can vary from state to state.
- The *remedy* for breaking the same law can vary from state to state.
- The *statute of limitations* for the same law can vary from state to state.

The point is, each state *can* have a different set of standards when it comes to the interpretation and the application of their laws. Therefore, the enforcement and the subsequent remedies that are provided to make the injured party *whole* can also vary from state to state.

Remedy is a legal term for restitution. Restitution is the act of restoring something back to its rightful owner, where the individual who had suffered the loss is put back to the economic position that he enjoyed before he suffered the loss.

In addition to that, the *statute of limitations* or the time allotted to bring forth a lawsuit can also vary from state to state.

- Controlling law *will* dictate how your relationship with the perspective licensee will both be interpreted and enforced in the event that the contract should be broken.
- Controlling law *will* dictate what remedies will apply should the law be violated.
- Controlling law *will* dictate the statute of limitations period to bring forth a lawsuit should the law be violated.
- Controlling law will dictate the law as it applies to any contract you sign, including the Misappropriation of Trade Secrets. Be aware that the states of NC, NY & MA *do not* participate in The Uniform Trade Secret Act.

This is how it works.

The various agreements that you might be asked to sign will be governed or controlled by a particular state's statutes. Generally, the party who drafts the agreement will specify or *cite* which particular state's law will govern the contract. This is known as controlling law or governing law.

For example, this is simply done by inserting a clause into the contract that goes something like this, "This contract will be governed under the laws of the state of New Jersey." Therefore, in this particular instance, the laws of New Jersey will govern how the *terms* of the agreement will be interpreted. The laws of any other state *will not apply* toward the interpretation of that contract.

Here is the significance. The law has three parts.

- The first component of the law is the law itself.
- The second component of the law is the enforcement.
- The third component of the law is the remedy.

The third part of the law will come to bear, should the law be broken and the guilty party is made to pay. Implicit in how the contract will be interpreted will also be how the contract will be enforced and what remedies are provided in order to make the injured party whole.

So here's what it really boils down to:

- All contracts will be governed by controlling law.
- Generally, the party who drafts the contract will specify which state's law will govern the contract.

I bothered to bring this to your attention, because more often than not, the ramifications of controlling law can get glossed over by the attorney who represents the inventor.

The reason for this oversight is quite simple. Controlling law will only come to bear upon the parties should the contract be broken. And when you're signing a contract, who's thinking about breaking it after it's been signed? Who's thinking about statute of limitations and damages? Certainly not the inventor and in most cases not his lawyer either. But let's see who might.

Some states are very strict when it comes to the violation of their laws. They will accordingly apply heavy remedies in the form of *damages* should their laws be willfully broken.

On the other hand, there are other states that may not take such a stern approach to the violations of their laws. Therefore, they may not apply the same remedies or adhere to the same statute of limitations.

The term *damage* means penalty. Damages means, that the guilty party must compensate the injured party with certain amount of money in order to make them whole. This penalty can range above and beyond what is owed to make the injured party whole. The amount of damages can range anywhere from one to three times the amount of the profit that was proved to be ill gottenly gained by the offending party.

So if the controlling law of a pre-license agreement called for *treble monetary damages*, the party who might be considering breaching the contract would have to factor in the consequences more carefully as opposed to an agreement where the state law does not provide for damages.

The first area of controlling law that I want both you and your attorney to be mindful of is referred to as the *counting of time*, or the *tolling of time* with regard to the *statute of limitations*. The statute of limitations refers to a period of time that a plaintiff is allowed to file a lawsuit with regard to the wrongdoer who broke a particular statute. This period of time can vary depending on the statute and the state that governs it.

The second area of controlling law that I want both you and your attorney to be mindful of is the remedy. Pay attention as to whether the controlling law provides for *restitution in the form of monetary damages* should the contract be broken.

For example, the statute of limitations for *breach of contract* in New Jersey is five years. If a plaintiff had filed a lawsuit for the breach of contract even one day after the five-year period, he would be disqualified or *barred* from bringing a lawsuit. As a result, he would be *forever barred* from bringing that particular suit, because the time had run out for him to bring such a claim. Even if he should only be only one day late! And there are no damages awarded for breaking a contract in New Jersey.

The statute of limitations for breach of contract *is not* the same in every state. So be mindful that each state can vary as to how much time they will allow to elapse before barring the injured party from bringing forth a lawsuit.

- There are different standards that will apply to both *contract law* as well as *intellectual property law.*
- Be aware that these standards as well as their remedies will vary from state to state.
- Both contract law and intellectual property law will apply to any contract or agreement that an inventor might be asked to sign.

So again, it's conceivable for a company who has violating a contract on their minds, might choose the state law that has a shortest statute of limitations period, as opposed to choosing a state that has a longer statute of limitations period for violating the same law.

It's also conceivable for a company who has violating a contract on their minds to choose the state law that provides for little or no damages, as opposed to a state that provides treble damages for violating the same law.

Allow me to pose a hypothetical question. Would it be a coincidence if a company's legal department favored a particularly weak state's law to govern their agreements when they are licensing someone else's technology for their own use?

In this particular instance we are referring to a company that is about to license your patent and perhaps your trade secrets. In this case, the company has decided to have your contract interpreted under the most liberal state law that they can apply. As such, they are going to choose a state that is *known* for having the shortest statute of limitations period and *doesn't* award damages to the injured party. In this particular case, the injured party would be *you.*

On the flip side, is it possible that a company's legal department would want to employ just the opposite approach if they were to license out their technology? In that case, they could easily accomplish this by citing the most stringent state law they can apply when they are *licensing out* their technology for another company's use. In this instance they would want to choose a state that has the longest statute of limitations period and awards the highest damages to the party who's been wronged. In this particular case, the injured party would be *them.*

To make it simple for you to understand:

- Companies will tend to favor *weak* controlling law when they receive information from an outside source.
- Companies will tend to favor *strong* controlling law when they give out their information to an outside source.

The game is such, that many times a company can accomplish this by the drafting the contracts and inserting the controlling law that best represents their position at any given time.

So let me ask you?

Do you think it's possible that these companies who have these various legal tools at their disposal, do such a thing? Especially when it comes time for you to license your patent and throw your trade secrets into the pot?

After all, it will be the companies and their lawyers who are going to draft these agreements for you to sign. Not vice versa. In many instances, these companies can have operations in many, if not all fifty states, so selecting the most favorable controlling law is not that difficult for them to do. Actually it's rather straightforward.

Any one of the criteria listed below is legal grounds for a company to select controlling law:

- The company must be based or *domiciled* in the particular state governing the contract.
- Or the company must conduct business operations or have sales of its products in the particular state governing the contract.
- Or one or more of the parties to the contract must be domiciled in the particular state governing the contract.

Again, just be mindful that when a company chooses a particular state to govern your contract, they might just be doing it for a specific reason. As a rule, most companies *are not* prone to give up the controlling law option during your contract negotiations either and that just serves to reinforce my point.

I bothered to share all of this with you, because what may appear to be nothing but meaningless legal jargon left in the hands of lawyers and judges, could one day rock your world in the event that the company decides to violate your contracts.

I tell you in advance, it's the wise inventor who monitors his relationship with the company by paying close attention to all of these details.

Just so you know, this was a real eye opener when I became embroiled in the lawsuit that I filed against Honeywell. So allow me to teach you in living color how important these documents can be to the inventor, should you ever find it necessary to institute a lawsuit against a dishonest partner.

When I brought my lawsuit against Honeywell, I had filed several claims against them. Here are some of the claims that I filed; *breach of contract, patent infringement and misappropriation of trade secrets, tortious interference with advantageous business relationships, fraud in the inducement.* One of my most solid claims was for the misappropriation of trade secrets.

Well over a year into my lawsuit, the judge saw fit to rule against me and threw out my claim for misappropriation of trade secrets against Honeywell. The claim was thrown out on a technicality, because the statute of limitations had expired some two months before I had filed the lawsuit. Though the court found the claim to have merit, it was thrown out due to a mere technicality. That means that my claim for misappropriation of trade secrets would never be presented to a jury, and as a result, it was stuck from my suit. All due to the fact that I had filed that claim two months after the time had tolled.

Here's how it worked. In my particular situation, I had signed two pre-license agreements. The first agreement was a Proprietary Information Agreement. The second agreement that I had signed was referred to as a Test Marketing Agreement. I had signed these agreements approximately five weeks apart.

It is important to note that Honeywell had drawn both of these agreements and the laws of Rhode Island governed both agreements. In due course, my attorney had reviewed both of these agreements and I had signed them like I was supposed to. By all appearances, nothing seemed out of the ordinary. The key issue here; is that my attorney and I had never discussed governing law with me concerning these contracts.

Just so you know, I was clueless as to what controlling law was, and how it could control my life in the event that I needed to file a lawsuit. As I said previously, who even thinks about breaking a contract before it's signed? All I can tell you is that I certainly wasn't contemplating breaking any agreement. Yet that was no excuse for my not understanding the ramifications of controlling law.

Here is what I didn't know at the time that I signed these documents. According to Rhode Island law, the statute of limitations for misappropriation of trade secrets at that time was *two years and it provided for double damages* for the injured party should the offending party be found guilty.

The point is this; both Honeywell and I were domiciled in New Jersey. So therefore it's not unreasonable to think that since both parties were domiciled in the same state, New Jersey law would govern the contracts. Yet Honeywell chose not to govern our contracts with Jersey law.

Why?

Upon further thought, Honeywell has manufacturing operations in many states and has *sales in every state*. So technically, they could have selected the controlling law from any one of fifty states to govern our contracts, yet they choose Rhode Island law to control these contracts.

Was the choice of governing law as innocent as Fram's business operations being located in Rhode Island? I can't say for sure.

But what I can tell you; is that there is something called *The Uniform Trade Secret Act*. Also referred to as the *Illinois Trade Secret Act*. At the time in which I brought my lawsuit, forty-five out of our fifty states had pledged to be governed under this unified statue. The Uniform Trade

Secret Act governs not only what a *trade secret* is, but also how the *misappropriation of trade secrets* are to be handled.

Under The Uniform Trade Secret Act, the statute of limitations for the misappropriation of trade secrets is *three years* and provides for *treble damages* for the injured party should the offending party be found guilty. The Uniform Trade Secret Act makes it quite clear that the misappropriation of trade secrets will be severely dealt with.

Coincidence or not, at the time, Rhode Island *had not allowed* themselves to be governed under this Act. Rhode Island was governed by their own statutes for the misappropriation of trade secrets.

Coincidently, at the time, the state of Rhode Island did not protect the injured party who has had his trade secrets violated nearly as vigorously as compared to the states that conformed to The Uniform Trade Secret Act. In addition to that, Rhode Island's statute of limitations period was one year shorter.

So based upon the controlling law of the state of Rhode Island, my statute of limitations for misappropriation of trade secrets had expired by just a couple of months before I had an opportunity to *file* my lawsuit. Had this contract been governed by the controlling law of any of the other 45 states that adhered to the Uniform Trade Secrets Act, this count would have gone to the jury and I would have certainly won.

As previously mentioned, 48 states have now adopted the Uniform Trade Secrets Act; the statute of limitations under this act is 3 years. Presently, New York, North Carolina Massachusetts and have not joined. At this time a bill is in front of the Massachusetts legislature sponsored by their governor to join these cooperating states.

- Make sure that you NDA is governed by one of the states that participates under The Uniform Trade Secret Act.

So why all the fuss?

This was a huge money claim for me, potentially worth untold tens of millions of dollars in damages. Remember, Honeywell made a hundred million dollars in profit off of the trade secrets in this dispute and the statute in the forty-five of the fifty states calls for treble damages. Now you do the math.

All this was lost due to a simple technicality. As a result, this was a monumental win for Honeywell and just served to reinforce that bad behavior towards inventors is worth the company's risk if you happen to have the right controlling law governing your contracts.

So remember, the art of the licensing deal is way more complex then you could ever imagine. And therefore it's way more complex than just going into business with a company so that they can make your product and pay you a royalty.

As a result, the licensing process should never ever be considered a given, no matter how honest you may perceive the company to be.

Just so you know, at the time, I was totally convinced that Honeywell, above all others was honest. Well much later on, during the Discovery process they would sadly prove otherwise.

Take a tip from the master chess players. You have to always be several moves ahead of your opponent if you ever intend on being successful. Likewise, you should take a tip from me.

Licensing is a minefield, yet all you need to do is take to what I am teaching you to heart, and then flesh it out with your lawyer before you ever breathe the first word of your presentation.

Simply put, it's the inventor's responsibility to know what these contracts really mean. That includes having a *comprehensive understanding* of the state law(s) that will *govern* or control any of the contracts that you may be signing. This means that you should know about your statute of limitations and your potential remedies before you sign anything.

To summarize, here are four good reasons why you should have a comprehensive understanding of what controlling law can govern:

- First. Controlling law will dictate the enforcement of the agreements.
- Second. Controlling law will specify what circumstances will constitute a breach of the agreements.
- Third. Controlling law will specify what the remedies are for the breach of the agreements.
- Fourth. Controlling law will specify what the statues of limitations are for bringing forth a lawsuit for the breach of the agreements.

As an inventor, you can *never totally eliminate the possibility of ever being a party to an intellectual property lawsuit*. Consider this fair warning as to the motivations behind the choice of controlling law, and how it could be applied in the event that the company should violate one or more of your contracts.

Some Things to be Mindful Of

So at least we know that before getting into this relationship we have to be mindful to keep at least one good eye on the company. As such, a typical line a company might hand you with regard to this instrument is that you need to sign it, *because it will protect the company from you suing them*. And indeed that is exactly why they are mandating that you sign it.

Yet, and you'll have to forgive me here, because I have to laugh... If the truth were known, they could give a damn if you ever sue them; in their eyes you're simply too insignificant to ever hurt them and they know it.

That's why I want to review some of the key elements in greater detail.

As I told you earlier, typically the company draws this document. So take care to have your attorney pay very close attention to what particular state has jurisdiction over this very legal and very binding contract.

Have the company fax this document to your lawyer first for his or her consideration and then take it from there. Don't give the company an opportunity to fax it, mail it, or e-mail it to you. Your refusal to personally receive this contract is the proper way of letting the company know that you have an attorney helping you and that you intend on dotting your I's and crossing your T's during this process.

Based solely on general principal, I don't want any of these documents ever being sent to you. They are legal documents and you're not a lawyer. Therefore, you shouldn't be playing lawyer; you're an inventor.

Rule number one. Do not personally receive any legal document directly from the company. For instance, if they should casually approach you and say, "Here is a document pertaining to our project and you need to review and sign it…" Just reply by pulling your attorneys card out of your wallet and give them his/her name and fax number.

Rule number two. Never sign any legal document offered to you without first having your attorney thoroughly look it over. This means that you only sign something after your attorney has made the necessary changes and has carefully explained to you *all* the ramifications of what you are signing.

Rule number three. This may blow your mind, but even the physical location or the state where you sign this document can have a future bearing on the jurisdiction that will govern this contract!

Rule number four. Make sure that your attorney has considered the jurisdictional repercussions of what particular states law governs this document. Have your attorney pull the controlling states statues covering the various laws that could affect your contract should the company beach your contract. Make sure that you get a copy of these statues and put them in your personal file.

There are several possible areas of law that may be violated by the company. As such, this agreement will be governed under the statues of the specific state's law's that will control the agreement.

The various laws to be considered by your attorney are the following:

- Contract Law, such as breach of contract.
- Trade Secret Law, such as the misappropriation of trade secrets.
- Patent Law, which covers patent infringement as well as inventorship rights.
- Copyright Law.
- Trademark Law, such as trade dress issues as well as ownership rights.
- Fraud Statues, such as fraud in the inducement.
- Tortuous Interference with Advantageous Business Relationships.

As such, I want your lawyer to concentrate on following three areas:

- The parameters that frame such causes of action.
- The tolling of time or the statute of limitations for each separate cause of action.
- The specific damages a plaintiff is entitled to under *each separate cause of action.*
- How to best protect your trade secrets.

This would also be the appropriate time to have your attorney make any modifications to the agreement that might be to your benefit.

Rule number five is like rule number four. Have your attorney look several steps ahead and have him inquire if the same governing law will control the next pre-licensing agreement and the final licensing agreement should one follow.

I don't care whom your lawyer needs to contact to find this out. It is far better to know the controlling law going into the relationship, as opposed to finding out during the lawsuit that you were either short changed on punitive damages or the tolling of the statute of limitations regarding any possible breach of the contract or the violation of any other statute that may apply.

Allow me to inform you that contract law; the laws governing fraud, and the misappropriation of trade secrets are all governed by state statute, and not by the federal statutes. On the other hand, federal statues govern patents, trademarks and copyrights.

Rule number six. Always consistently sign you name the same way on every contract. Do not deviate under any circumstances.

For example, let's say that you happen to be incorporated and as such, you are the president of your corporation. Seek your attorney's advice as to how you should sign this contract and the various contracts that will be presented to you along the way. Find out if you should sign these documents either personally or corporately. There is a big difference, so you better find out where the advantage lies for your particular circumstance. This may seem a small technicality, but you have no clue how big it can really be! There are legal standings and tax implications regarding settlement payouts just to mention two areas of rather significant concern.

Rule number seven. If you happen to have a corporation and you opt to sign your documents, John Doe, President of XYZ Corporation. Plan on keeping your corporation alive for the life of your contracts and possibly beyond, in the event you may have to file a lawsuit. If you get into a lawsuit down the road and your corporation has either been intentionally abandoned or has lapsed, you'll be mired down in a ridiculous fight over whether you actually ever signed the contracts on your behalf or not.

Simply put, their defense team will put forth the argument that since you signed the contracts as a corporate officer and your corporation no longer exists, then the contracts that you have signed are no longer valid! I'm just warning you, you cannot begin to fathom the legal hairsplitting an unlimited legal defense budget can bring to bear.

Rule number eight. In the event that you were awarded money from a lawsuit, you must plan on paying both state and federal taxes. That's unless you can claim personal injury due to mental anguish. However, in order to do so you must be able to substantiate that you've been under the care of a mental health practitioner. In any event, consult either a tax lawyer or a certified public accountant to know what your specific tax liabilities are going to be.

Rule number nine. Only specific types of corporations are allowed to deduct legal fees as expenses. Not private citizens! Again this is yet another area that you must seek the advice of your lawyer or accountant to know what your specific tax liabilities may be.

Rule number ten. The key here is this; even though you have been granted a patent and despite the appearances that you are supposedly going to be protected by a pre-licensing agreement I don't want you to *ever blindly place your trust* in any instrument that you might be signing to get you through this process.

Place your trust in being knowledgeable and playing a truly defensive game of chess. Just remember, the cobra isn't supposed to bite the guy who's sitting down cross-legged playing the flute either…, yet they tell me it happens.

If you have followed these simple instructions, in the horrible event that you might have to institute a lawsuit against the company that you've teamed up with, you won't have to spend the weeks and months trying to figure out your legal standing. By taking these prudent measures ahead of time, you will know what statutes govern your causes of action and where you stand legally.

This way if necessary, you can put the company on firm notice and eliminate any of the games that they'll want to play during the answer of your complaint and subsequent motions that they will file before the court. This simple preventative measure will save the judge an incredible amount of confusion and focus the attention on matter at hand. Such as what they did to you, instead of spending four or five years on splitting hairs as to what statue covers what.

As I've been doing my best to convey, I've personally experienced all of this and a hell of a lot more, as I faced off against a Fortune-Thirty Company and one of the world's top law firms as they spun their webs of doublespeak.

So..., if you and your attorney spend just a couple of hours doing this up front, it might just end up saving you the world!

Just So You Know

What I'm about to share with you next may very well keep you out of a lawsuit one day, instead of opening the door wide open and inviting one in. In this very foreign and sophisticated game of inventing, making the right choices is absolutely critical, because you will be living with the consequences of your actions for a long time.

I feel that it's best to use my personal experience teach you about this. Therefore, I want to run this one out all the way so that you'll know better what not to do.

During my relationship with Fram I had signed two pre-licensing agreements and I had signed these agreements approximately one month apart from each other. I signed my licensing agreement some ten months after that.

The first agreement that I signed was a *proprietary information agreement*, which was drawn by Allied's legal department.

Please follow the progression here. AlliedSignal drew the contract and Rhode Island law governed this particular contract. Allied then faxed it to me, where I had signed it in New Jersey and then faxed it back to them in preparation for our first personal meeting, which was to take place in Rhode Island.

Upon my arrival at Fram's headquarters, in Rhode Island, and after our meeting had concluded, I then signed the hard copy of the proprietary information agreement.

Now I want you to pay close attention here. This chain of events has several key details and I don't want you getting lost. So not only did I sign the document twice, I signed a faxed copy in NJ, and the original copy in Rhode Island after our meeting had taken place.

Just so you know, I did so with their complete assurances from Fram's upper management that this was absolutely proper, being that I had already signed the faxed copy in NJ. Also, the PIA was signed after the meeting had occurred, because I was whisked into that meeting and the original PIA, which needed my signature, was nowhere to be found prior to my arrival at their headquarters.

After I had given a successful presentation, I had to go to the office of the Head of Strategic Planning and World Wide Development to sign the original, which I did in her presence. Just to be absolutely clear, this high ranking company official had assured me that everything was in order and that I was absolutely covered by this agreement from the moment it was signed by me in NJ.

Oh, just one last thing to complicate matters. At the time that I signed this particular contract, I did so as Stephen Moor, President Trans-Eco. I had signed the PIA this way since I had formed a NJ Subchapter S Corporation to do my inventing under. So at the time, I thought nothing of signing my contract as the president of my corporation. Out of the three agreements that I had signed, I only signed this one as a corporate officer. The other two agreements I had signed personally as Stephen Moor.

As an aside I gained no real benefit by having a Subchapter S Corporation. Anyway, I am not qualified to counsel you in the area of corporations, so please seek your accountant or lawyer for that advice. Since we are on the subject, you should investigate whether it would be to your advantage to form an LLC to do your inventing under.

Getting back…

Two years after inking my license, not needing the benefit off my corporation any longer, I allowed my corporate status to lapse.

Now let's go back and review everything in the light of what I've just taught you. I want you to carefully take note of all of my missteps. All innocent mind you, but disastrous nonetheless when all these assurances made to you by the company have *the bright light of a law suit* shown on them.

That said, allow me to illustrate how these two documents can play into the devil's hands in an intellectual property lawsuit. As pointed out earlier, it was these documents that laid out the ground rules for the lawsuit that I would eventually file.

You see my starry eyed and unschooled inventors, things like personal assurances given to you by people in high places of responsibility, or the intent of the contracts coupled with your innocence, will only wind up tearing you a new backside once the lawyers come out to play, ...and to come out to play they will!

In my particular case, I had sent this document to my attorney and he had approved it. But he never mentioned anything about controlling law. Nor did he give me specific instructions on how, when and where to sign these documents so that they would all be done in a consistent manner. To the unschooled litigant this may appear to be splitting hairs, but based on what I've taught you thus far, you can readily see that it's not!

Our legal system as dumb as it sounds is designed for the best hair splitters to win any legal contest. Again, our legal system has very little to do with justice, concerning who is right or who is wrong. Or who did what, to harm to whom. Our legal system is an air castle comprised of split ends and I have to believe that many of you are all smart enough to realize that there's a good deal of truth behind that statement.

In the end your fate may very well come down to something as ridiculous as to how you may have signed your name. Or what state had controlling law. Or even what state you might have been in when you signed the contract.

Of course at the time, my attorney wasn't looking seven steps ahead like a Russian chess master either, because quite innocently or ignorantly on his part, he never foresaw that the relationship between Fram and I would result in an intellectual property lawsuit.

Just so you know, the patent attorney who represented me was a patent prosecution attorney and he came highly recommended. However, he was not by trade, a patent litigator.

Nonetheless, he should have known much, much, better considering that he was a practicing an intellectual property lawyer. As you can now understand, any such relationship based upon the licensing of intellectual property can boil over into a lawsuit for a whole host of reasons. Though I thought at the time that my lawyer was doing a good job of representing me, apparently he wasn't studying the chessboard as carefully as I'm now advising both you and your lawyer to do.

Keep in mind that there is a huge difference in qualifications between a seasoned IP litigator doing this for you, as opposed to a patent prosecution attorney. There's simply no room for a casual approach here. So be consistent.

The simplest and most innocent of things like:

- How you signed the contracts.
- Where you signed the contracts.
- What state law will govern the contracts?
- Whether you sign the contracts personally or corporately.
- Whether you signed a fax copy of the contract or the original.
- The order in which you sign the contracts.
- Acting on company's assurances in good faith.

Can all turn into a mini nuclear war that will follow you all the way to the eve of trial.

Just so you know, in my particular case, the judge allowed this fight over these stupid details to continue right up until the eve of my trial. We fought about everything that I just taught you about with regard to these pre-license agreements and their governing law for nearly four and a half years!

The never-ending hair splitting over the pre-license agreements can inevitably confuse the overall picture of how the company violated the contracts and stole your intellectual property to begin with. In the final analysis these contracts will affect:

- Your statute of limitations to file a lawsuit.
- Your ability to file any causable actions under the controlling states statues.
- Your ability to recover any damages as permitted under the controlling states statues.

So here's the key. Be ever mindful of all that I just shared with you. Keep these contracts consistent as to how you sign them, where you sign them, and as to the controlling law that governs them. If there are any variables and inconsistencies, it will give the company and their minion of highly skilled lawyers an incredible advantage to wreak havoc with any lawsuit that you may be forced to bring.

What may have appeared to be a very straightforward violation by the company will go totally ignored by the court. This can all happen, because depending on how smart and how diligent your judge is, the details can get so damned confusing that the judge can easily forget what the lawsuit was really about in the first place. I know mine did.

Chapter 13

LICENSING AGREEMENTS

Who's Invited to Your Meeting?

When the time finally arrives, you might be wondering, who's going to show up to this meeting anyway? I think it would be rather helpful if I could share with you who came to my meeting. In addition to that, I'd also like to give you a thumbnails sketch of what transpired so that you can get a feel for some of the dynamics. Since I've already told you that you can expect to be interacting with people from both the marketing and engineering side of the business, you might want to see what could happen.

Just so you know, assembled at my meeting were many of Fram's top filter engineers. They hailed from Rhode Island, Indiana, Ohio, and as far away as Canada. Fram had assembled at least a half dozen of their top oil filter engineers from both the automotive and heavy-duty side of the business. Not to beat a dead horse, but none of these guys had an oil filter patent on their resume.

Also present was, the senior VP of Fram, the Head of Strategic Planning and World Wide Development. The legal department was represented, and of course several high level individuals from the marketing department were present as well. As you can see this was no lightweight affair. It was a packed house, and to say that I was extremely nervous would be an understatement.

Right off the bat, my idea was met with great opposition from Fram's Chief Engineer and his counterpart, the Head of Filter Production. The top two ranking members of Fram's engineering staff hated my idea and they had no problem making that point abundantly clear to the entire assembly. Their vociferous objections were quite apparent as the V.P. of engineering said, "You never put anything inside of an oil filter. They aren't just made that way."

Also as expected, he brought forth front and center the *snake oil* objection. There were moments of shear insanity, and there were times that I was powerless to say anything in my defense. All I could do was to stand on the sidelines and take it all in, as the group bantered about my idea.

In retrospect, none of the oil filter company engineers that I had encountered along the way seemed to care that Slick-50 had been around since the late 70's. Or that Slick-50 had sold hundreds of millions of dollars' worth of their Teflon treated oil additives with no apparent fall out due to engine failures. Case in point, none of the filter engineers' industry wide had paid much attention to this burgeoning market, so in turn, most of what they had to offer on the subject was a negative gut reaction based on their total lack of information.

However, in the case of the Fram engineers it was different. Unlike the other engineers that I had talked to in the past, they had no excuses. You see, in order for me to be granted the opportunity give a presentation to the company, I first was required to deliver to the engineering department certified test studies that demonstrated that Teflon additives was not snake oil. My admittance to meeting with Fram was strictly predicated on the condition that I first supply the engineers the necessary scientific proof that Teflon additives had a beneficial effect.

As I've already told you, that was no light-weight task. I scoured the world looking for these studies and I did so at a time when the Internet wasn't available to the general public. Nevertheless, over the course of six months, I was able to secure several very scientific test studies. These studies proved my contention that Teflon when properly introduced into an engines lubricating system was beneficial.

The reason why the engineering department mandated that I produce these studies was twofold.

First, it was my idea and they were opposed to it. They made it clear to me that I not only needed to produce the sources of my information, but I had better be able to substantiate every claim that I would make about my invention.

Second, if AlliedSignal had commissioned these test studies on their own, it would have cost them over a million dollars to generate this kind of data. It was obvious to me that the engineering department wasn't about to sponsor something that they weren't going to support. In the end, the test studies that I produced were so authoritative, that Fram eventually relied upon my findings to bring the Double Guard oil filter into existence.

Yet, despite all of my best efforts to get this information into the hands of the Fram engineers and earn this meeting, the senior engineers reacted to my idea as if they had never even thumbed those promising studies.

Here's what I want you to grasp. The opposition from the engineering side was so great, that in an attempt to deal with all of their numerous objections, I began to volunteer information that was outside the scope of both my patents. I began to disclosing some of my trade secrets in order to close the deal with Fram!

Now understand something, in a perfect world I hadn't done anything wrong. Because from both a legal and contractual standpoint, I did what any normal inventor would do in that situation. My disclosures *no matter how secret*, were permissible under the protection of the *signed* Proprietary Information Agreement. So I sold my butt off and I threw in the kitchen sink in a heroic attempt to sell my invention. There was nothing new about that. Nothing out of the ordinary. Nothing that hadn't been done a million times, by a million inventors before me.

But sadly, we don't live in anything close to a perfect world.

Needless to say, I can certainly empathize that when your first meeting comes, you will want to pull it off too. I also realize that you may want this deal of yours to happen so badly, that it's conceivable that you could rather innocently give away the farm in the process too. That's what I especially want to talk to you about in this last chapter.

As I've already told you, this situation presents the opportunity for you to potentially disclose important information not specifically covered by the scope of your patent claims. Harmless as it may seem, as an inventor, you can easily get caught up in a spontaneous moment and expound upon the trade secrets behind your creation. What could have been something as innocent as trying to close the deal could later turn out to be disastrous.

Based upon my experience and what I've subsequently learned from researching the various lawsuits involving many other inventors, I have come to the conclusion that an inventor is taking a tremendous leap of faith if he/she places their trust in either the agreements or the company's word. My advice to you is simple. *Do not place your trust in either the Non-Disclosure documents or the company's word that they will protect your interests.*

Be prepared to do one thing, sell. But sell by exercising restraint, staying within the scope of your patents claims unless you have already put in place a specific action plan to protect yourself. Unless you have purposely put in place certain mechanisms to protect yourself, don't be selling anything that your patent cannot specifically protect.

Here's the wrinkle. Some of the information that you may be asked to disclose *will not* be protected under the scope of your patent. I find it rather impossible that all of it would. That fact brings us back full circle to the very reason why we obtained patent protection in the first place. And that's exactly why I have been schooling you on what trade secrets are, and how to best protect them.

So, as I've been preaching to you all along, document, document, document… That my friends, is where you can place your trust. What I'm about to share with you, is one of the most important lessons presented in this entire study. I want to teach you how you can best protect yourself from your new business partner during your first meeting and beyond.

It all boils down to this:

- There is right *time* to disclose closely held information or trade secrets.
- There is a right *place* to disclose closely held information or trade secrets.
- There is a right *way* to disclose closely held information or trade secrets.

You had Better Come Prepared

All I can tell you, is that in the final analysis I was not adequately protected. All the company's assurances failed. Honeywell's words and their ethics failed miserably. And the thing that hurt me perhaps the most, is that the legal system failed me.

Yet there is a simple way to for you to protect yourself and it was under my nose all the while, but I discounted its mighty power. Unfortunately for me, it took being a party to a Federal lawsuit for me to learn the reality of the inventing game. At least I will have the satisfaction of knowing that I can pass on all that I've learned to you.

So I've put together a simple list of what I feel would afford you the best protection during your first meeting. You can use any combination of these protective measures any time that you are going to disclose anything of great value that's not covered by your patent. I've taken the liberty of putting them in the order of what I feel will afford you the best protection.

First. Though I've already presented this option to you several times during the course of this teaching, it bears repeating. If you don't have to disclose your trade secrets in order to strike a deal, then don't! Keep your trade secrets a secret indefinitely or file for an additional patent for yourself. That would make you the sole inventor of you IP and not a co-inventor. The addition of second patent could further protect your patented product and could potentially increase your financial position later.

Second. In the event that you choose to disclose your trade secrets at your first meeting or any meeting for that fact, I would like to make a suggestion. To be afforded the very best protection, you would show up with your attorney and have a certified courtroom stenographer along with you to record your meeting. To absolutely make your presentation bulletproof, you could also hire a videographer.

Third. Bring your attorney. Of course you will have to pay his or her fee, but don't give that a second thought, because it will be well worth it. Attorneys are officers of the court. That means they have sworn an oath to uphold the constitution of this country. Therefore, their word, their notes, their recollection is readily accepted by the court as being both truthful and accurate. Simply put, the court presumes that they will always be truthful.

The very presence of a lawyer will lend credibility to your standing. Therefore, the company will have to think long and hard should they foolishly attempt to dismiss the fact that you had proper representation and documentation.

At some point during the meeting you should state for the record all of your trade secrets in detail. This will insure that it will go on the official record in the presence of your attorney. You should also follow up this oral disclosure by having your attorney send the company a letter. His letter should not only cover what transpired at the meeting, but should describe what you are claiming to be your trade secrets as well. This should prevent them from attempting to file a patent, and should they, you will have sufficient proof that they did so illegally.

Of course the downside of bringing your lawyer into the meeting might very well scare the company away. But after my experience, if a company is the least bit uncomfortable because an attorney is present, then there's a good possibility that they have something to hide.

Fourth. Hire a certified courtroom reporter. There are certified reporting services located everywhere. They are easily located and the arrangements are simple to make to have a reporter show up to record any of your meetings. The transcripts that they produce are certified to be accurate and are accepted by the court without reservation. In my opinion, they are gold!

Again after any meeting send the company a certified letter stating all of your trade secrets and disclosures in detail and in writing.

Fifth. Bring a tape recorder and place it on the table. The company may not like it, but too bad. As long as the parties agree, the recording can proceed. Make sure that at the very beginning of the recording, that the company acknowledges the fact that they are giving you permission to tape record the meeting. Make sure that during the recording that you disclose your trade secrets in detail.

Then have the tape recording transcribed. More than likely, you will have to use a *non-certified* transcription service to do this for you. I'm quite certain that a certified reporting agency *will not* do this for you, due to the fact that they were not physically present to make the recording. However, *you* should check with a certified reporting agency beforehand to see if they will do the transcription for you if you should decide to tape record the meeting.

Send a copy of the transcription to the company for their future reference. Whatever you do, don't let the original tape out of your possession! And make a few backup copies.

Again after any meeting send the company a certified letter stating all of your trade secrets and disclosures in detail and in writing to memorialize the fact that this information originated with you.

Sixth. Find out if the company is going to produce minutes of your meeting. Get a copy of the minutes as soon as possible. Here's where I have to draw the line. Although the concept seems good, don't rely on the notes that the company is going to produce. It's an unrealistic expectation for you to assume that everything that could take place during your meeting will show up in the minutes.

Seventh. Since it's impossible to be taking notes and selling your pants off at the same time, upon getting back home, write down from memory what both sides exchanged. Send a copy to the company certified mail memorializing what took place at the meeting. Make sure you list and describe your trade secrets in detail. Make sure that you put the company on notice that you are disclosing your closely held secrets and that you are sharing it with them in accordance with the NDA.

The sixth and seventh options are weak. Knowing what I know today, I wouldn't put my faith in them.

Just so you know, I never received a copy of the company's minutes after my first meeting even though they were produced. As a matter of fact, during Discovery I had requested Honeywell to hand over those minutes several times, yet somehow they never surfaced.

To my peril, I didn't have the presence of mind to send the company my own version of what took place at the meeting either. And I never concisely described my trade secrets and put them in writing to them either. This made it easier for Honeywell to throw their hat into the ring and claim authorship of my trade secrets and the subsequent inventions that they gave birth to with my IP.

Looking back, if I had even done the bare minimum, even if I had acted on the sixth and seventh options, I would have been in far, far, better shape in proving that I was the first true inventor and that there had been an egregious violation of misappropriation of trade secrets etc.

Just so you know, if were to ever do this over again, I'd at the *very least* bring either a lawyer *or* a certified courtroom stenographer to any meeting where I was going to teach the company anything. In my present state of mind, I would most definitely bring both!

A Very Important List

As the pre-licensing period draws down and the prospect of success is on the horizon, the company will then tell you that they intend to offer you a license agreement for your invention. That's great and that's in large measure what this journey has been all about. But before you start jumping up and down and begin counting your royalties, there is yet some serious work to be done.

When you reach the licensing phase, you should take a back seat and allow your attorney to handle all of the negotiations for you. This is a critical step and as such, that's exactly why I told you to have an intellectual property litigator do this for you. As we begin to explore this section, it will become clear why you should do just that.

There are two very important steps in the process that you need to complete before you should sign any license agreement. The first step is as follows.

- *Step one.* The inventor must strive to develop a firm handle on what the total opportunity costs might be to produce his value added product.

For the most part, you've already completed much of this step. Allow me to refresh your memory.

Remember how we devoted our energies trying to figure out how much it might cost the company to produce your product with your added improvement?

Remember how much energy we expended trying to figure out what the company's pretax profits might be?

Remember Goldscheider's rule where he stated that an inventor is entitled to 25% of the pretax profits?

Well here's the news. That was only the first step in the process as you begin to heading toward a licensing agreement.

The second step is as follows:

- *Step two.* The inventor must strive to ascertain the critical factors that will govern his long-term relationship with the company.

So before you sign this final licensing agreement, there are at least a dozen areas that you must be mindful of.

Allow me to set the stage.

By the time that you reach this juncture in the process, there should be a *minimum* amount of guesswork remaining as to where both you and the company stand with regard to your invention. I specifically mean that your working relationship should be well established and you should know how the company proposes to manufacture and market this product.

Just as important, you should be aware how the company plans on treating you. As you will soon see, how they propose to treat you ***should*** be embodied in the final license agreement. That means that all of the projections as well as the proper language should be made part of the licensing agreement as well.

Just a reminder, striking a licensing deal with a company that's capable of manufacturing and marketing your patented product isn't something that gets done overnight. It's conceivable that this process could take the inventor the better part of a year or more to successfully get through the pre-licensing period and accomplish such a sale. In addition to that, it could take additional months of negotiations to ratify the final agreement. It really boils down to the company's general attitude as to how they want to deal with an outside inventor.

So after all this time has elapsed, and you're finally presented with the company's first draft of the license agreement, there shouldn't be any surprises, right? Well not exactly. And that's what I want to draw your attention to.

Here are some critical factors that will put into perspective whether your long-term relationship with the company will be a healthy one or not. The key here is honesty and transparency.

First. Has the company shared with you how they propose to make your invention?

Have they supplied you with the detailed information as to how they are going to manufacture this product? This goes hand and hand with both ramp-up costs and the total opportunity costs to get the project under way. This information as it relates to their investment in the production of this new product demonstrate their commitment to the project and can be taken into consideration when they might try and offer you less than 25% of the pre-tax profits.

Second. Have both you and the company decided upon how the company proposes to market your invention? You should have a detailed knowledge of how they intend on marketing your value added product before you can in good conscience agree to a royalty rate. In addition to that, as the inventor, you should also have some input concerning the marketing plan since it was you who had first identified the emerging market.

You should be aware to what degree of effort they plan on investing, not only in the launch of this new product, but also in its maintenance throughout its life cycle.

Third. After you have been brought up to speed on how the company plans to manufacture and market your widget, have they provided you with the realistic calculations as to how many pieces they plan on selling?

Have they provided you with their best assessment for selling this item beginning at year one, and following it out five and then ten years?

Have they presented you detailed calculations as to your inventions life cycle, both near term and far term? Remember what I taught you about the trend waves.

This is critical information for you to know beforehand. Do not forget that you are being paid for every piece that they sell. Therefore, I would insist on getting these sales projections on paper and make them part of any finalized licensing agreement.

Fourth. Have you been told what all the related costs are going to be associated with bringing this invention to market?

Do you have solid figures as to what their gross and net profits are going to be on this item? Remember, ideally you are supposed to be compensated on 25% of their pretax profits. However, in the case that the company may offer you less than 25%, there are other important considerations that the company is responsible to make you aware of. They should do this to justify why they are offering you less than the 25% of their pretax profits.

As a reminder, I already told you that receiving 25% of the manufacturer's pretax profits isn't etched in stone by any means. As such you will be better able to decide what is a fair percentage for you to accept if they make should make *a rational case upfront for not being able to do so.*

Fifth. After the license is signed by both parties, what is your affiliation with the company going to be, moving forward?

For instance, once you sign this agreement, will your relationship with this product and this company more or less cease? Will your relationship with the company be reduced to the quarterly royalty check that they will send to you in the mail?

Or will the company invite you to act either officially or unofficially as a consultant on the project? Will your efforts towards the good and welfare of the product be viewed as something that you will do on a voluntary basis, or will you be compensated like any other valuable consultant?

Is the company willing to put in writing exactly what your relationship with them will be going forward, because if they don't put it in writing, you're probably *out.* It is a stupid company that doesn't utilize the vast storehouse of information that the inventor brings into the relationship. Yet it is a stupider company that pushes the inventor aside after the license agreement has been signed. Honeywell distanced themselves from me immediately, and at the time, I couldn't fathom why.

Sixth. What is the length of the licensing agreement that they are offering you?

Is this license to be run for the existing life of your patent or some other specified *shorter length of time?* If the term has been shortened, then my best advice is that you had better be on the lookout for smoke on the horizon.

Is this license agreement exclusive to just this one specific company, or can you seek out other companies to partner with?

Has the company that you are entering into the agreement with compensated or weighted your royalty rate to reflect the fact that you are giving them an *exclusive right* to your patent?

As you might expect, because your patent is going to give this company a competitive edge over *all* their competition, they aren't going to be too keen on accepting anything less than an exclusive license. In my experience, *unless you have* a patent on a value added product that many manufactures would be clamoring for in order to conduct their future business, don't expect to be entering into license agreements with multiple companies.

A perfect example is the bar code invented by Jerome Lemmelson. In case you're wondering, the bar code is that series of numbers with all those funny straight lines underneath them that are found on every single item that is sold. Mr. Lemmelson was arguably one of the craftiest and wealthiest inventors of all time. I would certainly look him up if I was in your shoes.

Seventh. Is the company going to pay you an upfront sign on fee for the privilege of going into business with you? In my opinion the company should pay the inventor something. Keep in mind that both company CEO's and professional ball players alike earn huge sign on bonuses. Well in my book, inventors deserve a sign on fee as well. This fee should be realistically based upon your entire contribution and what this product will generate in *potential future earnings* for the company.

Unfortunately, I don't have any hard and fast rules for you to calculate this figure, because there aren't any formulas that I'm aware of. This sign on bonus is just something that you and the company are going to have to work out amongst yourselves based upon the total value of your contribution. Nonetheless if you have a valuable idea, you should be expecting to receive a sign on bonus.

This sign on bonus could also be viewed as an earnest money deposit of sorts, something that the company will put up that in order to prove to the inventor that they are going to perform.

Just so you know, I received a fifty-thousand-dollar sign on bonus from Fram and I thought it was pitifully small as compared to the market I placed them in. In my opinion if they were playing fair, it should have been closer to a million dollars. Remember, they probably made in the neighborhood of a hundred million dollars off of the emerging markets that I was responsible for placing them in. So if you like, at least a couple of percentage points of what the lifetime gross might be, is a realistic sign on bonus. And that's only if you can agree upon what your product is going to generate over the course of its life.

Eighth. If other improvements are made along the way, do you automatically become a co-inventor to those subsequent patent applications as specified under 35 USC §115 &116? You most certainly should! In any event you should be recognized as the co-inventor of any new-patented improvement that your value-added product should give rise to. Also in the event that additional revenue streams were the outcome of such future improvements, you would in turn receive a proportionate share of the additional revenue generated as well. If a company is willing to put this in writing, they are telling you ahead of time that they don't have any intentions of trying to go around your patent or your trade secrets.

Just so you know, this was one of the very first things that I asked for, and AlliedSignal flatly rejected this request right out of the box. Under no circumstances would Allied make me a partner to any new product improvements or any subsequent patents as specified in the license. Hence, they did what they did with all my trade secrets. Yet they made a major miscalculation that I'll share with you momentarily.

A word to the wise should be sufficient here. A refusal of this kind is a harbinger that your business partner might have other plans for your relationship on down the road.

However, if you are fortunate to team up with a company that's willing to make you a co-inventor and will put it in writing upfront as part of the licensing agreement; then you'll really have something great! This is what I'm hoping will be your experience and as such, this honesty should bode well for your future relationship with the company.

So take my advice. Ask for this commitment right out of the gate. If they come back with a yes then rejoice, because you just might have something great!

On the other hand, if they refuse to acknowledge your partnership in writing, then go on red alert!

Just so you know, this was a huge mistake that both my attorney and I glossed over. Honeywell rejected such a partnership right out of the box. At the time I was way too naïve to realize what Honeywell was telegraphing as to what they might be up to in the future, and quite frankly, so was my attorney.

Ninth. Is the company going to seek patent protection outside of the United States? Are they going to file for patent applications and add you as the co-inventor to the foreign applications once you assign your patent over to them?

Do they plan on using any of your trade dress for the marketing of your product? If so, are they prepared to acknowledge you as the co-owner of any such designation or registered mark since you will be assigning it to them?

The company should always add you on as the co-inventor and co-owner if they are honorable. Again, Honeywell refused this option and as a result filed for at least six patents around the world and made tens and tens of millions of dollars without having to be directly accountable to me.

Tenth. Be very mindful of the language *made* or *sold.* If you get paid for what they *make*, then you get paid for every piece that rolls of the line whether it is housed in inventory, shipped out the door, sold or thrown in the garbage.

If you get paid for what is sold, you become a partner with the company. You're then on the hook for thefts, defects, returns, packaging problems or anything else that could arise. In my opinion, that's not your responsibility as the inventor. And that is exactly why the company earns the lion's share of the profits and why you as the inventor earn the smaller portion. In my view it was your job to bring the patents, the trade dress, the trade secrets and the business plan for the emerging market. The final execution is the company's responsibility and they have no right to include you in any of their screw ups.

Just so you know, Honeywell originally agreed to pay me for what they made, but during negotiations they retracted it. Eventually they insisted that I accept being compensated on what was sold. Subsequently, I became their partner to packaging, theft and inventory control problems of their doing. This was clearly their responsibility and as a result, I lost hundreds of thousands of dollars in royalties in their theft and repackaging fiasco in Walmart.

Eleventh. Are they promising to put forth their *best efforts* to market your product? Or are they going to employ their *reasonable efforts* to market your product? Both of these are legal terms relating to standards of performance and there is a huge difference between the two standards.

I know that I explained this earlier to you, but it definitely bears repeating again. It all comes down to performance and accountability as to how the company is going to manufacture and market your patented product.

As the inventor, you will have very little power over the destiny of your product once you sign your licensing agreement. What little power you have, will be derived from two little words… *best efforts*. Be aware that there is a vast difference as to what legally constitutes *best efforts* as opposed to the much-watered down language of *reasonable efforts*. If you end up accepting reasonable efforts, I can assure you that your ability to hold the company accountable for their performance will all but be lost.

Just so you know, Honeywell promised me verbally on several occasions that they would employ the standard of **best efforts.** But once it came down to putting it in the final agreement, they reneged and insisted that I accept the reasonable efforts threshold.

Twelfth. There is little phrase that will be found in nearly every contract, it's called the ***entirety clause***. The entirety clause means that once you sign this contract, this contract will become the entire sum total of your relationship! That means that no other documents and no promises, either written or otherwise, can influence or come to bear against this final contract. What it really means is that this contract will supersede everything that either you or the company has ever agreed upon to prior to signing this document.

To keep everyone honest, this is an excellent time to have their business plan and their marketing projections inserted into the final contract, because now what you've been promised by the company will be irrefutable. So make sure that any secrecy agreements; trade secret agreements, confidentiality agreements and the like are directly incorporated into this agreement as well.

What I am telling you is this. You want everything that was agreed upon in your pre-license agreements embodied in the final Licensing Agreement. You don't want those agreements left hanging out there on their own, due to the scope of Entirety Clause.

Just so you know, my final licensing agreement did not have a confidentiality section included in the final document. And although the entirety clause of the final license agreement stated that the agreement that we were signing was the final agreement, the TMA which I had signed eleven months earlier stated; that *unless* the final licensing agreement had a confidentiality section included in it, [which it did not] the TMA would be in control until such time that its authority expired. The TMA's authority lasted for four years and still had control over my final license agreement as to the confidentiality of my trade secrets! So, I have only God to thank that my final license agreement *did not* extinguish my TMA.

Just so you know, Honeywell filed two patents while this NDA / TMA was in place and while I was still being paid royalties. And while under the protection of these two separate documents, I did not receive any credit nor any compensation for these two patent applications. What I did get was a surprise and heartbreak, because they did this regardless of the law!

Here's my point. In the worst-case scenario, if you find yourself embroiled in a lawsuit with your partner, and you have multiple documents governing your relationship instead of one complete contract, the hair splitting that will ensue over these various documents will follow you the four or five years that it will take you to get to trial.

So make sure that your final license agreement contains a complete and simple to understand confidentiality section that will extinguish all your prior confidentiality agreements that were embodied in the PIA and TMA. It will make any necessary litigation go much smoother. Again, this was something that a seasoned intellectual property attorney should have caught from the very beginning, but again, mine didn't. As a consequence of that simple misstep on his part, I had to dance with satin himself over this cluster fiasco for over four years.

By not having one complete document govern the relationship gives the company's defense team a supreme advantage. I tell you that the waters will get so muddy from all the hairsplitting that the simple fact that they stole from you will get gobbled up. The end result will be that the illegal act that they have committed will go virtually ignored. That's unless you really have a no nonsense judge, and a really brilliant lawyer who is representing you during your legal proceedings, but you better not count on that one either. This fact alone makes your job of monitoring the construction of these contracts all the more important, while you still have some control.

There is an old expression that sums up this inventor-company relationship quite nicely. It usually has to do with sex and marriage, but to my way of thinking, it fits here as well. It goes a little something like this, "Why buy the cow if you can get the milk for free?"

Turning the Tables

Try and get all of the information that I just laid out in the twelve points in writing beforehand. At least get as much as possible, as soon as possible. I would also advise you to get your attorney involved with regard to this checklist as soon as the second pre-license agreement has been signed. After the Test Marketing Agreement has been signed, the typical company will require anywhere from three months and upwards to a year or more to be capable of launching a new product.

In light of my experience, I would think it's rather prudent to have a check list outlining the various points that I covered prepared by your attorney and placed in the in the hands of the company well in advance of them ever offering you their version of a license agreement.

The timing of this is critical and you certainly don't want to do this too prematurely.

First. I would only present them such a list or version of your licensing agreement only if you are fairly certain that they are going to offer you some sort of proposal.

Second. You should base your version of the licensing agreement upon the performance goals that the company has already communicated to you.

I can tell you that in all likelihood that the company won't take too kindly to you presenting them a contract first. This is because you will have taken away their control, because the offering of a contract has "first strike" advantage. But so what. You have to be preemptive and proactive where your interests are concerned especially during the licensing phase.

Here's my rational. If you wait for the company to offer you their version of a license agreement first and then your attorney presents this list to them afterwards, this list will only appear to them as one big afterthought. Thus, this list of yours will only have the impact of some sort of counter-offer on your behalf. As a result, I'll bet you dollars to doughnuts, that everything that I just listed will be refused by the company in a rather long and drawn out, offer and counter-offer fashion. In the end, the chances are good that you will be left with nothing that was on your original list!

The inventor must enter the licensing phase armed with the knowledge that the company is not his friend and that they are not going to offer him the world to begin with. So it's in the inventor's best interest to make his expectations known early.

In anticipation to what I've just said, I'd like to suggest that your attorney to prepare *your version* of a license agreement and present it to them first. I realize that this tactic might get them upset, but it also telegraphs to the company that you are coming from a position of strength and not from a position of weakness. I can assure you that it is far better for you to enter into a relationship, which is relatively fair and balanced from the beginning as opposed to getting into a lopsided license such as the one that I became entangled with.

So! The list that I just presented to you is crucial and shouldn't be viewed as an afterthought by either you or your attorney. If you have a problem communicating this to your attorney, provide him/her copies of the various pages of this manual that addresses any of your concerns. Don't be bashful; I'm giving you my permission in advance to do so.

Make no mistake, you have entered the money stage of the process and it's this stage where your royalty rate and your relationship with the company will be determined. As such there are three critical areas for you to keep in the forefront of your thinking. Therefore, some of what I've already mentioned, bears repeating.

First. The underlying performance of the company where your product is concerned is of paramount importance. Their ability to perform will directly influence your royalty stream. If they fail to perform, you may as well have sold it to them outright from the very beginning for the largest onetime fee you could get out of them and be done with it.

Second. *You have to come as close as possible to receiving a guarantee in writing* from the company that they will perform on the sale and the marketing of your product. This language will be contained in the license agreement under the *performance clause*. As such the company will have two choices. The first choice is a promise to use its *best efforts* to market this product. This is significant verbiage and is the best guarantee as to performance that an inventor could hope for in a license. This language will actually mean something should you ever have to go to court to enforce this contract from a performance standpoint.

On the other hand, if the company is not sure of the product or better yet, not sure of their ability to perform where the sales and the marketing of this product is concerned, they will opt for the much weaker verbiage, and will promise to use *reasonable efforts*. This language, which promises to use reasonable efforts, is limp-wristed at best. And folks, that's precisely how the courts will view it in these situations as well. As a consequence, you will *never* be able to hold a non-performing company's feet to the fire in a court of law once this language is inserted in the contract and agreed upon by you.

As I already explained, Honeywell promised me verbally to use best efforts during our conversations, but when the written contract was presented to me, reasonable efforts is what appeared in print. It's a long story, but Honeywell failed to exert their best efforts to market my invention and I was powerless to enforce that aspect of the contract. That was a huge bone of contention, which I had to endure during our relationship.

Here is my advice to you. In the event that a company is not willing to put in writing right up front that they will use their *"best efforts"* to market and promote your invention, I would seriously consider backing out of the relationship before it's too late.

Allow me to reinforce something. If the relationship going forward looks as if it's not going to fly, then now would be the time to get out. That said, you can certainly get out with your patents intact. As for your trade secrets and all your secret sauces, you may have already disclosed them during your interaction with the company. But don't panic, because if you've signed an NDA and you've documented your IP beyond any reasonable doubt, then all of the IP that you disclosed is yours. Any company or individual that attempts to capitalize on *"your IP"* will therefore be running a grave risk should they be tempted to produce this product without you!

I don't care how the experts may want to water down this relationship that takes place between the inventor and his chosen company, but I warn you, this relationship is as close to a marriage as you can get. Both parties bring their respective strengths and weaknesses into this relationship. And if that weren't true, then why would there be any need for this relationship to form in the first place. Right? So to my way of thinking, why would you want to enter into a relationship that gives the party that you're about to marry an *escape clause* before the relationship ever gets off the ground?

Third. Are you going to be paid a royalty for the widgets that are *sold* or *made*? I realize that I've already mentioned this, but it bears repeating here. The language that's applied in your contract does matter. There is a world of difference between what *made* means as compared to what *sold* means. This is a hallmark fight that takes place in every inventor's licensing agreement.

Let me put it to you this way, are you going to receive a royalty for every piece as it rolls off the assembly line? M*ade?* Or are you going to receive a royalty after the customer receives the physical product and actually sells it? *Sold?*

On the surface there doesn't appear to be such a great distinction. Under both scenarios it certainly appears that at some point, the inventor shall be receiving his royalty, right?

Well, not exactly. For example, if the inventor gets paid for every widget those rolls of the line *made*, you receive a check for that amount. No if's, and's or but's.

On the other hand, if you were to receive a royalty for every product *sold* when does that occur? Do you get paid when the retailer booked the sale or when the retailer received the physical item? Where does that leave the inventor where a recall or the loss of inventory control of the item is concerned?

Keep in mind a product can be recalled for defects, or inadequate packaging etc. Should the inventor share equally in the financial responsibility that is clearly the company's responsibility to oversee? Think about how much inventory the manufacturer eats when they deal with the big box retailers.

All I can tell you is that I personally lost hundreds of thousands of dollars in lost royalties, due to the theft of the Double Guard oil filter and the related packaging issues. I had my quarterly royalty check go from 50K a quarter to $700.00 a quarter without so much as a whisper from the company beforehand.

All over what you might ask? Theft and packaging. I was instantly made a partner to something that Honeywell; a Fortune-Thirty-eight company should have been able to get right all by themselves, but yet they couldn't.

Again, this all happened because I had allowed them during the course of negations to pressure me into accepting the language that went from "made" to "sold."

So to recap, the licensing agreement contains several parts, but the most important elements are threefold:

- How you are going to get paid?
- How much you are going to get paid.
- And most importantly, what are your guarantees for getting paid in the future.

Just so you know, my licensing negotiations dragged on for well over four months, and there were some seven versions of this licensing agreement that were presented to me. Each time that I was presented a new version, Honeywell would find yet another reason to change or take away something important that we had already agreed upon.

So right about now you certainly might be wondering, "Why didn't you walk? The answer is I should have, but I was too scared. I was too scared to walk away from my trade secrets and I wasn't given the proper counsel on how to do so!

Remember, you have to keep in mind I hadn't written this book yet and as a backyard inventor I was flying nearly blind amongst the clouds. You on the other hand don't have to be too scared to walk, because this book not only teaches you how to protect yourself, but it teaches you how to build the evidentiary means to defeat a dishonest partner in a court of law. At the time of my negotiations, this was a major tool that was not in my tool box.

As mentioned, I did not know many of the things that I just told you about before I entered this phase of the odyssey, nor was I ever warned by anybody! I'll be quick to point out, just like the nuances of obtaining a patent, in most cases an attorney is not going to be too quick to point these critical things out, until it's too late. So as I've told you in the past, now that you've hired an expert and you're paying his/her fee, ask questions.

- This is yet another reason why the lawyer that represents you must be both an IP litigator and an expert in contract law!

As a result of my ignorance, I took way too much of my interaction with the company on faith and trust. I based way too much on the verbal assurances of the high level company employees that I worked with on the project. As a result of this trust, when I had received their first copy of the licensing agreement I was alone. I was in Fram's corporate headquarters and I didn't have an attorney present.

Just so you know, I was a fool for ever putting myself in that situation. Therefore, I am telling you that your attorney must be at your side for any license agreement negotiations or signing.

In addition to that, I placed way too much faith on the hype that I was working with a world leader. My advice to you here is very simple, don't you be so gullible.

Here's a fact for you to consider. If and when your license agreement ever makes its debut in writing, and it finds its way to the president of the division, or their chief patent counsel, or the company's chief general counsel or to the CEO, the gloves will come flying off and you can kiss any semblance of personal interaction and good-will goodbye! At that time, it will be all about the good and welfare of the company. Your contributions as the inventor who discovered the emerging market and who holds the patent[s] will be all but forgotten.

After the dust had settled, I lost precious tens of millions of dollars during the course of my relationship with the company that I chose to go into business with. The theft of the product and the company's *lack of best efforts* were mainly to blame, compounded by the fact that my royalty was only 10 cents per filter sold instead of ¢60 cents that Goldscheider's 25% rule calls for.

Honeywell's gross net profit on my improvement was $2.50 per filter and I was the inventor of the final product they were offering for sale since it was made under my patent and my trade secrets.

Much of what I suffered was the direct result of this licensing agreement that I should never have signed. So here's my point, I screwed up. My question to you is simple. Based on all that I've taught you thus far, are you going to get played when your moment in the sun arrives? I certainly hope not.

Aftercare

I wouldn't be doing my job if I didn't tell you that after you've signed your license agreement it's your responsibility to monitor your partner company's patent applications. Make sure that they haven't filed any patents that may encompass any new claims or improvements to your widget without first coming to you and designating you as the co-inventor. By the way, this clause should appear in the final licensing agreement.

Just so you know, this was one of the very first changes that I proposed to Honeywell, since this clause was glaringly absent in the original contract that they presented to me. I fought like hell over its inclusion, but in the end they would not agree to have this inserted into the final agreement.

I wonder why?

So learn a lesson. With the wonderful advent of the Internet and the interphase it gives the inventor to interact with the PTO's database, it would be a terrible shame for you to let your guard down, because you became too happy and as a result grew sloppy.

During my lawsuit, I had Honeywell dead to rights on the Misappropriation of Trade Secrets. Under Rhode Island law, the statute of limitations was 2 years and entitled the plaintiff to double damages. That means that if the company were found guilty of violating this statute, I' d be entitled to at least twice the amount of their earned gross profits generated by the sale of the Double Guard oil filter for violating this statute. If a judgment had gone in my favor they could have been ordered to pay me on the order of eighty million dollars on that count alone. Now you can better understand why they brought in the world's top guns to dispatch with a lone backyard inventor like myself.

As it turns out, Honeywell filed for two patents while we were yet under the control of the pre-license agreements. Not only were they in direct violation of those agreements, but also they were in flagrant violation to 35 USC §115 & 116 where the Federal statues clearly define the guidelines for inventorship.

To make a long story short, I never checked the Patent Office regarding Honeywell's patent filings during the first several years of our relationship. So by the time it came to my attention as to what they had done, my statute of limitations had run out. As a result, I lost this most valuable count, not on a substantive basis, because they were guilty, but I lost this due to the tolling of the time. As such I missed out on having this count come against them, because I was too late in filing a formal complaint by just a couple of months.

Just so you know, during this time frame there was no internet to facilitate any checking up on Honeywell's patent activity where my trade secrets were concerned. Actually, back then I would have needed to hire a professional search service to do this for me. You have the internet. Enough said.

Now here's the kicker. And this is in great part why I have endeavored to craft this book with such attention to detail. You see, from my judge's viewpoint, it did not seem to matter that Honeywell was my business partner and that they had engaged in activities such as filing multiple patents with my trade secrets in violation of our NDA. As strange as that may sound, that truly wasn't important as far as the judge was concerned. And furthermore, he seemed to gloss over the obvious fact that they breached not only one, but two ironclad confidentiality agreements.

Now here's what was important to my judge, and herein lies one of the most important lessons that I want you fledgling inventors to come away with. At the end of the day, the judge felt that it was my personal responsibility to check the Patent Office to make sure that my business partner wasn't involved in any such illegal patent activity. In his view, it was my job to make sure that they weren't using my confidential information inappropriately.

It didn't seem to matter to him whether there were agreements in place forbidding such behavior on their part from doing so. And it didn't seem to matter to the judge that both federal and state law prohibiting this behavior was clearly violated. It just didn't seem to matter that my business partner was in clear violation of both patent law and contract law.

What did matter to this particular judge was that the statute of limitations on my claim for the misappropriation of trade secrets had expired by two months and that it was my personal responsibility to have monitored my partner's interaction with the PTO. Holy S…!

Needless to say, be prepared to monitor your product as it begins its life out in the market place. See what venues it's selling in and try and determine why it might not be selling in others. Monitor your business partner's efforts in this area. Try and make a determination whether they are either helping or hurting the sale of your product. Monitor the Patent Office.

Some Final Thoughts and One Last Lesson

Every teaching worth its salt should have a meaningful conclusion. So in keeping with that, I feel that it's crucial that I share a couple of final thoughts with you.

So hang on… The last bit of your climb is just around the bend. At this time, I realize that some of you are getting off this mountain for good, while some of you are committed to press on towards the summit.

As you can recall, I've often times said, *"It was my hope that you've invented is something valuable."* And I truly meant it.

In the final analysis what you believe is valuable and what I believe is valuable may be two different things. Over the course of our association, I never once bragged that I made several million dollars from my inventing career. Well now that we are parting ways, perhaps it would be more meaningful if I told you that I have.

It's equally important for you to know that the lion's share of my earnings got eaten up by both legal costs and taxes. And of equal importance for you to know, is that the vast majority of my time, my money and my energy was consumed by trying to get back what was mine in the first place!

So here's the deal…

If you can discipline yourself to follow the game plan that I've laid out, and you're convinced that your efforts can earn you at *minimum;* a hundred thousand dollars, with an upside potential to make much more…, *then you should consider following through with your idea.*

But…, if for any reason *you cannot commit* to following the blue print that I've laid out, then I suggest that you cross this particular experience off of your 'bucket list.' Now don't be disappointed. Rather, consider yourself lucky that you experienced this journey in the comfort of your living room and you got away with it for the price of a cheap dinner.

Many of us are not capable of climbing Everest, and by the same token most of us do not have what it takes to trek across the Amazon. It's a fact, we all have limitations and it's something that we all must come to grips with. So…, there's no shame if you decide to pass at becoming an inventor. As you now know, becoming a successful inventor doesn't just happen. It takes a lot of hard work and dedication to reach this summit. Now that you've taken the journey with me, I'd gladly meet any one of you back at base camp and we'll raise a glass.

As for those of you who *truly possess a valuable idea* and are committed to do what the job requires to reach this summit, I have one last lesson before you can hoist the flag.

It's not the most uplifting thing that I could share with you, but it's what can frequently play out in the real world, so it's my job to make you aware of it. Again, it's not the kind of scenario that the *Voices* are going to tell you about, but I will.

The case law is brimming with examples of inventor's who have gone through the process of dialoging with a potential licensing partner. Now on the surface, that seems innocent enough.

During that association the inventor would have signed either *a non-disclosure or trade secret agreement,* only to be told sometime later by the company that they are no longer interested in their[your] *protected* idea.

- NDA's get signed whether your idea is patented or not.
- In many, many instances a business relationship never materializes as a result of the two parties meeting and signing an NDA.

Now here's the part that's really going to hurt. Usually in about a year or so, you *might* end up seeing your IP embodied in some product that's now available in the marketplace. And that product just so happens to embody the very same IP that was protected under your NDA. As your heart begins to drop to the basement, you soon realize that it's being offered by the very same company that just got done telling you that they were no longer interested in your idea.

So for those of you who have the summit on your horizon, I want you to understand the details contained in following cases. They are representative of what a typical violation of a nondisclosure agreement looks like and how they can play out in an inventor's life. Keep in mind, that every one of these cases was settled on the Federal Appellate Court level. So that means that each case represents an investment of millions and millions of dollars in legal fees and a good 10 to 15 years of an honest inventor's life in order to go after this now tarnished pot of gold.

SEE

X-IT Products vs. Walter Kidde CIV. A. 2:00CV513. 155 F.Supp.2d 577 (2001)
Celeritas Technologies vs. Rockwell International 150 F.3d 1354 (Fed. Cir. 1998)
Alling vs. Universal Manufacturing Corp. No. A049088. First Dist., Div. Three. Apr 30, 1992)
Injection Research Specialists vs. Polaris Industries No. 90-C-1143. 759 F.Supp. 1511 (1991)

Just so you know, I was such a victim at the hands of Honeywell. My story and how it played out, though similar in many respects, had one glaring deficiency. I lost my most valuable count; The Misappropriation of Trade Secrets, because my statute of limitations for this cause of action had lapsed before I filed my lawsuit. Nonetheless, Honeywell violated two NDA's and as a result of that, they went on to file 17 patents with my trade secret information… and that was just for starters.

If you happen to be on the cusp of entering into a licensing deal with an entity more powerful than yourself, it would behoove you to read my book, *The Greed of a Dime*, which documents my entire journey as an inventor. The book recounts in vivid detail everything that led up to my licensing agreement, and covers all of the details that transpired both during and after it. So if you have a desire to know what the misappropriation of trade secrets looks like as it happens to the inventor as it's going down, then the "Greed of a Dime" is a must read for you.

Believe in Yourself

What I've really been trying to drive home during our time together is twofold:

First. You are personally responsible as to how your inventing odyssey is going to turn out. In the final analysis, you are the one who's going to be responsible for everything and everyone who participates in this journey alongside of you. So being responsible and being several moves ahead of everyone else on the chessboard is going to be key.

Second. Inventing is a lot like love. In my estimation it is far better for your soul to experience inventing's unbridled thrills with all of its unpredictable twists and turns, than never to have experienced it at all. Therefore, if your invention is real, I urge you to pursue it with every fiber of your being! So believing in yourself and believing in your invention at all costs is yet another key.

Just so you know, when I had first set out to write this book, my goal was to provide you with a detailed roadmap of not only how the inventing game is framed, but how it's actually played. I'm proud to tell you that after a hard year of writing and a tremendous amount of soul searching and multiple hundreds of hours of polishing, I've finally accomplished this task.

You are in possession of the roadmap now. My advice is that you go out and discover the next great emerging market. Be true to yourself and follow your dreams. Get the patent, get the proper trade dress, build the proper team, and then go out and strike your deal!

You can bet that the next time I get a good idea; I'll be doing the same.

THE
END

Epilogue

I really had no plans to write an epilogue…, none whatsoever. But on the eve of going to press, a story broke that I just couldn't resist bringing to your attention.

I found it sad, yet ironically, I found it most validating. It has to do with the fourth mountain that I climbed during my inventor's journey. It's the very mountain that I've done my best to keep you away from. It's the lawsuit mountain.

Case in point: Miller UK LTD. vs. Caterpillar Inc., decided November 20, 2015.

Miller just won a $76 MM verdict in Federal Court for trade secret theft committed by Caterpillar.

I was totally disappointed that my favorite class 8 truck engine and heavy duty equipment manufacturer just got caught with their pants wrapped around their ankles..., but they did. By no means can I say that I'm shocked, just disappointed. A far as I'm concerned, Cat's actions just earned them a place in the annuals of disreputable trade secret violators. How sad, how greedy…, and how stupid for a company of that stature to stoop so low.

You would think that their prominence as the world leader in the heavy equipment arena would preclude such behavior, but it didn't. Setting my personal experiences aside, we all have witnessed time and time again, the incessant drive that possesses these powerful companies to grab every last penny. Remember, if you invent a game changer, the penny that I'm talking about might one day be yours.

The operational tactics prevalent amongst many of these large corporations leads them to believe that they can do whatever to whomever, under the delusion of earning greater profits in order to please their shareholders. As a consequence, they don't fear any of the laws, and contrary to what you may believe, they really don't give a flip about public opinion.

As I warned you about in the beginning, it's always about the money, and it always has been. As put forth, the mission of this book was to educate all inventors both great and small, about their vulnerabilities during the journey. Simply put, there's no depths to which a trade secret violator will go to pull off their schemes of unjust enrichment. So never forget that as an innovator, your misplaced trust in any business partner could result in grave trouble for you later on down the road.

If your idea is valuable, you must do things right from the very start. Let's take a look at the newest case.

Miller UK LTD. vs. Caterpillar Inc. Misappropriation of Trade Secrets

As it turns out, Miller didn't just fall off of the turnip truck. They've been in business for over 30 years. Over time, due to hard work and innovation they have become the world leader in quick release coupling devises for digging buckets and related attachments. Their products are available globally through various dealer networks and have been adopted as OEM fixtures by such company's such as Volvo, CNH, Komatsu and Caterpillar. As their website states, "We are the world leader in quick coupler design and manufacture. Protecting our innovation is a serious business, with significant investment in both design registration and patent application. Miller always ensures that both our trademarks and our product designs are legally protected in all relevant countries worldwide."

"As we celebrated our 25th year in business, we became an approved OEM pin pick-up coupler manufacturer with a supply agreement to 'factory fit' quick couplers. This contract meant that we had become the supplier of choice to Caterpillar Inc. for its quick coupler requirements. Our unique Bug coupler invention was exported directly to Caterpillar's North American and Japanese machine assembly plants and was branded as the Cat Pin Grabber Plus – 'The CAT PGP'2003.'"

Miller had established an intimate business and manufacturing relationship with Cat, and according to their mission statement, they pride themselves on protecting their IP. Now that's not so hard to understand, right?

So let me ask, 'Didn't I have an intimate relationship with Honeywell? Didn't I take the right steps to protect my IP?'

According to DueDil.com, Miller grossed over $35 MM in 2015. That said, I'd like to make this point. To sue an outfit, the size of Caterpillar is beyond the comprehension of most mortals, and apparently, even for a multi-million-dollar company like Miller. The fact is, Miller presented their case to several litigation funding firms before they were able to secure the necessary funding for their lawsuit. It's hard to fathom the monetary costs, but despite earning tens of millions of dollars a year, it's still not enough to run both a business, and to mount a proper legal campaign against a mega corporation like Cat. Now something is terribly wrong with that picture.

And just so you know, it wouldn't be enough to sue a company like Honeywell either.

In Miller's case, things worked out, and I am extremely happy for them! According to court documents, "Miller received financing from Juris Capital LLC, a privately held commercial litigation funding firm in Chicago, and Highland Park, Illinois-based Arena Consulting LLC," enabling them to team up with a law firm out of Chicago. As a matter of fact, this particular law firm has twelve offices located throughout the world. And as it turns out, the law firm chosen for the job was none other than Kirkland and Ellis, one of the largest, most prestigious and powerful law firms on the planet.

According to the legal masthead for the case, which you can view at Leagle.com, Kirkland had at least eight attorneys that were credited for working on Miller's case. Despite all that muscle behind them, it still took Miller five very grueling and expensive years battling Caterpillar in order to get to trial. And again, that's with a powerhouse like Kirkland and Ellis pushing their sled!

As mentioned in my introduction, I faced off against Kirkland and Ellis' New York office. That office boasts 150 partners and fields an army of over 400 attorneys.

To keep things in perspective, I'd like to remind you that there weren't any lawyers on my team for the first couple of years, and that there was never a possibility of obtaining litigation funding for my case, since that sort of help was in its very infancy back then.

In order for me to sue Honeywell, I had to mortgage my home that had been paid for free and clear. I had to quit my job, so that I could train myself to become a lawyer, and I had to prepare myself to handle the avalanche of legal filings that would threaten to bury me alive. My decision to play the game at this level banished me to wander the lonely and terrifying wastelands of high-stakes litigation for five very precious years of my life. I won't deny that going after Honeywell put the future of my two young children and the serenity of my family in jeopardy, because it certainly did! However, that was a risk that both my wife and I were willing to take at the time. And if we hadn't…, I'm not certain whether either of us would have been able to live with our inaction.

Like Miller, it also took me five very grueling and expensive years to get to trial, accept by the time I got there, I had only one gutsy thirty-something lawyer by my side. Make no bones about it, my inventors journey was mind-boggling enough…and yes, my legal experiences were harrowing, but without that hard fought experience, both of my books would hold no value for you, the reader.

I invented a billion-dollar baby, and that's precisely why my partner had to have it for their own. And that's of course, only after they finally had the smarts to figure out what I had brought them.

You see my friends, inventing can be like a double-edged sword. If you should be blessed to invent something so valuable, your business partner[s] will inextricably want it for their own. This happened to me, long before Miller entered the news. And long before I entered the game, it happened to Dr. Kearns, *The Flash of Genius;* who invented intermittent windshield wiper that Ford, Chrysler and GM were compelled to steal.

The take away message here is this… Though the struggles and the indomitable drama behind each one of our cases are different, we as innovators share one thing…, our IP was exceedingly valuable and was worth stealing. As a consequence of being subjected to this greed, each one of us was put through our own individually tailored version of Hell. Those of us who choose to fight back, take on this monster knowing that in the end, we're only going to recover *just a fraction of our inventions' equity.*

There's no doubt in my mind, that had any one of us had read this book prior embarking on our journey, each one of us would have fared much better.

For me, the Miller case couldn't be more timely or validating. It's yet another clear-cut case that reinforces everything that I've tried to prepare you for. As you can see, Miller was by no means a babe in the woods. They were a financially healthy company and they were a world leader in their space. They were also a company that was savvy enough to have the necessary safeguards in place in order to protect their IP. Yet despite their best laid plans, their IP came under attack by one of their biggest and most trusted business partners.

As we now part ways, I leave you with this...

I traveled through the lite side of Hell in order to bring you the truth about what the dark side of inventing in America can hold for the uninformed individual or company who wants to compete with a valuable idea. If you have a valuable idea or invention, you owe it to yourself to get informed before you go out and play with the big boys.

May God Bless You, in all of your future endeavors.